THEY CALL ME
MR ENGLAND

THEY CALL ME MR ENGLAND

Mr England Publishing

Published in 2014 by
Mr England Publishing

Copyright © Peter Cross 2014

ISBN 978-0-9931091-0-2

Twitter: @mrenglandrugby

Printed and bound in Great Britain by
Short Run Press Limited, Exeter, Devon

FOREWORD
by Jason Leonard OBE

Peter asked me if I would write a foreword for his book. Given I am RFU President for the year the World Cup is to be played here at home, I have obviously reflected on what is so good about our game and of course it is the people involved at all levels in the many ways one can be.

'Crossy – Mr England' is the uber-fan and a feeling of continuity for the players who turn out for England. A figure that epitomises the character of the game in all its facets. I commend this story to you, it is a good read from a proper rugby man.

Thank you also Peter for directing proceeds of this book towards The Atlas Foundation which means it will benefit those who need our support the world over where Rugby is being used as the link to crystallise such help and hope for the future. You are everybody's 'Mr England'.

THE ATLAS FOUNDATION

Rugby gives much to those that play, administer, act as officials and watch the game. One of the stand out cultural elements of the game is its philanthropic and charitable nature in assisting those who need a helping hand. In this spirit the offer by Peter to support The Atlas Foundation by contributing proceeds from this book is fantastic.

The Atlas Foundation provides the financial support to worldwide charities that use the game of rugby as a facilitator to improve people's lives. These rugby based charities have an enduring problem funding their activities. As an independent charity funded through sponsorship, fundraising and donations allows such charities to focus on delivery rather than funding their activities. By seeking out and securing tailored grant funding from large UK corporations and matching these funds to charitable organisations, the foundation will advance and promote the efficiency of rugby based charities around the world. Allowing them to apply their resources in a more effective manner towards carrying out their charitable purposes.

The Trustees thank Peter 'Mr England' Cross most deeply.

ACKNOWLEDGEMENTS

First I would like to acknowledge the hard work and hours spent by my nephew Simon Jones in writing my life story. We have both had great fun over the past two years putting it together. The remote 'Turf Locks' a great pub on the banks of the River Exe was generally our meeting place. Simon would cycle from Exeter and myself from Dawlish. We would eat, drink and have a great laugh and invariably be the last to leave the pub, before cycling about 8 miles home in the dark.

I would also like to thank Richard Prescott and Sarah Swayby of the RFU for having the vision and foresight to appoint me. Also, Keith Webster, Head of Security at Twickenham, without his trust and confidence my position would just not have happened.

Thanks to Paul Bettesworth who did the first 'proof read,' my good mate Bruce Priday, the second read and Paul Ackford for doing a 'critique'. Photographers Dave Rogers of Getty Images and Jeremy Rata, plus Ian Court of Westec, Dawlish for reproducing old pictures. Thanks also for the help of Vincenzo and Lawrence Dallaglio, Jason Leonard, Mike Cleary, Jamie Kingsley and Mark Couch of Short Run Press, Exeter.

Dedication

I would like to dedicate this book to my wife Pam, daughter Ali and her family. To all my mates who have helped, not only make my life great fun, but have been massive rocks in my moments of despair. To every England supporter and finally to my special son Simon, who loved life and sport. We all miss him massively and we will never get over losing him.

Pete Cross
Mr England

CONTENTS

WOAH, I'M GOING TO BARBADOS

I've ended up with a job that is not a job; It's a passion! The question everyone always asks me is how I ended up becoming the man they call 'Mr England'. Well here is the story . . . or at least my version of it.

Initially, let me tell you about my experiences of watching England play cricket against the once all conquering West Indies team in the beautiful Caribbean. I will take you back to the Commonwealth Games in Kuala Lumpar and the Olympics in Atlanta, before telling you a little bit about my upbringing, my family and my friends. Let me explain how I became the official England Rugby Union mascot after following the British Lions to South Africa and supporting the English Rugby team all over the British Isles, Ireland, France and Italy. Come with me behind the scenes and discover how it felt to know some of the England players, management and families before and after their momentous World Cup victory in Australia. Share with me in the glorious World Cup celebrations and some of the highs and lows England have enjoyed since.

Through my privileged position let us look at how England have rebuilt a winning formula and allow me to identify some of the special characters I think you should look out for in the new England team. Join me as we look forward positively to hosting a memorable Rugby World Cup in England in 2015 with Stuart Lancaster's men hoping to emulate, that historic moment in English Rugby's history. We know the supporters at Twickenham have a massive role to play, the atmosphere at the stadium is reaching new highs and I am honoured to be part of that wonderful support.

My first ever introduction to the magnificent island of Barbados came when I was playing with Torquay Rugby Club's, 'Pilgrim Fathers.' We toured the island for two weeks, shortly after I had retired from playing first team rugby, at the age of 37. I had the good fortune to be invited by the Pilgrim Fathers to tour with them and boy did we have some fun. The tours had been set up two years previously for recently retired players to visit glamorous locations around the world and play rugby.

Three matches had been arranged against the full Barbados national team. The first game we played was only a day or so after arriving. I can't say we were that well prepared as we had spent most of our time making the most of the local hospitality on the beach. The Barbadian national team ran the ball from all over the pitch and really surprised us with their skill, pace and quick hands and they comfortably beat us. We re grouped and went into the next two games with our heads screwed on. By playing total forward rugby, putting the ball up our jumpers and not allowing them any possession we found they couldn't compete with us. We were comfortable winners in both games.

During that, my first tour of Barbados I just fell in love the place and I vowed to myself that I would visit again with my wife Pam. Sure enough the following year I returned to Barbados with Pam and she was as captivated by the beautiful island and its people as me. One of the first things we did when we arrived was to join the local hash running club, it was a brilliant way of meeting many of the locals and ex pats. The boozy evenings we enjoyed enabled us to really understand the local culture and find out first hand where the best restaurants and bars were on the island.

One day, Pam and I went down to the Kensington Oval to watch Barbados play cricket in the Red Stripe Shield. When the cricket was over, we set off walking back into Bridgetown where we were going to get a bus back to our hotel. Out of the blue a ramshackle taxi held together by string pulled over and the driver asked, 'do you want a lift' we said, 'no, no thanks we're happy walking.' The driver persisted, ' No, I'll give you a lift, I'm a cricket man!'

So we conceded and accepted his kind offer of a lift to our resort 'The Rockley Resort and Golf Club.' It was about ten miles away and neither of us expected the taxi to complete the journey. We chatted to the driver and found him to be a really nice guy, probably about twenty years older than us. He introduced himself as Mr Bennett, although we subsequently got to know him by his first name Wyatt. The Barbadians are very respectful, traditional people full of personality and Wyatt was no exception. A few days later out of the blue Wyatt turned up at our apartment and had a cup of tea with us.

We built up a really good friendship with him and even asked him to take us back to the airport on our final day in his clapped out old taxi! The next time we visited Barbados we couldn't wait to touch base with him again. We didn't go out with him socially, but we loved him popping in to see us at our apartment, the bonus for me was he was cricket mad. Wyatt knew many of the legendary West Indian players, legends such as Joel Garner and Sir Garfield Sobers personally. He could talk forever about the game and I was fascinated; I loved spending time with him.

I often went down to the Kensington Oval by myself to watch Barbados play cricket and that's when I discovered many of the local characters. I quickly realised that if I went into a bar or a rum shop and started to talk cricket it was a guaranteed way to get into a conversation with the locals and make friends. It was at the Kensington Oval that I first came across two very well known Barbados cricket followers.

Matt Fingle, a local school teacher, together with a dozen or so of his pals would play reggae music as the cricket slowly unfolded and the sun shone down. Many more of the locals would join in, gather round Matt and his band and gyrate in time to the music in that beautiful Caribbean style. Mums, dads and children all used to get into the calypso mood. I was enthralled, captivated, it was party time. I fell more and more in love with the Barbados people, their culture and their absolute passion for cricket. Their wonderful spirit and love of life was infectious!

King Dal was another brilliant character, a lovely old Barbadian who would never miss a match. He was an ordinary guy who had a massive love of the game and supported Barbados and cricket with a total passion. He always stood out from the crowd as he dressed in an array of red, pink or yellow suits, brightening up any occasion. I found it a privilege to sit next to him, buy him a beer and listen to his yarns. Back home in England I had seen glimpses of him on the television as he watched the West Indies playing test cricket, now I was sat with him, it was a joy to be in his company. As I got to know King Dal, I was pleasantly surprised to discover that he was a big supporter of the English cricket team too and that he had been over to England to watch us play test cricket. Generously, Ted Dexter, the former England captain and legend had paid for King Dal to travel to England to watch the West Indies play test matches against us. What a truly memorable experience that had been for him, one that he told me he would never forget.

It was in February 1994, while I was on holiday in Barbados with Pam and my grown up children, Ali and Simon, that I got caught up in the buzz and excitement of the ex pats and locals talking about the upcoming England cricket tour of the West Indies. The series was due to start in April and I could feel the sense of anticipation. The prospect of the tour was too much for me to resist, I had to be there! An English guy, Julian, who played in the jazz band on the waterfront suggested to me that I could rent a room from him for £25 a night. What could I say? I spoke to Wyatt and he said he could get me tickets for all five days of the test match. It was done, sorted! I don't think Pam was too impressed but I just couldn't resist the opportunity. All I needed to do was book the flights and in eight weeks I would be back in Barbados and Antigua (it would be rude not to visit Antigua), for three weeks supporting my beloved England cricket team, my childhood dreams were coming true!

Wyatt gave me a phone number of a friend of his in Antigua who he said may be able to get me tickets for the Antigua test. Upon returning to England I duly phoned Dr Charles and asked if he could get me tickets. His words were, 'any friend of that mad taxi driver Bennett is a friend of mine.' I gave him my phone number and he said, 'leave it to me.' I casually mentioned my plans to some friends in Dawlish and before I knew it, four younger guys approached me and asked if they could join me. They suggested they could book a package deal to Barbados and meet me over there. I agreed and phoned Dr Charles to ask if he could get hold of more tickets and without hesitation he readily agreed to get tickets for all five days of the test in Antigua. He also mentioned he knew an apartment very close to the cricket ground that would accommodate all five of us and he would book it! I was so grateful, Dr Charles was a star, purchasing tickets and booking accommodation for five people over five days and I had never met him!

I flew out to Barbados, with the boys due to join me on day four of the test. I still needed to arrange some tickets for them for the fifth day's play. Fortunately, I was able to contact, 'Spamy', who I knew from the hash running club. She was the secretary of the Rockley Resort and Golf Club where the England cricket team were staying. On the conclusion of day one of the Barbados test, Wyatt took me to the apartment where Dr Charles was staying to introduce me to him, as he'd come over from Antigua. What a perfect gentleman and an absolute cricket aficionado. He cooked us a great barbeque and treated us to his famous, 'Dr Charles Rum Punch' as we shared cricket stories. During the evening, I discovered that he was an eminent Doctor in Antigua who had worked for many years in Africa and was a world authority on tropical diseases. Furthermore, his son was a top doctor in Antigua and his sister Dame Eugenia Charles was the first woman female Prime Minister of Dominica and the second ever to be head of a Caribbean country.

What a fantastic test match the Barbados test turned out to be. England had just flown in from Trinidad where we had been skittled out for 46 and absolutely annihilated.

In an amazing turnaround we won the fourth test, a first England win in Barbados for 74 years and the first by any visiting side for 59 years. Man of the Match, Alec Stewart, was in imperious form, scoring majestic centuries in both innings. Angus Fraser brought some much needed, steel and determination to our attack, taking eight West Indian wickets for seventy five runs in their first innings. Andy Caddick took a five for 'in the Windies' second innings, while Phil Tufnell wheeled tirelessly away -eventually taking three for a hundred. Tufnell, who was generally a shite fielder, put the icing on the cake when he actually held on to a catch in the deep, to dismiss Brian Lara, a pivotal moment in a famous victory.

My four Dawlish friends, Nigel (no legs), Jim, Lee and Steve celebrated long and hard at Barbados Cricket Club's Members Bar, the joys of which, I'd previously been introduced to by Wyatt. The five of us and loads of local cricket fans enjoyed a brilliant evening surrounded by pictures of some of the most legendary West Indian cricketers.

Next up was the Antigua test match, where I met some smashing lads, most of whom were young enough to be my son and like me totally dedicated England followers. I guess those guys were the fore runners of the Barmy Army. I spent time listening to them and how they funded their tours, what kind of strategy they had and what their future plans were. They revealed they always took their Union Jack or cross of St George flags bearing their favourite football team's name, town or city they were from or even their local pub. They explained they always tried to place them in the most prominent position where they could be seen on television. In a way I clocked it all. Nowadays it seems obvious, but in those days . . .

1994 was proving to be a monumental England tour of the West Indies. I feel blessed that I was present when Brian Lara played his sublime, magical, record breaking innings of 375 at Antigua (surpassing the great Sir Garfield Sobers long held world record of 365), a highlight I will never forget. Lara's innings took twelve and three quarter hours to complete. The scenes of jubilation at the Antigua recreation ground, St Johns were incredible, with many of the crowd rushing onto the pitch to mob Lara. Play was held up for about seven minutes. I was so pleased to witness Sir Garfield, a true gentleman, strolling out to the wicket to shake Lara's hand. I am delighted to recall that I greeted Sir Garfield when he walked back to the pavilion. I'd walked onto the outfield and had the honour of shaking his hand, my own little bit of history.

During the Antigua test I came across another fanatical West Indian fan. Gravy, (real name, Labon Kenneth Blackburn Leeweltine Buckonon Benjamin), was very much an exhibitionist. He voluntarily entertained the Antiguan faithful with a variety of antics over a twelve – year period. Life was never dull with Gravy at the cricket ground. One day he would be dressed up as a cricketer, the next he would be dressed as a woman. He was more of an acrobat and showman than King Dal or Matt Fingle, always bringing a lot of colour to the occasion. He was fun, an eccentric, the authorities even afforded him a stage on the boundaries edge, where he would writhe and swing from the rafters. Outside the stadium there were lots of food stalls and rum shops, where after the days play we would partake in the odd drink and chat with the locals, who included Gravy and the Prime Minister!

Pam is convinced that it was all those wonderfully passionate Caribbean characters like Matt Fingle, Gravy and King Dal who inspired me, giving me the ideas and motivation to become a fan who likes to be noticed. In meeting the colourful personalities that followed the West Indian cricket team and the young Barmy Army fore runners, maybe Pam was right and the seeds were being sown for me one day to become Mr England. It's true my thirst for not being just another English supporter was ignited. Why couldn't I be an instantly recognisable and memorable fan, a figurehead able to galvanise England's army of followers? I am a big believer that if all the supporters are positive they can help inspire the team.

One evening at the end of play during the Antiguan test Dr Charles invited me to his home to meet his wife and have tea. His other guest was to be his old friend Christopher Martin Jenkins. I was really pleased as over the years I had read many of his cricket articles in The Daily Telegraph and was looking forward to meeting him. Unfortunately, Christopher Martin Jenkins didn't make it as there was a mess up with the arrangements regarding time and place. Dr Charles lived quite close to Sir Vivian Richards and as we drove past Sir Viv's house we chatted about him. I was aware that Sir Vivian was an icon for the island and was interested to learn more about him. Overall, I was surprised, I got the feeling that Dr Charles was not a big fan of Sir Viv's personality.

During Lara's historic innings we had been listening to the local radio station and I heard there was going to be a massive celebration party at a local sports field, organised by The Lions of Antigua. When we visited the local rum bar after the day's play, I asked one of the locals whom we'd got to know, 'where is the big do tonight?' He told us where it was and one of the guys came with us to show us the way.

When we got there, hundreds of people were all gathered in front of a big stage. We managed to negotiate our way through the throbbing crowds to the front near the stage where all the West Indian players were. Three or four of them, including Richie Richardson had their own band and they were playing calypso music. Various people made speeches congratulating Brian Lara on his innings, including Sir Vivian Richards who came on and congratulated Lara. Richards was Lara's idol. At the end of all the presentations, which were not formal by any means, Brian Lara came to the front of the stage and shook our hands.

The next night we were drinking in the rum bar again when the locals announced 'there's a party tonight, it's open to anybody!' Again, two or three of the Antiguan guys took us up to where it was all happening. It was a typical Caribbean street party anyone could go. There were little kiosks selling burgers and some free food available. The party was around Sir Vivian Richards mum's house and Viv was present. I got talking to him, he was my idol, I'd watched him play many times for Somerset at Taunton, an absolutely fantastic cricketer.

Dr Charles was such a delightful man and his hospitality was so typically West Indian. Pam and me vowed that on our next Caribbean holiday we would spend a few days in the tropical rain forest country of Dominica; a country that was renowned for being one of the last unspoilt rain forests in the world. Dr Charles had spoken so enthusiastically about the country that Pam and I just had to go. After all, how could we refuse, his sister was the Prime Minister and he had pledged to arrange our stay. Dr Charles booked our accommodation, taking great care of all the arrangements, including having a driver waiting at the airport to meet us. The driver was a charming bright young man who would collect us daily and show us around the island. Dr Charles even offered us the opportunity to meet his sister Dame Eugenia and to have afternoon tea with her at her official residence. Pam felt that was going a bit too far, but I would have liked to have met Eugenia.

Pilgrim fathers in Barbados

Simon with his Mum

Barbados

9

Hash House Harriers

OVER LAND AND SEA

I wanted to make a massive statement in support of Great Britain's competitors at the Atlanta Olympics 1996, so I decided to wear a bespoke British uniform. As I flew to America with my Union Jack design Arabian robe packed safely in my luggage, I was quietly confident that my meticulous preparations would pay dividends.

Prior to travelling to Atlanta, I decided that I would watch a diverse selection of sports that I knew I would enjoy. I made sure I had booked tickets for all the main athletic events, gymnastics, tennis and swimming. I was particularly keen to lend my support to the British competitors competing at some of the more traditional amateur sports, so I had arranged tickets for the boxing, badminton, hockey and table tennis too. Despite my best efforts I could not secure tickets for the cycling events because the demand was so high. Originally, I did have tickets for the synchronised swimming, (I wanted to study the form), but something else came up so I never made it, shame!

The first event I attended in Atlanta was the women's hockey, which was very well supported. Approximately 15,000 people watched, although there didn't seem to be many British fans present. I'd got my outfit organised in a little bag and as I sat there surrounded by hundreds of spectators I remember thinking to myself, 'well, I've brought the gear with me, I've got to wear it'. I popped to the toilet, got changed and returned with a little trepidation to my seat. Within a minute I noticed the television cameras and photographers were focussing on me and I guess that's where it all started. People have asked me, if I enjoyed all

Atlanta Olympics with Howard and Sam

of that attention. To be honest, on that first occasion I was a little bit embarrassed, but I could cope with that.

Credit has to go to my sister Margaret and her friend Eileen for making the Arabian outfit that became my own recognisable brand for the Olympics. I had originally planned to wear a Union Jack suit in the same mould as the Mr England gear I wear today. Thankfully, I decided that in the sweltering heat of Atlanta it wouldn't be practical, so I asked my sister to come up with a much cooler Arabian style design. It proved to be an excellent decision, as I could sit in the baking sun for hours watching the various events and I was always comfortable. Pam, had expressed concern that some Arabs may take offence at my costume. However, I was very positive and open minded and felt that this was an outfit that respected both Atlanta's conditions and the practicality of Arabian clothing.

At some of the events I attended there seemed to be only one man and his dog watching, leaving large open expanses of space in the vast stadiums. Personally, I saw this as a massive opportunity. Dressing up was certainly making me stand out, as was my Union Jack flag with 'Dawlish' emblazoned on it. It was easy for me to offer the highly visible support and encouragement to the athletes of Great Britain that I'd always intended. As a result I was fast becoming one of the most high profile supporters present at the 1996 Olympiad and I was certainly the proudest. My hopes and aspirations were coming true.

My mate, Howard Rowe, was also over in Atlanta with his son Sam, watching the Olympics. Howard, had a very soft spot for Denise Lewis, so even though we were staying at the same hotel, Howard and Sam had their own itinerary, usually involving Denise. We did spend lots of time watching the athletics together, while I also went solo to many of the less 'glamorous' events.

After I returned from watching the women's hockey on the first day, we all met up in a bar for a beer and a bite to eat. Two days before leaving for Atlanta, I had read a newspaper article written by Steve Cram, in which he recommended this particular establishment. On arriving in Atlanta, we had discovered Steve was booked in the same hotel as us. He'd obviously travelled to the States early to report on the lead up to the Games. In his article, Steve had given an insight into the facilities in Atlanta and what the travelling British supporters could expect to find when they arrived. Having read Steve's interesting piece, I decided there was one place we must visit, the bar just around the corner from our hotel with the topless waitresses!

Despite the distractions, pleasant as they were, we sat and watched the television coverage of that day's Olympic highlights. We were all excited to see my image popping up on screen on numerous occasions. Later that evening, I appeared on various American news channels and as I witnessed the fantastic reaction of the locals sat around me in the bar I realised that all my preparations had been worthwhile.

I remember Howard saying that night, 'I wish you had told me you were going to dress up, Sam and I would have liked to as well.' I hadn't dared to mention anything about it to Howard previously because to be honest I wasn't 100% sure until the last minute that I would carry it off. Throughout my life I had never enjoyed dressing up at fancy dress parties. This was different, dressing up in a sporting context I didn't have the same misgivings, I wanted to be seen supporting Great Britain.

The next morning Howard, Sam and I got on the coach to go to our selected days events. Once again, I was dressed in my Arabian gear and still feeling slightly self conscious. As I took my seat, people on the coach, (not just the Americans), stood up and started applauding me, much to the amusement of Howard and Sam. Unbelieveable! I had definitely captured people's imaginations and this really was the beginning of something very special in my life.

In time, most people in our hotel started to recognise me as the guy in the Great Britain outfit as they had witnessed me leaving the hotel in the mornings. Purely by chance, we were staying in the same hotel as the Radio 5Live commentary teams including John Inverdale. As a rugby man, I was particularly excited to see Cliff Morgan, the legendary Welsh rugby union player and original team captain on 'A Question of Sport'. At breakfast it was all quite casual and you could sit more or less wherever you fancied. One morning I sat with Cliff and Sean Kerly, the outstanding goal scorer and gold medal winning GB hockey player from the Seoul Olympics. Sean was debuting as a commentator for BBC sport.

I remember the three of us discussing Sean's future. We agreed it could be quite a lucrative career, analysing the sport you loved and had excelled at. Cliff was very high up in the BBC at this stage, an extremely shrewd operator, yet I could tell he was a man of the people. Cliff explained sympathetically that although Sean had all the attributes and persona to be a great commentator, hockey would only attract large audiences at the Commonwealth and Olympic Games and therefore was unlikely to ever have the consistent mass appeal of football or rugby. In conversation I cited Nigel Starmer-Smith, as an example of someone who had incorporated commentating on hockey having been established for years as a commentator and presenter of Rugby Special.

Sharing breakfast in the company of two sporting legends was allowing me a fascinating insight into the world of sport and media. What struck me most was that they were both incredibly decent, ordinary people. Cliff Morgan was a true legend, one of the worlds greatest ever rugby players and a really intelligent and articulate man, it was an honour to spend time with him.

As the Olympics unfolded it became increasingly apparent that Great Britain were not enjoying their greatest of games. We had so few genuine medal prospects and successes were very thin on the ground. I was over the moon to see Steve Smith take a bronze in the high jump, but after that early British triumph I did begin to wonder where the next medal was going to come from. I made a conscious decision to visit events that were not on my original itinerary. I listened to the pundits to see where they rated our chances of glory.

One of the first spontaneous events I attended was the rowing. I hired a car and set off on my own on the two hour journey from the hotel in Atalanta City to Lake Lanier in Georgia. Thankfully, after queuing for ages I managed to get a ticket and I was richly rewarded, witnessing a wonderful regatta in which the GB coxless four team picked up a bronze medal and Redgrave and Pinsent secured what would ultimately be our first and only gold medal of the entire games in the coxless pairs.

All the drama unfolded right in front of my fantastic position on the banks of the lake, overlooking the finishing line. My Union Jack robe and Great British flag ensured I attracted a lot of attention personally, while adding highly visible support to our competitors. After Redgrave and Pinsent had won the race they rowed right past me and they both gave me a thumbs up, a moment I cherish.

Moments later, a knackered Steve Redgrave who had just won his fourth consecutive gold medal gave a lakeside interview, where he uttered the immortal lines, 'If anyone sees me going anywhere near a boat you have got my permission to shoot me.' The relentless training and effort the rowers had put in to achieve their goals had made them true heroes of our nation. I was ecstatic for them, at last, I thought, Great Britain were off the mark and I was there!

I was becoming more and more comfortable in my new skin and I was finding watching the events dressed in my gear more enjoyable with every day that passed. My uniform ensured that I was becoming instantly recognisable myself and as a consequence I was being approached more and more. People of all ages and races were coming up and having their pictures taken with me, engaging in conversation and I loved it. Momentum was building, the more events I went to the more coverage I received, I was so proud to be 'representing' Great Britain.

Americans randomly approached me, said 'hi' and introduced themselves; they were typically American, so positive and supportive, whooping and hollering. British compatriots loved to sit and chat about what part of the UK they were from, tell me what their plans were and discuss what the weather was doing at home. Perhaps some realised that by sitting next to me, they were increasing their chances of featuring on the television coverage. This was a chance for them to be seen by their families back home, an opportunity to say 'hello mum' and announce, 'I was there.' I for one could identify with that!

These days we have become accustomed to peoples faces lighting up when they appear on the big screen in a stadium. Whether it's at Twickenham, on Henman Hill, at a football fixture or at the Twenty Twenty cricket, sports enthusiasts love nothing better than waving and smiling or even kissing the badge of the team they support when they get their moment of fame. It is noticeable these days how many people are prepared to dress up in all manor of guises to attract the attention of the cameras. For me it adds to the colour and the spectacle of the occasion, people having fun, that's what it's all about.

In 1996 at the Olympics I was unique amongst Great Britain supporters and had the attention to myself. It was really enjoyable meeting the hundreds of interesting and fascinating characters I encountered in Atlanta and I absolutely loved it. I'm a people person and this attention and friendliness was a lovely unexpected by product of my new found notoriety. Meanwhile, Great Britain were still not having the best of Olympics. As time passed, a desperate nation was craving for Great Britain to win another gold. Millions of sporting enthusiasts back home were still hoping for the best while watching and cheering on our guys and girls.

I had watched some of the tennis at the Games and needed no encouragement to go it alone again when it came to the Men's doubles final. There was a faint hope that Great Britain could win gold against the strong favourites the 'Woodies', Todd Woodbridge and Mark Woodforde. Whatever, we were guaranteed a silver medal and I had to be there. Tim Henman and Neil Broad had been catapulted into the spotlight with their heroics in reaching the final. Prior to the Olympics they had only played together once and that match had finished in defeat. The boys had done really well in defying the odds to reach the final and although they were massive underdogs I knew that win or lose it would be a very special occasion.

I happily queued for hours to get a ticket to watch the match in the sweltering 100 degree heat and was feeling very privileged to be present at Stone Mountain for the final. I was grateful that Margaret had made me such a cool outfit to wear the heat was so intense. I thought to myself, the weather was bound to be more to the liking of the Aussies, handicapping our boys even more. As I took my seat inside the stadium some fellow British fans sat around me and we did our best to support the lads, chanting GB throughout the match, all hoping for a miracle. During a break in sets, I went for a comfort break and was stopped by a gent', who introduced himself as John Barrett from the BBC. We had a brief conversation, John asked me a number of questions about myself and what I was up to.

Sadly our boys lost the final to the Australians and I was gutted for them and all of the British supporters. When I later heard from some friends at home that the legendary tennis commentator, John Barrett (who was married to Christine Trueman) had mentioned me during his commentary, I felt a lot happier. Apparently, John said something like, 'there is Peter Cross from Dawlish in Devon', as the cameras zoomed in on me. I'm told John continued, 'we have christened Peter 'Mr GB' as we see him at almost every event here at the Olympics'. I was so pleased to have been recognised for my support. Inadvertently, John and his colleagues had provided me with yet more inspiration and incentive to continue chasing my dream to become the nation's biggest sporting supporter.

I'm sure some people might think that I am an attention seeker, but I don't even contemplate that. Maybe I am guilty of being naïve, again I disagree. I am just a positive person who sees the good in everything and everybody, someone who happens to be massively passionate about his country and adores meeting people. It's an attitude to life.

Back in Atlanta, as I left the tennis stadium, I was stopped again, this time by BBC Radio 5's Clare Balding who I'd never met before. Clare was just starting out in her presenting career and I remember it was an absolutely brilliant interview, she really put me at my ease and made it easy for me to respond well to her questions. The interview went out live on BBC Radio 5 and Clare asked me various questions including what was my job back home and what I'd thought of the game. After the interview was finished, Clare asked what I was doing that night and would I like to go out with them all for a drink. I would have absolutely loved to gone out with them, but I had tickets for the athletics in the main stadium that night and had already arranged to meet Howard and Sam.

Since that original meeting I have met Clare at quite a few Rugby Internationals as her career has developed, she is a smashing person. Once in Ireland, some of my mates and I were in a pub enjoying the craic on the Friday afternoon before the international game at the weekend. Clare suddenly appeared and was looking to do some live interviews. Before I knew it, she had made a beeline to us and interviewed the boys and me. The next day I was at the stadium waiting for the England team coach to arrive. I noticed Clare was there too with her crew filming. After the team had disembarked and entered the stadium, Clare approached me, linked her arm in mine and said, 'come on lets go in the stadium together!'

When I got home after the Atlanta Olympics I became aware that I had received a lot of attention in the local media while I had been away. I saw photos of myself in the national newspapers, the Western Morning News and the Dawlish Gazette. Many of my friends and family told stories of how they had spotted me at the games. Westcountry Television were making a programme about entertainers in the South West which was being shown live weekly and was presented by Nick Owen, who had previously hosted some sports shows. Nick interviewed local celebrities, whether they were singers, dancers, or whatever. I received an invite to appear on the show and I travelled down to Plymouth wearing my Union Jack gear as had been agreed. I was introduced as someone who had become famous at the Atlanta Olympics. Nick interviewed me and I can remember thinking, I can't believe how nervous I am. I suppose I'd never done anything like that in my life before. Anyhow, it was really good fun and I'm told that the interview was well received.

After the success of my Atlanta Olympics experience and the joy of meeting some wonderful people, I decided I was going to make a conscious effort to become Mr Great Britain in a similar manner to Ken Baily. Ken was famous for being at many England soccer and rugby games at Wembley and Twickenham in the 60's, 70's and 80's and was a memorable figure to most sporting fans of my generation, instantly recognisable in his John Bull outfit. My instincts told me the country needed a figure like that again and lets face it I'd had a ball in the States. Like so many people, I am massively patriotic about England and Great

Britain. I felt my support had made a difference in some small way in Atlanta and I wanted to build on that.

I vowed that I would support Great Britain at as many sporting occasions as I possibly could. Amongst other things, I attended the Riverside centre in Exeter dressed up in my full Arabian costume to watch Great Britain play an international badminton match. I was determined to do everything I possibly could to be recognised as Mr Great Britain. I went along with my friend Howard and a whole group of his friends from Seaton, they all helped me not to feel quite so conspicuous.

Every Summer I went to the England cricket home test matches at Lords and Edgbaston. I was also a regular supporter of Exeter Rugby Club, who were in the third tier of the English leagues in those days. I had played for Exeter myself when I was younger. When I watched Exeter I took a large Union Jack flag with Exeter Rugby Club written on it and I would carefully place it in the most conspicuous position near the tunnel. I even wore my Arab outfit at some of the 'must win games!'

In 1998 part of my ongoing campaign included dragging my wife Pam, who is not at all interested in sport, all the way across to Kuala Lumpar, Malaysia for the Commonwealth Games with my mate Howard and his girlfriend Kathy. Howard, Kathy and I dressed in Union Jack gear for the Games; Pam ended up acting as unofficial photographer.

We had a brilliant time supporting all the home nations in their quest for medals and we were lucky enough to secure front row seats for all the main events. I'll never forget, just after Denise Lewis won the heptathlon gold medal, she was joyously running around the track doing her lap of honour, as she came past where we were sitting, she suddenly made a beeline directly towards us, screaming 'yeah' as she came, Howard was wetting his pants!

We watched all the athletic events and the hockey and everywhere we went we took the great big six foot wide Union Jack flag that I'd had made up with, 'Exeter Rugby Club,' emblazoned on it. Howard and I would each hold an end up. The attention we created for ourselves was amazing, wow!

A couple of parents of some Scottish competitors approached me at one event and asked me, quite seriously, 'How can you be English and wear a Union Jack?' I answered, 'I am supporting England number one and Scotland, Wales and Northern Ireland second, I am supporting all of the United Kingdom athletes. I think I must have sounded like Eric Morecombe when he famously responded to Andre Previn's criticism by saying, 'I'm playing all the right notes-but not necessarily in the right order!' England managed 36 Gold medals, Scotland 3, Wales 3 and Northern Ireland 2 and we were very pleased for all of our teams.

After the closing ceremony, it was absolutely chaotic leaving the stadium. We couldn't get a taxi or a bus for love nor money. Pam had had more than enough after a full week of sport, so in the end I suggested we all walk up the slipway towards the motorway which was above stadium level and see if we could get a lift from there. A car eventually stopped as we held out a thumb, it must have helped that I was in my full uniform. The passenger asked where we were heading, we told him the name of the hotel we were staying at and he asked us to jump in. It turned out to be a chauffeur driven car and the gentleman that had asked us to hop in was the Minister of Tourism for Malaysia! We had a great chat about all the arrangements and things and the best bit was, they didn't charge us for the ride!

RULE BRITTANIA

The first time I wore an outfit at Twickenham for an England Rugby match was in November 1996 for the Argentina fixture. I must have looked a right prat as no one dressed up to attend rugby internationals in those days. I wore the Arabian style Union Jack robe that I had worn in Atlanta at the Olympics. Back in 1996, rugby was as traditional a sport as you could imagine. Many of the spectators wore Barber jackets and green Wellington boots and certainly didn't dream of taking a flag to wave at the games. There was hardly any sign of sponsorships at that time, the Cotton Traders range of rugby shirts were the closest thing you would get to today's branding and professionalism. I have to say, it did take a lot of guts and soul searching before deciding to give it a go, but I was determined to throw myself into it.

I arrived at Twickenham dressed in my bespoke Union Jack Arabian outfit and went to meet the team coaches feeling more than slightly conspicuous. For moral support I had a few of my mates with me. I did try to encourage them to dress up too, but none of them were interested.

Looking back, I'm so happy that I made the decision to go for it. Who could have guessed back then where I would end up? I stood nervously for what seemed an eternity in my now familiar position in front of the main west stand and awaited the arrival of the England team. When the team coach finally drew up, I made a point of greeting all the players individually as they stepped off the coach. I will never forget the England captain Will Carling saying, 'well done,' as he passed me, that definitely made me feel a bit more comfortable. I had arrived! (I understand as the team arrived the television commentator said something about me being the guy that was at the Olympics)

We excitedly entered the magnificent stadium and immediately headed down to the tunnel area to soak in the atmosphere and to be as close to the action as possible.

I was on a massive high, flushed with the success of greeting the England team and seemingly meeting with their approval, my confidence had soared. The adrenalin rush I had first experienced in Atlanta was again coursing through my whole body. I felt surprisingly at ease, as if I were part of the event, the same sense of belonging had returned.

Unsurprisingly to me, given my Olympic experience, a few fellow supporters came down to have a chat with me. Fans universally seemed to like having someone they could identify with, share their views with, whether it was the rugby, the weather, my outfit or the atmosphere in the stadium. I really appreciated their interest in me. The pin badges I wore on my uniform were often the catalyst for conversations. People were fascinated to learn what other events I had been to and were interested in learning more about my dedication and commitment to supporting our sporting teams around the world. Some supporters asked if they could have their photos taken with me, reminding me again of that special Atlanta feeling, further lifting my spirits and confidence. I was buzzing!

Two stewards, coincidently both called Colin, patrolled the tunnel area at Twickenham in those days and they both approached me and questioned me about my outfit. Colin Buckle shook my hand and chatted with me, checking me out a bit I guess. After about five or ten minutes Colin commented, 'you're going to go a long way Peter, make sure I'm your agent!' Those early conversations with Colin Buckle and Colin Whitford led to a very special relationship that has borne a lot of fruit over many of the intervening years.

Indeed, not long after that initial encounter I was at another international and Colin Buckle invited me into the tunnel area for a warming cup of tea with him and a policeman. This became a bit of a routine and I began to recognise people like Richard Prescott, the RFU Director of Communications, Sarah Swaby, the Press Officer and other officials who were passing by in the vicinity. Colin regularly invited me into the tunnel area for a chat and a cuppa and I soon encountered Richard Prescott again.

My great mate Colin Buckle

I was still unaware of Richard's position within the RFU when on this occasion he approached me. He looked at my pin badges and said, 'you don't have this one' and promptly gave me the official England pin that the players were wearing. I was so chuffed! Richard would have a massive part to play in the future.

After the games ended, my mates from Devon would routinely come with me to the pub in Twickenham used by Colin Buckle and his mates for a few drinks. If we travelled up on a Friday night we would join Colin and his friends and all go out together. I was becoming a really good friend of Colin and his mates, in fact we all thoroughly enjoyed being in their company. Periodically, Colin would suggest to me that he would like to be my agent, he definitely recognised the potential of my role.

One evening, Colin enquired, 'where do you park Pete? My mum and dad live near to the stadium, you can park there if you like on match days.' Brilliant! I had a priceless parking space very close to the stadium that I went on to use for many years, courtesy of Colin's parents. Years later, as a small thank you, I gave Colin's mum, the only existing replica of Billy the Bulldog for allowing me to park on their drive. I believe she's still got it in her house now. I'm still friendly with Colin, even though he

1999 World Cup with Lawrence D'allaglio

hasn't been a steward for about ten years. He lives in Twickenham and I meet up with him from time to time and have a drink the night before a game. I remind Colin that he wanted to be my agent all those years ago, therefore, he owes me thousands of pounds in expenditure costs that I have incurred, the very least he can do is buy me a pint!

In those early years of being an unofficial mascot I received terrific support from so many people. Two England rugby legends were exceptionally supportive, Lawrence D'allaglio, who like me is someone who wears his heart on his sleeve and Roger Uttley another former England captain who is a massive patriot. Lawrence has always been a top man and not just with me. I have witnessed Lawrence giving his time to complete strangers and showing a genuine interest in them. Lawrence is such an articulate, intelligent and friendly guy. The English rugby supporters were brilliant too, the best in the world. It is an honour for me to be recognised and appreciated by such enthusiastic, passionate, England rugby fans all over the world. Long before the days of smart phones fans would come up to me and ask for a photo with an ordinary digital camera. To this day, I am approached by men and women who excitedly show a picture of me with them when we were both clearly a lot younger.

In 1997, when the Lions toured South Africa, buoyed by my successes in Atlanta and at Twickenham I decided to go on the full tour with my mate Jack Smith, Pam and Jack's wife Mary. I didn't really have a clue how to organise the tour or how to get tickets, so I rang one of the guys who I'd met on the plane to Atlanta, a member of the soon to be Barmy Army and asked, 'How could I get tickets for the Lions tour?' He replied, 'Pete we are going places and we are really into our sport, but we haven't really got any contacts to help you with rugby tickets and travel'.

The Barmy Army and I were all starting out at similar times, but we were still in our embryo days. Sometimes, I had considered my own future, wondering whether I may be better as part of a group. Again and again I'd come to the conclusion that I wanted to be an individual and do my own thing. I didn't want to be part of a group. I often meet some of the original guys from the Barmy Army, when they come over and greet me warmly outside Twickenham. We have a good laugh and reminisce about how we all started years ago. They are all really good lads who love their sport, just like me. It's incredible how we have all made such an impact, doing what we love, following our Countries sporting teams around the world.

We eventually booked up our South African trip through Gulliver's travel, arranging tickets for the matches and the flights, but booking our hotel stops independently, that way I could placate Pam a little by seeing and visiting some of South Africa's landmarks and stunning country.

This was our first Lions tour and it coincided with the first professional Lions tour ever, the professional era had only started some two years previously. In many ways the Lions were massive underdogs. However, we had some warriors who were unknown to the Springbok's. Professionalism meant some rugby league boys had been introduced into our union teams and the selectors picked quite a few of them. The squad had a compliment of exceptional ex-league players who would prove to be crucial throughout the tour, John Bentley, Scott Gibbs, Scott Quinell and Allan Bateman to name a few.

The first test was in Cape Town and on our flight to South Africa we realised there were some British Lions legends including Dean Richards and Robert Jones on board. They were flying out to participate in a golden oldies legends game. Jack and I had been very thorough and meticulous in our planning, although for some reason we had failed to mention to the girls that on the day we were due to arrive in South Africa, there was a midweek Lions fixture in the afternoon!

Deano

We arrived in Cape Town after a fourteen hour flight, picked up our hire car and I started driving direct to the stadium. The girls naturally assumed we were heading to the hotel. As we approached the stadium the astonished girls exclaimed, 'blimey, it's busy, look at all the Lions fans that are staying at our hotel.' Up until that moment I hadn't had the heart to tell them I'd got four tickets and we were going to watch a game of rugby! We gently explained to them our devious and cunning plan and waited for the inevitable reaction. They were visibly shocked, but probably too tired to complain too much. Jack and I were buzzing. We had successfully plotted to slip in a game of rugby before we'd even reached our hotel, the girls could not believe it!

Our hotel was in Stellenbosch and we eventually arrived there after the game in the early evening. The girls were still reeling from their 'surprise' so we set about earning some brownie points. We promised them we would visit all of South Africa's iconic locations, perhaps do a safari, things for them would only get better. Climbing Table Mountain would be the first adventure on the agenda a few days later.

As usual we were meticulous in our planning, ensuring the climb was conducted in the morning, leaving plenty of time to get back to the hotel and get changed in preparation for the Golden Oldies game that was being played that night. It was a really enjoyable ascent, although because we were approaching from the rear of the mountain, (the easier route), we were unaware of what awaited us. We were joined by hundreds of other Brits all with the same agenda. The atmosphere amongst us was superb. We'd heard that you could climb to the summit of the mountain and catch the cable car back down, which was a blessed relief considering the age of most of us, and the state of our hips and knees. We finally reached the top and were immediately informed that the cable car was closed. We had no choice but to walk all the way back down, there might have been some swearing!

The Golden Oldie Lions were playing the South African Oldies in Stellenbosch and we were seriously worried we wouldn't make it in time. To save crucial minutes, we all decided we would have to descend down the steepest part of the mountain, following the cable car route. It was really quite hilarious. There were loads of Lions supporters, all of a certain age staggering down the mountain as quickly as possible. We made it to the match in time and as the game kicked off we were still laughing at the sight of so many of our fellow fans hobbling about rubbing their knees.

Soon, the First Test match would be upon us. The big one and I was ready for it. I just hoped the team was. I was going to be wearing a new outfit; a top hat and tails in a Union Jack design, which once again I had had made especially by my sister's friend Eileen. I had invested a lot of time and effort into developing the right image and the suit was perfect for supporting the Lions.

On the way to the stadium in Cape Town before the match, Jack (who had also dressed up) and I were stopped and interviewed by Phil Edwards the Sky Sports reporter. You really feel as if you are part of the occasion when this happens. Back home in the UK the interview went to air ten minutes before the match kicked off. Lots of our mates were out and about in Dawlish and throughout Devon watching the coverage in rugby clubs and apparently there was quite a reaction. 'Look, there's Crossy and Jack!' people shouted. I'm aware that there are some people who like to say they know me, or that I am from their town. In a way they are sharing in my enjoyment I guess? I'm pretty comfortable when it comes to giving interviews I quite enjoy them. Having played the game for years and watched hundreds of matches I am confident in my ability to analyse

Lions tour, South Africa

a fixture. In this instance, I suggested to Phil that the Lions needed to stand up to the massive front row of the Springboks and if we could do that we would win. As it was, we picked a small front row, the players were short and squat and they managed to get under the big animals of South Africa and out scrummaged them.

That First Test was a momentous occasion. The rugby league boys brought with them extra dynamism, power, fitness and a massive will to win. It was a fantastic game to watch, the lead changed hands regularly and the physical battle was brutal. Scott Gibbs led the charge when he took the ball into contact with Os Du Randt, bosh! He steamrollered the Bok's mammoth prop and knocked him arse over tit, an iconic moment in Lions rugby, which fired up the team and provided great momentum. Meanwhile, Neil Jenkins (playing totally out of position at full back) was superb throughout the game. In fact, Neil continued that brilliant form throughout the whole tour kicking almost 100% of his opportunities. Matt Dawson won the game for the Lions with a brilliant individual try. He threw an outrageous dummy, skinned the South Africans captain and number 8 Gary Teichmann and scored in the corner. I've got to know him a little since then and that try was typical of Matt who was a typical scrum half, very talented, confident and a bit cocky. What impressed me most about Matt Dawson was that after games he had time for the supporters wanting autographs and photos, I liked that.

Back in South Africa, the team and the supporters were euphoric, I was

28

buzzing, what a result! For the rest of the tour we developed a pre match routine we hoped would ensure maximum coverage. Jack and I arrived at the venue nice and early for every fixture in our outfits, making sure we were there to greet the team coach. It wasn't rocket science, but it worked. We were getting to be known by the players, the media and our fellow supporters and we loved it!

One night, between the Test Matches, we were travelling from Cape Town to Durban and we stayed in this little place in the middle of nowhere called Hogs Hollow. Pam had read about it in the paper and it was highly recommended. When we arrived we immediately noticed about eighteen people sat around a communal table. Jack recognised Micky Steele-Bodger CBE, a true rugby legend who he'd met previously at an event in Redruth, Cornwall organised by Bill Bishop who was the President of the Rugby Union in 1995/6. Micky is the long standing President of the Barbarians, had been President of the RFU in 1973/4, Chairman of the International Rugby Board and was an ex England back row forward.

We were invited to join them all at the table and much to our surprise we found ourselves alongside the rugby correspondent of the 'Daily Telegraph', Mick Cleary. Owen Slot, who became current chief sports reporter of 'The Times', but was then writing for the 'Telegraph', covering for Paul Ackford who couldn't make the trip. Also present were a couple of other ex players, while I had the pleasure of being sat next to Micky and his wife Muff, whose father used to run Edinburgh Academicals -another famous Barbarian type team.

We had a brilliant evening chatting away all night. They were really friendly, interesting rugby people and we loved their company. Micky had great pleasure in announcing that he recognised us, saying, 'you are the two silly buggers who dress up and greet the players off the coach looking like prats!' Sure enough when we welcomed the Lions players off the coach at the next game Micky and Muff were there. They came over and were shaking our hands, saying 'well done boys' and taking the piss.

South Africa is an absolutely stunning, beautiful country but we had been left in no doubt when we were in Cape Town, to be extremely careful in certain townships as we travelled to Durban. Travelling with male companions all over the world I have always felt totally safe, but when you are with ladies who are very important to you it can be a stressful time.

When we travelled to Durban and en route passed through the area Nelson Mandela had been raised, The Transkei, we had been advised not to stop the car for anyone as the threat of car jacking was extremely high in that province. Jack was driving and he followed the advice to the letter. If anyone came anywhere near the car Jack pressed his foot down on the accelerator and whoosh we sped off!

When we were finally flagged down at a real police road block, I remember screaming, 'stop' at Jack as we approached it. I was really worried he wasn't going to stop because we were so afraid of encountering bogus police officers, but these were genuine! Thankfully, Jack came to a halt just in time as the police pulled him over and we followed their instructions. I don't mind admitting I was still shaking by the time we got to Durban, what a journey! On arrival we booked into a superb hotel that had been recommended to us by a sports physio we knew from Torquay who was working in South Africa. Opposite the hotel was a cracking bar with loads of stunning waitresses to look after us. Touring with the Lions was still great fun.

We were full of excitement as we got to the stadium for the second Test in Durban, a win would secure the series. The arena was vast and the stands were incredibly steep. It felt as if you were on a tight rope climbing the steps up to your position in the stand, really precarious. Scanning the stands I clocked a big guy I thought I recognised, yes, it was John Fiddler who had played for Gloucester and was an England player too. I went over and introduced myself to him and explained that I had played for Exeter and had played in matches against Gloucester, John was a great bloke, we got on really well and exchanged numbers. John proved to be a great contact as he is a close friend of John Hall owner of Gullivers travels.

The match was a really tight affair. Jenkins was kicking his goals, keeping us in the game. Jeremy Guscott dropped a goal near the end of the match to put us in the lead, I don't think I'd ever seen Guscott drop a goal in my life. The South Africans launched a typically ferocious fightback and Lawrence D'allaglio put in a tremendous try saving tackle as we held on. We'd won the series and we were on a massive high.

When we left the stadium the defeated South African supporters were still enjoying their barbeques by their cars as is common practice. A couple invited us over to join their party, probably because we stood out in our

Union Jack gear. Although we'd never met them before we had a brilliant time and in conversation we mentioned we were going to be travelling up to the Drakensburg mountains when we left Durban. They immediately said, 'on your way up, come and join us on our farm', so we did! Two days later we turned up at their farm in the middle of nowhere and stayed the night. Once again their hospitality was brilliant, rugby people the world over are like that.

Due to some heavy snow in the mountains we reluctantly had to reroute our journey. It wasn't so bad as we were able to earn some brownie points by taking the girls to Rorke's Drift, scene of the Zulu massacre. Following on we went to St Lucia on the coast and stayed at a bed and breakfast. Our host regaled us with many stories about life in Africa. St Lucia is known for being home to large numbers of hippopotamuses. The most humorous story he told us was, when one evening whilst he was in his garden, he heard screaming. He looked up to see a local villager, in his words, pedalling like fuck on his bike, up the street. He observed the villager being chased by an extremely quick hippo' and he continued that the expression on the poor soul's face showed he felt his judgement time had come! Our host never discovered the fate of that poor chap, but he did explain that locals were often killed by hippopotamuses.

Next up for us was the compulsory safari we had promised the girls. After hearing that story we decided we would keep our distance from the wildlife and enjoy the memorable scenery from the safety of our jeep.

The tour was going brilliantly. The rugby had been immense and we were having the time of our lives in beautiful South Africa. By the time we reached Johannesburg, the Lions had already secured the series and the party was just beginning. Johannesburg, located in the north of South Africa, has a reputation for violence that is well documented worldwide. We stayed in the relatively safe area of Sandton prior to the Third Test. Nevertheless, we were advised to be very careful and make sure we booked our taxis to the game via the hotel.

The anticipation before the final test was huge, could we win the series three nil? First things first, we had to get there safely. Scary stories abounded about people who were picked up by, 'taxi drivers,' who pretended to get lost, before proceeding to a hostile location where the victims could be robbed, raped or even murdered. It was extremely intimidating but we listened to the advice we were given and arranged our taxi through the hotel. Our recommended taxi driver turned out to be a really nice cheery fellow. He dropped us off at the Coca Cola tower, agreeing we would meet him at the same spot soon after the game. We were dropped off in one of the roughest, most frightening suburbs of Jo'burg, immediately opposite the stadium.

We made our way to the stadium and waited outside, ready for the coach to arrive and to greet the players. When the team arrived, we were shocked to see team manager Ian McGeechan had a crew cut. He'd agreed with the squad to have his head shaved if we won the series. The players were in really good form and Jack and I were chatting away with some of them as they walked into the stadium. Before we knew it we had entered the stadium. We had no official accreditation, yet we were walking around the pitch with the team, nobody had challenged us! Eventually, when we had gone half way around the pitch I said to Jack, 'we shouldn't be here mate, we had better break away from the group before we end up in the changing room with them.' It was brilliant! No one had questioned us, even as we walked back out of the stadium. Looking back, it was another sign of things to come for me personally.

We went into the game with a depleted squad and finished up losing a very open game. It didn't matter, we were totally happy, we'd won the series! When the game was over we were pleased to join the Gulliver's crowd at a reception they were attending. Their departure from the reception coincided with when we were due to meet our taxi. We were relieved we would be in the safety of a large group as we walked across from the stadium to their pick up point, which was thankfully adjacent to ours. Unfortunately for us, the Gulliver's posse were quickly collected and were on their way, leaving Pam and me, Jack and Mary waiting nervously for our taxi to arrive.

We waited and waited, the taxi was late, 'where the hell was he?' we all wondered. I was becoming increasingly worried. Were we going to become the latest victims in that notorious ghetto? I felt like a sitting duck dressed in my Union Jack attire, I was very afraid, it was dark and you could smell the danger in the air. Feeling extremely vulnerable myself was bad enough, but I also felt a massive responsibility for Pam, who lets face it didn't really want to be at the rugby in the first place, for Jack and

Mary as well of course. It was surreal, moments earlier we had all been celebrating an historic test series victory over South Africa, now suddenly that euphoria had been put sharply into perspective.

The relief when the cheery taxi guy finally turned up was immense. We could all relax again and look forward to a big party back at the hotel. What happened next was unbelievable. The driver got lost. We couldn't believe it. We sat in his taxi shitting ourselves. I'm sure we were all thinking of the plots we had been warned about. I looked in his eyes for clues. His expression had changed, he looked and sounded terribly scared and he repeatedly blurted out, 'uuurgh, I'm lost, I'm lost'. Pre planned or not, we were in serious peril and we knew it, the colour was draining from our faces. Our destiny was in the taxi driver's hands and he was clearly as worried as we were. Nervously, he negotiated his way through dimly lit, frightful, back alleyways, in the heart of one of the most notorious parts of the city. Eventually, he did manage to navigate his way out of downtown Jo'burg and we made it back to the hotel. After tipping him generously we all headed straight to the bar and boy did we down some beers! I said, 'there is no way am I leaving this fucking hotel tonight!'

Soon after that experience, to treat the girls and compensate for the stress we had put them through, we decided that while we were in Johannesburg we should travel to the Victoria Falls in Zimbabwe. We knew they would love the opportunity to see them. By that time, we all felt that we didn't want to spend any more time in Johannesburg than was absolutely necessary. We booked our flights and accommodation, ensuring the timings allowed us to return and immediately connect with our flights home to the U.K. While walking around the Victoria Falls we bumped into a guy called Bill who I knew well from Old Merchant Taylors Rugby Club. He was a senior club member and had been coming to Teignmouth Rugby Club on the annual Easter tour for years. Coincidently, I had bumped into Bill years before at an Antiguan test match. Small world!

IN ENGLAND'S GREEN
AND PLEASANT LAND

Travelling the world and meeting so many interesting people, some of them quite famous, appeals to me and is an enjoyable bonus of what I do. Why do I think I have this great desire to mix with people and socialise, to be recognised, or be seen on the television? I honestly can't answer that. I had a fairly normal upbringing, a relatively happy childhood. I've never felt the need to consult a psychologist!

I was born in Oldham during the Second World War, my sister was born at the end of the war. The first house I remember being brought up in was a three bedroom terraced house, similar to the ones you see on Coronation Street or in a Lowry painting. My mum Edna, my dad Ray, my sister Margaret, my grandad and myself all lived there under the same roof. There wasn't an indoor bathroom or toilet in the house, so when you went to bed you would take a jerry pot with you and keep it under the bed in case you needed a pee in the night. The proper toilet was in the garden. It wasn't a flushing toilet, there was a tipping pan down a big hole. When it got heavy it would tilt and tip the contents. This was real austerity, the period of rebuilding just after the war. There were few of the home comforts we all take for granted these days, no automatic washing machines, no soft toilet paper. We hand washed our clothes and tore newspapers up and down into squares when we had the call of nature, unbelieveable! Once a week we would fill a big round tub, which was about three foot high, with hot water, get it to the right temperature and

Hello, Hello. Dad on left patrolling the Penny Rush at Watersheddings

put it in front of the fire. One at a time, we would all get in the same bathwater, scary.

Prior to the war, my dad had worked at Metrovix. He'd been an electrical engineer working on aircraft. During World War Two my dad met my mum, they got married and he was called up to serve in the Navy. Myself and my younger sister Margaret were born during this time. I spent the first year of my life living in Plymouth where dad was stationed. After leaving the Navy, dad became a policeman in Oldham where for many years he was a motorbike rider in the force, later becoming the Coroners officer. At home, I remember dad having his own bike with a sidecar, he used to take us out for rides, great fun at the time.

After giving birth to my sister Margaret, my mum became very depressed and dad has since informed me she found it very difficult coping with family life. Mum spent a lot of time going in and out of mental homes to be treated. In those days, people with problems were often quickly diagnosed as having a mental illness and treated appallingly. They were put into mental institutions and treated like prisoners, which is so difficult to understand nowadays. I was about ten when mum and dad got divorced and dad got custody of Margaret and me. As you can imagine I was utterly devastated. However, dad was now our custodian and we were already used to him doing so much with us, when mum was not around, so we had kind of got used to it.

At Roundthorn junior school in Oldham I remember most of the

Mag on Dad's motor bike and sidecar

Me, 3rd row from the back, 3rd right

kids wore clogs (I don't recall Lowry painting us matchstick men though!) because they were so hard wearing. I struggled with English lessons, although I was always very good at Mathematics. In order to help improve my English, dad encouraged me to write to far flung football clubs, with exotic names like Partick Thistle and Wolverhampton Wanderers, asking for autographs or programmes, anything these fascinating institutions in my imagination could spare. I threw myself into writing with a passion that only a sporting connection could inspire. Impatiently, I would

Mum and Dads Wedding

wait for the next day to arrive and the postman to deliver a package. I watched excitedly as the postie walked towards our house with a letter and my heart would sink if it wasn't addressed to me. I'd soon bounce back and would be full of optimism again, tomorrow, I will be lucky, I'd tell myself. I was lucky and I received numerous responses from famous football clubs and players. My English certainly improved as I developed more imaginative ways of securing a reply from those distant heroes.

In my early teens Greenacres Church in Oldham was at the centre of my social life as I was growing up. On a Sunday I would go to the church service in the morning, Sunday school in the afternoon and the service in the evening. After Sunday school I remember going back to a friends house and snogging with girls. The church owned their own cricket pitch and the team played in the Oldham leagues, which was my first introduction to senior cricket. There is no doubt the church played a big part in my upbringing and had a massive influence on family life in Oldham back then.

When I was about thirteen the church were trying to raise funds and encouraged the youngsters to come up with ideas. I came up with the idea off buying off cuts at the local sawmill which I then chopped up to make fire wood. I knocked on all the doors in my local neighbour-hood and was amazed at how much I sold on behalf of the church. This led to me starting my own little business supplying cut firewood which I dragged round fully loaded on my home made 'bogey' (go kart). Part of this entailed me cohersing my little sister Margaret into spending hours in our back yard chopping the wood. I seem to remember paying her with the occasional bag of sweets. My parents often said that they thought it was the start of my selling career, although they did think I took advan-tage of my younger sister.

Dad took Margaret and I on some wonderful holidays to North Wales and the Lake District on his motorbike. He would shove Margaret and me and all the camping equipment in the sidecar and off we would go, looking like a scene out of The Last of the Summer Wine! I remember how all the mills and factories, offices and schools all used to close down for the Wakes weeks, Oldham would come to a stand still and everybody in the town would go away on their holidays. Years later in 1963, I was amazed when walking the beat in Torquay that I recognised dozens of friendly faces from my hometown enjoying the annual getaway. If you couldn't afford to go away in Wakes weeks there would be some compensation for the children left at home. The fair would visit Oldham and those children left at home would flock to the fairground in the centre of the town.

Once, dad took us all the way down to Wembley in the twin sidecar to watch the Rugby League Challenge Cup Final. It was a massive pilgrimage for the folk from the North and I loved the colour and vibrancy created by both teams' wonderful fans. The 1953/4 final between Warrington and Halifax ended in a draw, four all, in front of over 81,000 people. The replay was at the Odsal stadium in Bradford. I didn't go, although over 102,000 people did. Incredible.

Many years later, when dad was enjoying his retirement in Bournemouth with my step mum Alice, I ended up making my own annual pilgrimage to the old Wembley stadium with a crowd of blokes from Dawlish and Teignmouth. We would all go up on the train to watch the Rugby League Challenge Cup Final. The main driving force for me was the opportunity of being able to invite dad and my sister's husband Roger along too. We'd meet them at Paddington station, I would book some of the best tickets

Rugby League Challenge Cup Final Day

available in the Olympic Gallery and treat my dad to a grand day out. Dad loved his rugby league probably more than me. The Challenge Cup Finals provided him with many memorable experiences during his lifetime, it was such a massive weekend every year for all the Northern fans.

The most memorable final my pals, dad, Roger and I attended during this period was when Teignmouth's very own Jim Fallon represented Leeds against the all conquering Wigan team in 1994. Jim was up against the legendary Martin Offiah on his wing. This was the era of Wigan domination. They were a tremendous team, packed full of international superstars. Andy Farrell, Shaun Edwards and Martin Offiah to name just a few. Leeds had a great team too, Ellery Hanley, the Iro brothers, top players, plus Jimmy who a lot of my mates had played with or against when he was starting out with Teignmouth. I only came across Jim the once myself, when I was playing for Teignmouth Vets. We had a training session a week before we were due to host a touring vets team from Sydney. Jimmy was about eighteen at the time and he was in the opposing team. It was only a training game, but it was a proper match. I remember tackling him and I felt so much power coming through his body, I thought the best way of surviving was to let go! I can clearly remember thinking what a powerful boy he was. Jim went on to play rugby union for Bath and England A. Apparently Dick Best told him he'd be in the England first team the next year, but he signed professionally to play for Leeds in rugby league.

That year was like any other, we always did it in style. It wasn't just a day to treat dad, my pals and I liked to make it an occasion to remember too. The Friday evening before every final, my mates and I would go to Marks and Sparks and buy loads of booze and put together some top quality food to complete a luxury picnic hamper. We'd take table cloths, napkins, serviettes, proper wine glasses, bottles of vodka, bottles of gin, loads of bottles of wine and pack it all in wicker baskets. Once we arrived at Paddington we would leave most of it in left luggage, keeping some aside for dad and Roger. Then we'd go and meet them as they got off their train from Dorset, before all heading off to Wembley together to watch the match.

We would always have a brilliant day at the final but the Wigan versus Leeds final in 1994 was so memorable. John Ware's report from the Herald Express local newspaper will give you a flavour of how the match and our support of a local favourite panned out. Published with the article was a photo of Jim Fallon scoring a try and another of me and some of my pals soaking up the atmosphere.

'South Devon rugby star Jim Fallon may have been on the losing side in the Wembley cauldron at the weekend-but at least he had his name emblazoned in lights at the famous stadium. Thousands of fanatical Leeds supporters and a couple of dozen from the Teignmouth area erupted with arms raised and whoops of joy as the burly winger scored a brilliant try to put his side back in the match against Wigan in the Rugby League Cup Final.

The name J Fallon was flashed up on the giant scoreboards at either end of the world famous ground. Millions of television viewers at home and around the world were able to savour his storming run to the line in slow motion and from different camera angles. And the fans were even more ecstatic when Fallon set up the pass for his team mate, Great Britain skipper Gary Schofield to burst over to take Leeds within two points of the league champions in the second half as the temperature on the pitch soared to nearly 100 degrees F.

For a time it seemed the mighty, all conquering Wigan were reeling as Leeds piled on the pressure, but the Lancashire club survived the onslaught and struck back to finish clear winners at 26-16, thanks to some moments of magic from their ace paceman Martin Offiah, who was named man of the match.

But the small but vocal Teignmouth contingent who watched one of the most exciting and entertaining finals for years, were not disappointed.

Fallon was always in the thick of the action in both attack and defence and achieved a unique double – the first player to appear in rugby cup finals at both Twickenham and Wembley. He was in the Bath side that took the cup at Twickers two seasons before.

His father, Terry, a former Irish international and mum Sue, who now run a hotel in Teignmouth, were there in the crowd with the rest of the family, including Jim's twin sister, Julie, who flew over from Belfast. Unlike football, there was no segregation of fans at Wembley and no trouble. Leeds and Wigan supporters, including a large number of women and children, stood shoulder to shoulder with their banners and flags. Although the banter flowed constantly between the two deadly rivals, it was all good natured with everybody enjoying a thrilling game of rugby played in brilliant sunshine. It was a great day out.

Fallon started his rugby career at Bitton Park, Teignmouth and locals who were lucky enough to obtain tickets said his performance was first rate. Dawlish gift shop proprietor Tony Welsh said, 'We must have been Leeds' most southerly supporters and their fans could not make out why a bunch of Devon lads were screaming just as hard as them. When they shouted 'Yorkshire' we yelled 'Devon' but nobody cared because it was a carnival atmosphere.' A drained Jim said afterwards 'it was a great game and the Leeds fans were great. 'Thanks to all my old mates who made the journey up from Devon.'

What a brilliant day we'd had and yet as was the case for every final we went to, the fun had only just begun! Having bade a fond farewell to dad and Roger we recovered our stash, boarded our train for the journey back to Devon and prepared to party. Before the train had even left Paddington we had found our reserved seats, cleared the tables and put on the tablecloths. By the time we'd reached Reading, we would have had a few gin and tonics and some hors d'oeuvres. It was brilliant. People walking past our picnic would see what fun we were having and start talking to us. Often we would offer them a glass of wine and invite them to join us. If a pretty girl walked by we would offer her a glass of our wine and a bite of our pasties, so to speak!

The journey used to go so quickly. By the time we had arrived in Exeter, our destination for changing trains to take us home to Dawlish and Teignmouth, we were so merry we didn't want it to end. We would say, 'oh fuck it, we are having such a good time, we'll stay on the train until Newton Abbot', just to get another half an hour of partying in. Then we would have to get the last train back again to Dawlish. You would have thought we had had enough, but those trips were such good fun and time just flew!

It's funny how events over the years connect together. Years after watching Wigan in some of those classic Challenge Cup Finals, the present day England union coach and father to England fly half Owen, Andy Farrell got off the team bus at Twickenham and said 'would you mind giving this shirt to Martin?' It had been pre arranged for Andy to give me a signed shirt to give to his good friend and ex Wigan team mate Martin Hall, the ex Wigan hooker who now lives in Teignmouth and is a friend of mine too. At the after match reception I got talking to Andy Farrell, I said that I had seen him and Martin play in many a final. Commenting on how I had sometimes socialised with Martin in South Devon I said, 'Martin is mad, I've been out drinking with him,' Andy replied, 'we were all like that in those days.'

I'd once asked Martin Hall if he had encountered Jim Fallon as they'd both played rugby league for massive teams up north and Jim was an ex Bath, Richmond and originally Teignmouth player, (a Teignmouth boy really). Had they ever met each other? Martin replied with a passion, 'we never even spoke to each other, it didn't matter who the opposition was you hated them, you had to win at all costs, all we were interested in was winning the game,' interesting!

Dad had remarried a year or two after divorcing mum, so I acquired a step mum, Alice, and two step brothers, Peter and Graham, and later a half sister, Joan. As a teenager I worked for Stanton's travel agents in the centre of Oldham in the days when you used to sell the rail tickets with the holiday. It was my first selling job. We used to have competitions on Saturday mornings to see who could sell the most holidays. Although I was only fifteen or sixteen I would often sell more than the established weekly staff.

Like so many parents in those days, mine encouraged me to look for a job with career prospects and a pension, so I got a job in the Borough's Treasury Office working for Oldham Council in the Rating Department. I'll never forget my boss explaining to me that one of his assistants was a homosexual and he had a conviction for committing indecent exposure or something in the local toilets. It came as quite a shock to me. Things were very different in those days and I'd never heard of homosexuals up until that moment. My boss advised me to be on my guard, especially on the upcoming Saturday, when I was going to be working with said assistant alone in the office. Sure enough as I sat diligently at my desk, the guy came over to offer me some advice and placed his hand on my thigh, whack! I was ready for him. 'Don't you ever . . .' I blurted out, he definitely got the message!

During my spell in the office to get some extra fitness training (not because I was being chased) I would run home for my lunch in the allocated hour. I ran really fast, making sure I had a scarf around my mouth to protect me from the smog of the Cotton Mills. When I got home and took the scarf off, I could see all of the black bits of smog covering it, Oldham was lovely in those days! It is hard to imagine now exactly how thick and dense the smog was, incredibly in 1952, 12,000 people died in the Great Smog of London which paved the way for the Clean Air Act of 1956.

Time moved on and I began to lose contact with my real mum, Alice and dad took good care of us all and I just got on with my life. By the time I started a new chapter in my life by leaving home and heading down to Devon to join the police force, I had totally lost contact with mum. I immediately loved everything about the fabulous county of Devon and just forged on with my life.

Many years later my step brother Graham told me that he had tried to trace my mum but without success and understood that she must have passed away. Thirty years or so on I received a letter from the Salvation Army asking if Edna Tindell was my mum. Incredibly for me, it seemed that mum had remarried and was living in the Manchester area. I asked my sister's daughter Sue who lived in the area to find out from the directory all the 'phone numbers of people with that surname. I spent a whole Bank Holiday weekend ringing the numbers asking the people I spoke to if they were they related to Edna, but I didn't have any luck with my enquiries. Soon afterwards the Salvation Army responded to a letter I'd sent them informing me of an address they had for mum.

Pam, my sister Margaret and I headed straight to that address. It was a care home for people that couldn't cope with life which was located in Pendleten, Manchester, not far from Old Trafford. We learnt that mum had married a chap who had come back from the Burma War with Post Traumatic Stress Syndrome or something similar and that they had met at one of the institutions she'd been in. We discovered that mum had lived a totally normal life with her new husband and had even been the carer for her new husband's father for a while. Unfortunately, when her husband passed away, mum had broken down again and this explained why she was back in a care home.

Mum was living in this fantastic house, it was like a Manor House, sub divided into lovely apartments surrounded by beautiful gardens. It was awesome meeting her. She was well enough to understand exactly who I was and it was incredible. We visited mum on a few occasions after that first reunion and on one of our early visits she mentioned she liked a glass of whisky. The next time we went to see her we gave mum a bottle of whisky, she was delighted and immediately poured herself a glass. Whoosh, down in one, she knocked it back! The next day we had a phone call from the home saying, if ever we took any alcohol in for mum in the future, could we give it to them, as they'd found mum flat on her back on the floor after we'd left!

After we were reunited with mum we were lucky to be introduced to her extended family and got to know them all. They were able to fill me in on a lot of mum's past. She had enjoyed a really good upbringing, her parents had owned their own shop and apparently she had been a very religious lady. My cousin Janet, (my Auntie Nellies daughter), told me that mum was a star in many productions, pantomime's and the like. She would write poems that would get printed in the Manchester Guardian and she had been a really talented woman before the depression had struck. Sadly, mums', sister, Nellie, by now had had a stroke and had been in a coma for two years. We met her husband Bill who was a lay preacher and a really lovely man. Pam and I went to see her in hospital and I leaned over and said 'Nellie, it's Edna's son Peter,' tears started rolling down her face and a smile crossed her lips, incredible.

Mum died some four years later, aged 87, and we all went up to the funeral service which was conducted by Bill, Nellie's husband. There were only about twenty people there, some family and some carers, but it was the best service I had ever attended. Bill knew mums whole life history from childhood and it was evident mum had been part of a very well respected family. Margaret and I were terribly proud as we listened to the moving Eulogy. It was only then that my own childhood memories came flooding back and it all began to make sense to me again. I recalled how when mum had first started going into care, Margaret and I had stayed with this beautiful family who looked after us both really well. In a way, I think I'd shut those childhood memories out of my mind up until then. I had just got on with my life after mum had left. Margaret agreed, she too shared the same feelings.

My dad didn't play any sport in my lifetime, although he told me he had enjoyed playing sport at school. However, he was a real sporting enthusiast. Maybe not a nutter like me, but he loved his sport. I remember him taking me to Old Trafford to watch Manchester United, the Busby Babes, play when I was about ten. He would also take me to see Manchester City in the Bert Trautman era. We had some brilliant times together.

When the Manchester United team were sadly decimated in the Munich tragedy, I remember reading about it in the local newspaper. My hero Duncan Edwards, the midfield dynamo I used to adore was gravely ill, struggling for life in hospital. From memory I believe that because Duncan was such a fit, strong man he fought to cling on to life with enormous bravery. The tragedy was such a very sad and emotional time for everyone in Manchester, Lancashire, Great Britain and the World beyond. It touched everyone who loved sport. I'm pretty sure this was the period when I decided I would be a United fan, rather than a City fan. My son Simon followed suit and we never regretted it!

Spending all my one and six pocket money when I was twelve or thirteen and watching the famous footballers of that era play was fantastic. I would get on the bus from Oldham to go to Manchester and then get on another bus from Manchester along the Salford Road to Old Trafford. As a young lad I was overwhelmed by the atmosphere around the ground. I could sense the excitement in the air as I was caught up in the enormous tide of people all moving in one direction towards the huge stadium. Everything and everyone seemed enormous to me in those days. Once inside, I was relieved when the adults lifted me over their heads and passed me down the terraces to the front rows so I could find a space to watch. The waves of noise the crowd generated in support of United was unbelievable. After the match I would join the masses of people walking back from Old Trafford into Manchester before getting a bus back to Oldham and that was my pocket money for the week gone.

As much as I was into all my sports, I loved rugby league more than any other when I was growing up in Oldham. At the time Oldham were probably the best team in the country. Rugby league was the only game in town in Oldham. If you wished to get on in sport you just had to play rugby league.

In the Summer of 1957 Oldham were rugby league champions. They had seen off the mighty Hull in that season's championship final at Odsal before over 62,000 paying customers, having already bagged the Lancashire Cup and Lancashire League Championship.

Bill Doran the Oldham Chronicle's match reporter at the time wrote:

'Not for a long time on the field of rugby have so few brought so much colour into the grimy Oldham life. Off the field, too, Oldham have managed to keep things heated up in the world of controversy. Whichever way you look at it – Oldham's rugby team has given Oldham plenty to talk about. Honestly, I tremble when I think of the disasters Oldham have managed to avert this season. Retirements, transfer requests and revolts have all helped Oldham to be the most talked about team this century. But Oldham will be best remembered for its rugby – its charming, hair-raising, spine tingling, heart straining, honest – to – goodness fan – winning rugby.'

In those days, Oldham used to play Rugby League at Watershedding's, which sadly is now defunct. At one end of the stadium there used to be a terrace called the Penny Rush. Only children and pensioners were allowed in that end of the ground. There was always a fantastic atmosphere

amongst the thousands of spectators. When the opposition were taking a goal kick, we all used to bang the metal railings to create as much a din as possible to put the kicker off his stride. My dad would always be at the ground, usually in his police officer capacity. There wouldn't be a lot of trouble in those days, so he could stand and watch the game like the rest of us. The bonus for me was if dad was on duty I could watch the game for free and save a penny!

Up until age ten I had never even heard of rugby union. It was only when I was walking to meet a friend one day and passed a field and saw someone lying down with his hand on the top of a rugby ball as a kick at goal was being taken did I begin to realise that union existed. This was a totally different world, I thought, what the heck's going on here?

At school, I loved playing sport but I didn't manage to break into any of the school teams until I was in the third year. Eventually I managed to get selected for the school rugby team and I never looked back. My school was full of working class children who always wanted to get one over you. Although very brutal, I got stuck into it and I dealt with it. I started to make an impact for the school cricket team around the same time, playing a year up for the fourth year. I'd developed suddenly and had got a lot bigger, so while lots of boys were dropping out from playing, losing interest or discovering girls, I was revelling in my new found strength.

At sixteen, I played for an exceptional Oldham team called Strinesdale. We won everything. We had some really talented players like Terry Fogarty who went on to play for Great Britain and Jimmy Russell who captained Great Britain Under 19's. In fact we had lots of quality players who went on to carve out professional careers.

I had two trial matches before the start of the Under 17 season against a team who were all a year older than us. I had previously played at full back, but I was picked at prop for the trial, I had never propped in my life. It was well known that in rugby league players were expected to be versatile and capable of playing in various positions. The first scrum I went down in was one to remember. The older more experienced opposing prop playing in his normal position thumped me, whack! He continued to thump me throughout the game, I just had no idea how to react, at that stage I wasn't at all street wise.

At the end of the game we came off the pitch and I had tears in my

Strinesdale, under 17s. Top right, Jimmy Russell, England age group captain;
next to Terry Fogarty, future GB Rugby League International star

Saddleworth Rangers, under 19s, 1962

eyes. The guys in my team tried their best to console me. They said, 'don't worry about it, you're a good rugby player, when we play next week, (we were playing the same team again) if he thumps you, thump him back.' When I got home I was a complete wreck, not only emotionally, but physically too. My step mum rubbed me with ralgex and sympathised with me. Sure enough the next week we faced the same opponents, with the same ugly prop. At the first scrum, he thumped me, I don't know why but I was waiting to see if he would do it again. I steeled myself and in the second scrum of the game I thumped him back, as hard as I could. He never thumped me again. That season, we won the Cup at Oldham's Watershedding's ground and we managed to win the league trophy too!

At under 19's level I played for Saddleworth Rangers. We had a very good team featuring some players who went on to play professionally. The season I left for Devon our senior team won the Lancashire cup and I'd managed to play a couple of games for them. The experienced rugby league men used to say to me that having played at the level I did in league, I could easily play union for England and they meant it.

In hindsight, none of them had probably ever watched a game of rugby union. They knew absolutely nothing about the sport at all, living in Lancashire, they were in a cocoon. All they had ever known was league and they were totally focused on it. Union didn't exist as far as they were concerned, they believed they were a class apart.

My rugby league coaches demanded you had all the ingredients, you learnt the basics, passing, tackling and all the core skills. I was to learn later in life that in rugby union there were more specialised positions to be mastered. Rugby league provided me with a tough introduction to the world of rugby. The games were hard, physical and extremely competitive, played by working men, but I loved testing myself against the best. When the games finished there were never any shower facilities at the ground so we used to go to the local pub for a shower. There was no social side for me to enjoy, there wasn't a culture of drinking. We were not always old enough to have a pint anyway. You trained, you played and you went home.

When I'd played for the Oldham Under 19s town team, we used to train at Watersheddings and were coached by the professional first team coach on the evenings the first team were off. One night, the first team, who all had full time jobs by day, changed their training night and I will always remember having the opportunity to train with them. I mixed it with some exceptionally talented players. The thing that stood out the most for me was the quality in the timing of their passing and running angles.

My passion for following cricket had been ignited when dad took me to watch England play the 1953 Australian touring team at Old Trafford in the Ashes series. We loved to sit on the grass by the boundary rope and when the ball came towards us all the kids would compete to see who could field it first, usually before it had reached the boundary. In the Summer months, Dad would often take me to Oldham Cricket Club to watch them play. They were in the Central Lancashire League and would welcome some of the best players in the world. I saw some brilliant professionals at Oldham Cricket Club, playing for and against them. I particularly remember watching a guy called Polly Umrigar who was a professional for Oldham, was a captain of India and a really good batsman. The brilliant South African, Basil D'Oliveira, also made an appearance. I'd never seen a player hitting the ball as cleanly as he did. I used to sit and romanticise about international cricket teams and imagined one day being able to have the opportunity to go and watch the West Indians in the Caribbean sunshine.

ENGLAND IS A NATION OF SHOPKEEPERS

In the Summer of 1962, I decided on a change of career and applied to join the Devon police force. Since the age of one I had never been back to the south west, although my parents had always enthused about holidays in the West Country. I joined the police force on Boxing Day in 1962, ready to go to Chantmarle training school in Dorset. After completing my training, my first post was Torquay. I was delighted. What a great posting, a young Oldham boy, working in one of the premier holiday towns in the UK. On my first weekend off I decided to go to Torquay Rugby Club to watch a game of union.

On arriving, I became aware that they were looking for players to play in the match. Torquay's opponents were a couple of players short, so rather than watching from the sidelines, I quickly volunteered to play. They asked me, 'have you got any gear?' I said 'I do, but it's back at Torquay police station', they quickly drove me back to the station and I picked up my gear. I ended up playing for the visitors, Brixham III's against Torquay III's. I'd never played a game of rugby union in my life before and Brixham were still three men short. Despite all of that and losing the match, I thoroughly enjoyed myself. I played at fly half and scored three tries. I realised that, one: it was a totally different game and two: contrary to what I'd been told, there were players in rugby union with massive talent.

Both Brixham and Torquay invited me back to play for them. I decided

Police Training College at Chantmarle, Dorset. Class 125,
December 1962 to March 1963

I would like to play for Torquay, as it was my local club. It was near the end of the season so I only played a couple of games for the second team before the season was over. That was enough for me to realise that rugby union was right up my street. The camaraderie and spirit of the union boys was what I had been looking for.

As I became immersed in the rugby union culture, I began to notice that rugby league was a bit of a taboo subject. There was a definite nervousness surrounding the game, an apprehension that the best union talent would be scouted and whisked off to the northern league clubs. I remember an ex rugby league Welsh International player watched every Torquay fixture, as his son played for Torquay. Everyone knew that at the same time he was keeping an eye open for stand out performers. All the Devon clubs were aware that league scouts were watching the best players religiously and it really bothered them. I was encouraged not to talk about rugby league by all the players and management at Torquay, to put my past behind me. I know that I was scouted, probably because I had already

53

On the beat in Torquay

played a lot of league rugby, but I couldn't imagine ever wanting to go back to Oldham or anywhere up north. I was in love with Devon, I was in love with the fresh air, the companionship I had found amongst my new team mates and the social events that came hand in hand with rugby union.

Before long I was doing some really intense pre season training with a guy called Mike Davis. Mike was a local Torquay boy who had just come back from an England rugby union summer tour of Australia and was studying at St Luke's College in Exeter. Mike, a second row forward, later went on to coach England to a Grand Slam victory in 1980. Mike had obviously learnt a lot of coaching techniques while he was playing for England and we all benefited from his know how. I was in my element, learning the many differences in the rules of union like rucking, mauling and releasing the ball as you were tackled. Best of all, I was increasing my fitness levels with the regular intense training. That season we became a really strong and fit side.

During the first week in September, the Torquay club traditionally held a rugby festival week at their gloriously located seafront ground, named The Rec. Touring teams would come from all over the country and that season the county champions Warwickshire played Devon. Warwickshire had a whole host of international stars in their ranks, it was a carnival atmosphere to the start of the season.

My second game of that season was my first team debut for Torquay and I was picked to play on the wing. We were up against a very strong Exeter St Luke's College team. St Luke's had lots of excellent sportsmen at the time going to university in Exeter and representing them. Mike Davies played in our team that day as a second row forward. I didn't really understand the significance at the time of making my debut alongside a current England international. I can't imagine that happening today.

My abiding memory of my first season was the great camaraderie and fun that we had at Torquay, which was in stark contrast to my time in rugby league where you were lucky to even get a bath. After the games we would enjoy a nice meal, a few beers and a great laugh. It was a brilliant social life suiting my personality down to the ground. It was an amateur game then too, so win or lose all the players on both sides would have a drink and enjoy the social side together, I certainly did.

The following season I was transferred with my job to Topsham, a picturesque village outside Exeter on the banks of the river Exe. I was to be the local, 'bobby,' It was a plum posting for someone still in his probationary period. I decided to continue playing rugby for Torquay and commuted to games. The club generously paid me ten shillings a week, 50p in today's money, that covered my petrol money and a beer or two!

One Friday I got a call from the rugby club. Could I play for the first team the next day against London Wasps? At the time I was on a secondment to Exmouth CID and wasn't due to finish that night until 1am, but there was no way I was going to miss the opportunity to play Wasps. I got to the pick up point in time for 6am and got on to the team coach at Countess Wear in Exeter, having walked about two miles. We journeyed up to London, getting cat naps wherever possible. I played on the wing opposite a guy called Andy Hurst who had played for England the previous season. They had two or three internationals playing and in a close game we lost narrowly. I recall that we signed autographs for lots of children after the game, a new experience for me. To cap it all we then had a great post match meal of steak and chips, definitely a step up from rugby league! Ironically, the club booked us into a hotel for the night so we could enjoy the attractions in the big city. Today the reverse would

On pub patrol with Special Constable, Don Wreford, Topsham

happen, clubs would book a stay in the hotel, the night before, to make sure the players were fresh to play!

The following season having moved permanently to Topsham I decided to play for Exeter. I used to drink in the Lighter pub and that's where I met the landlord's son Tony Hopper, the Exeter and Devon scrum half. Tony talked me into joining Exeter, taking me along to pre season training and I soon discovered what a super player he was. That summer, through Tony, I got to know Tony Lee who also lived in Topsham. Tony had recently retired from rugby having been a very successful captain of the Exeter first team. Exeter had a reputation for not being one of the best social clubs, but as one of the best teams in the south west. I soon discovered only half of that statement was correct!

I was selected to play for Exeter in a sevens tournament in Tiverton. Tony Hopper was in the team and Tony Lee was involved in the management. After the tournament I remember going for a drink with them and they left me for dead within about 30 minutes. Could they drink! Given the standard of rugby, I was amazed at how they partied and it dawned on me that it wasn't such a bad move for me after all! Tony Lee later became the Devon representative on the Rugby Football Union's council; one of the original 57 'old farts' as Will Carling famously christened them. Tony Hopper's son Matt is, as I write, the current Harlequin and England Saxons centre.

My most memorable game for Exeter was an October evening kick off under floodlights against Bristol at The Memorial Ground. I had come into the team as a late replacement for ex England winger Martin Underwood. Our preparations were disrupted by our journey to Bristol. It was before the motorways had reached the south west and due to half term holiday traffic we were late arriving, just making it in time for the kick off. We had all got changed on the coach en route and when we arrived we just dumped our things quickly in the changing rooms. We ran onto the pitch to be greeted by a crowd of over five thousand people.

Bristol had a team packed with internationals, it was a really pulsating, tight game and the home crowd were really vocal. We lost 19–16, although I had enjoyed my best game ever. One moment I will never forget is when Richard Sharp, the legendary England international, who was playing for Bristol at fly half kicked the ball down the wing. I recovered the ball near the touchline and ran back up field. Sharp was my immediate opponent as I sprinted up the wing, I side stepped him and left him for dead! John Baxter who was a really good second row forward in our team said, 'Crossy, you left Richard Sharp for dead with that side step.' Our lack of time for preparation meant I'd gone straight into the game without having any time to be nervous and maybe that had suited me?

In those amateur days one of the best things for me was that the really talented players played for their local team, unless they got moved up country with their job. Therefore, the standard of rugby in the West Country in my day was excellent. Over the years Devon and Cornwall has a proud record of producing international players. From my time, memorable players such as Dick Manley, Mike Davis, Stack Stevens Richard Sharp, Roger Hosen, Paul Ackford and John Scott to name a few. More recently, outstanding players such as Phil Vicary, Julian White, Trever Woodman, Lee Mears, Olly Barclay, Jack Nowell and Tom Johnson have all represented their country. Add to these all the excellent players that have played for England that hail from Gloucestershire and Somerset and it makes me realise the abundance of talent in the south west.

When I was in the police I was very ambitious. In fact, I was a very ambitious young man. From the very start I applied myself and I used to get top marks in the examinations I took. I'd worked in Torquay for twelve months before being stationed in Topsham. I loved the responsibility of having my own beat, you were more or less on your own. A typical day would be patrolling the town and neighbouring hamlets on my police official 'sit up and beg' bike. Every hour on the hour, I would be expected to be at various red telephone boxes on my patch, where I could be contacted by an officer who was based at Budleigh Salterton approximately ten miles away. Having had the call I would often find myself having to cycle like hell in full uniform to deal with an incident miles away.

Despite the majority of Topsham residents being extremely respectable, the beat still had it's challenging times. Not least on Friday nights when the local hall played host to live bands and dancing. Topsham was equidistant from the Lympstone Royal Marine barracks and the City of Exeter, without fail lads 'representing' each would meet on the night and it would kick off. The Exeter boys would arrive looking for trouble and the Marines were only too happy to oblige! It was a tough town to police, especially at weekends. I was on my own with no walkie talkie and you were expected to get amongst them, it was the law of the jungle.

After serving a really interesting 12 months in Topsham, I was moved to Middlemoor, in Exeter, which was Devon and Cornwall's police head-quarters. I worked in the admin office for two years. Another great move for me. Working in the admin' office meant I learnt a lot about the bosses and what was going on in the force. While at Middlemoor I became the fixture secretary for the police rugby team and also looked after the admin' for the cricket team. Having served 3 years, I was able to take my sergeants' exam, which I did and my results were in the top two hundred in the country. I was seen as a potential high flyer and I was still only in my early twenties.

As a consequence, I went for interviews in London to go on a twelve month 'Special Course' for rapid promotion. Being situated in the admin office meant I was perfectly placed to see the glowing reference the Chief Constable had given me before it was sent to the selection committee. Armed with this knowledge, I was full of confidence when I attended the interviews in London, only to find myself not selected when the results were declared. I had learnt a lesson that has stayed with me for the rest of

Teignmouth RFC

my life. Never again would I be complacent in interviews or meetings. I reasoned that you only had one opportunity to sell yourself and I have stuck to that principle ever since. The Chief Constable had given one of his own men a good reference, nothing more than that.

After my three years at headquarters I was transferred to Teignmouth to work in CID to gain more experience. Having moved to Teignmouth I decided to leave Exeter rugby club and join my local rugby club as it was where I would live and work. I figured it would be an ideal way to meet and make friends and get to know the local characters. As a family, we really settled in Teignmouth. It was an interesting fishing town on the mouth of the River Teign with bustling docks. We were living a minute's walk from the beach and by now Pam and I had started a family, so it was an ideal location to bring up our young children, Alison and Simon. I made many friends in the area, mostly through rugby and the family became really settled. We had moved home an awful lot in my seven years in the police and I was ready to put down some roots.

I decided to change my career and seek a job as a sales representative. I was extremely fortunate to get the first job I applied for with Pedigree Petfoods, one of the top companies in the grocery trade, a subsidiary of

Taking an order from Barbara

the chocolate giants, Mars. The interviews were extremely intense and demanding, but having learned from my failed interview for entry to the police 'Special Course'. I was positive, confident and sold myself. I was to work all of South Devon, parts of East and mid Devon and from Bude in Cornwall to Lynmouth in North Devon. What a beautiful area to cover. Everything was going well and we decided to buy our own home in Teignmouth, although as it transpired we eventually bought a property in nearby Dawlish.

Pedigree Petfoods were renowned for being one of the top training companies of their salesmen in the country. This change of focus had a massive influence on my working career. I was with Pedigree for four years, it was really hard work, but great fun too. After a brilliant grounding in the world of sales I reluctantly resigned from the company and took the big decision to go and work as a salesman with a family company in the gift trade.

Leaving the police did seem to family and friends a gamble that I might regret. I had totally enjoyed my seven years in the police. I had met some great people as a result of playing lots of sport. I had represented Devon police at tug of war, cross country running, cricket, life saving and most importantly rugby. Most of our games were mid week and we played some Naval and Marine teams, playing at the Britannia Royal Naval College for officer training in Dartmouth and The Royal Marines Commando Training Centre, based at Lympstone, along with College teams, including St Luke's and Seale Hayne Agricultural College. More interestingly for me, we played against other County Police teams, including Hampshire, Dorset, Cornwall, The City of Plymouth and the top side at the time, Somerset. It was well documented that Somerset had recruited many officers from South Wales after they were demobbed. These included an ex international fly-half and a number of county players. It was at one of these games where I first encountered Ray Robinson, Andy's dad. He was a great scrum-half with a never say die attitude. Ray represented Somerset at both cricket and rugby, a great all rounder. Andy obviously inherited many of his dads' genes!

My abiding memory of police rugby was in 1969 a few months before I resigned. The force side were to go on a week's tour of Berlin. A squad of about twenty left for Berlin on the police coach with a volunteer driver and some rugby nuts, including a few senior officers. The whole trip cost £25 a man, including accommodation, but not food. We stayed in the famous Spandau Police Barracks in Berlin. The route necessitated travelling through the then East Germany. One of our leaders, a legendary detective called Den Steer who had a reputation for knowing everybody and an uncanny ability to get in everywhere, assured us we would have no trouble getting through border control. Wrong! Armed guards entered our coach and proceeded to detain us for about three hours. We finally arrived in West Berlin at around midnight and went straight to a hostelry opposite Spandau barracks. After being fed and watered we left the hostelry and were amazed to discover it was daylight! Where had the time gone? We were due to be playing our first game that afternoon!

In those days, The Brandenburg gate was isolated and inaccessible immediately next to the Berlin Wall, still dividing the East from the West. Some of our party, including Den Steer managed to get the local police to take them to the Eastern side of the city for a tour. I chickened out, feeling safer in the West!

Having moved into the gift trade, I quickly realised that there were lots of opportunities to become a freelance, self employed sales agent. Manufacturers and importers were regularly asking me to work as a sales agent for them. One of my mates Buster Crabb a real Devon boy and a good rugby player helped me out at trade shows and we worked as a team selling across the west country. He was the funniest guy I have ever known, no one has made me laugh as much as Buster. Between the laughs, we worked really, really hard, calling in every gift shop in every town to sell our wares. Buster was also one of the most predictably unreliable guys I've ever met, so generous with his money that I would often have to bail him out. Tourism was booming in Devon and Cornwall in the seventies and I was ready to make the most of the opportunities that came my way. It was seen as a massive gamble at the time leaving the police, as I had a young family, a big mortgage and not much in the way of savings. Pam was at St Luke's teacher training college in Exeter, doing a three year degree. I had to go for it. Yes, it was a gamble, but I would be working in the area I loved and now called home.

The work was very laid back, the shop owners were very friendly and many of them became good friends. I socialised with some and even stayed with them at their homes to cut down on the travelling. I got to know and deal with some of the biggest businesses in the area, learning all the time whilst on the job. I've always shown an interest in people and like to think I am a good listener. Some of my mates have commented over the years that they cannot believe how I remember people's names. It is true, I have always had a capacity to remember names and faces, I believe I learnt an awful lot on the intense Pedigree Pet Foods training course, not least to do things professionally and with intelligence. In a way the skills I learnt in my early business career have proven useful to me in my quest to be England's most prominent sporting fan. I tended to deal with characters I liked, could trust and most importantly for me, have a good time with socially. My philosophy of working hard and playing hard has in no doubt given me the opportunity to follow my dreams and the sport I love.

In time, as I became more and more accustomed to the gift market, I started to purchase my own shops. Soon I owned a shop in Teignmouth and another in the popular Cornish seaside town of Looe. Around this time, I formed a partnership with one of my biggest customers John Hambly. Our company manufactured gifts and souvenirs and I sold the products directly into the shops myself, while also employing agents across the rest of the country. Meanwhile I formed an alliance with another gift shop proprietor Howard Rowe. The partnership with Howard (who was to be my companion at the Olympics in Atlanta) and his wife Rita gave us more buying power at the Trade Fairs. Buster was on board too and would become our chief negotiator, he had such a brilliant way with people, he would always secure a great discount.

In 1978, three years after starting on my own, I had the good fortune to buy the freehold of a shop in Widecombe in the Moor, a tourist 'honey pot' on Dartmoor. Pam had only recently obtained her teaching degree and then, wham! she was facing a life in the gift trade. For the next twenty five years, Pam travelled the forty mile round trip daily from Dawlish up to Widecombe on Dartmoor. It was an extremely busy shop but we would close from November to Easter. Pam loved it and really appreciated the five months holiday every year, that was even better than teaching! Widecombe proved to be a brilliant decision, it was great fun, Pam worked throughout the Summer season and I would join her on my day off on a Sunday.

We got to know lots of the local characters and found out that the village had only had electricity supplied since 1961, just 17 years previous!

Shortly after arriving in Widecombe, we noticed that there was an elderly lady who would always be sat on the green opposite our shop under an old chestnut tree. Miss Harvey was a carbon copy of the 'grandma' character in Giles' cartoons. She loved to talk to the tourists, telling them many tales, real and exaggerated. Once, when asked by a visitor what the locals did in the Winter when the holiday makers had gone, she replied, 'Well my dears, us sits by the fire an' us laughs and us laughs and us laughs at all the silly buggar's that comes up 'ere to look at us in the Summer!'

One chap, who had been the local postman when Miss Harvey ran the post office, told of overhearing her giving directions to two walkers who were unsure of their route. When they had left, he questioned Miss Harvey, 'Why had she sent them the wrong way?' 'Well, me dear, she answered, 'If they don't know where they be gwyn to, 'ow the 'ell am I

Widecombe Fair

sposed to?' Incredibly, Miss Harvey had also been been the village school mistress!

Queenie, another local Dartmoor lady, who was well beyond retirement age, used to religiously clean the public loos, which became known in the village as Queenie's castle. She would regale us with stories of her growing up on the moor. She told of how she and her siblings were, at the onset of Winter, smothered in goose grease and sewn into their winter underwear. She also informed us about her granny, who was a witch and would cast spells. Queenie said she had inherited her grannies ability. She took pleasure in explaining how a school master had reprimanded her daughter and she had cast a spell on him. The next day he broke his leg. We always made sure we kept in Queenie's good books!

The highlight of the calendar year had to be the annual Widecombe Fair. A one day event immortalised in the song, 'Widecombe Fair' 'Tom Pearce, Tom Pearce lend me your grey mare, Old Uncle Tom Cobley and all', are just some of the words of the famous folk song written down by the Rev. Sabone Baring-Gould. The earliest written record of the fair is in 1850 when it was described in the Plymouth Gazette as a 'cattle fair' Held on the 2nd Tuesday in September. Today it has grown into a massive event with clay pigeon shooting, gymkhana, dog shows, tug of war, tossing the hay bale, stalls and the all important beer tent! The tiny village is inundated, but the local fair committee do a wonderful job in keeping everything flowing. Plenty of fun is had by all, copious pints are drunk and pasties consumed.

It was a privilege to have met and worked amongst such interesting people, we shall never see their like again.

Meanwhile, while I was in my late twenties I rejoined Exeter rugby club in order to play at a higher level again. I'd previously played for them in the three quarters or on the wing. During my time at Teignmouth I had successfully converted to playing in the back row. On my return to the Exeter team, I managed to play a number of first team games in the forwards at number eight. One of the games I remember well was against Exeter St Luke's College. They were a very good side with lots of future Internationals, England's John Scott, Mike Rafter, Mike Sleman. Welshman Jeff Squire played opposite me at number eight, along with centre David Burcher who later captained Wales. It was a really close game, we dominated in the forwards, but they just had too much firepower outside and they beat us by three points

Around about four years after going self employed, I was with one of my old police mates and best man John Essery and he asked how I was doing. I told him I was loving my job, it was really hard work, but it was great fun, with nice people, it's not like work really. He asked, 'are you earning all right?' I said to him, without boasting, roughly how much I was earning and he said, 'you're joking!' I said, 'no, no', he went on, 'that's more than the Chief Constable earns!' I had been doing really well in the force and a lot of people had said to me when I left that I would regret leaving, but I knew I had the fall back option of going back if I wanted to within a certain amount of time.

Into my thirties, I returned to play rugby for Teignmouth. In those days it didn't matter who I was playing for or where we were playing, Bristol, Cornwall, Forest of Dean, or more locally against, Newton Abbot, Brixham, Paignton or Torquay. We would always have a coach to the game and have a good old drink in the bar afterwards. We would love to mix with the opposition players and their supporters and then all go out socially afterwards, have an almighty piss up and a sing song together. Wives and girlfriends back home would always be asking, where the hell have you been?

Teignmouth Rugby Club played host to many touring teams over the years. Old Merchant Taylors' Rugby Club, a public school just outside London would play us every Easter. They would arrive at our little rugby ground on a Thursday night in their Rolls Royces and Porches. They were a good team who played a high standard of rugby, quite a few of them had played at county level. Their itiniery would see them play us, Plymouth Albion and then Bath on the way back to London. They were so wealthy they used to take over the Ness Hotel at Shaldon and as time went on they used to stay in the Burgh Island Hotel, on the island famous for its references in Agatha Christie stories. We used to have some brilliant times with those guys and they still come down to Teignmouth every Easter, I am led to believe it's the oldest running tour in rugby.

THE ITALIAN JOB

After serving my apprenticeship at the Atlanta Olympics and the Lions tour in 1997, I was still totally committed to wearing my Union Jack outfit to as many sporting events as possible, concentrating particularly on following England at rugby home and away. In time I began to clock that people would comment and make little observations about me being in a Union Jack outfit when England were playing Wales or Scotland. I realised that the time had come for me to have a custom made St Georges Cross England outfit, if I was going to be solely supporting the English rugby team.

I had my Mr England uniform specially made for me in time for the Five Nations campaign in 1999 and I wore the outfit from the start of that tournament. Wearing it for the first time at Twickenham, I was quickly spotted by Dave Rogers of Getty images as I walked down the terraces and in an instant he demanded, 'Pete, on the pitch!' He wanted a photo, there and then, I stepped onto the pitch and Dave took some photos, before saying, 'It's brilliant, I reckon you have made it now!' From that day, I wore my new outfit to every Five Nations game. I was really excited at the prospect of the World Cup being staged in England, Wales and France later that year.

I went to every England match of the 1999 World Cup dressed in my England outfit. For the group stage match against Tonga at Twickenham, I took a friend Ian Court who was a massive Manchester United supporter. He followed United all around the world. Ian could not believe the camaraderie amongst the rugby fans, how the English fans clapped the Tongans when they did something good. After the game the Tongans did a lap of honour and the England fans rose to their feet to give them a round of applause. Ian really couldn't believe it and remarked that you would never see an opposing team receive a reception like that in football.

England qualified for the quarter final and my mate Roger Cowie and I arranged to travel down to the game in Paris by car. When we arrived at our hotel I sat on the bed and opened the Daily Telegraph. I was stunned when I saw on the front of the sports supplement a full page picture of myself and Billy the Bulldog.

England played South Africa in the Quarter Finals in Paris. I remember it was Jonny Wilkinsons first World Cup campaign, Clive Woodward selected Paul Grayson the Northampton fly half ahead of Jonny for the crucial tie. The game was famous for Jannie De Villiers dropping 5 goals (a world record at the time) and we were knocked out. Clive had said 'judge the team and me on our performances at the World Cup!' luckily the RFU had seen enough and Clive remained as coach.

It was during the 1999 World Cup that I watched one of the best games of rugby I have ever seen. New Zealand, most peoples red hot favourites to lift the cup, were playing France in the semi final at Twickenham. New Zealand led the French comfortably at half time with the irrepressible Jonah Lomu scoring. Dressed neutrally in my union jack outfit, I was sat directly behind the French substitutes. As the French management started to make substitutions I could see in their body language that they knew they had the beating of New Zealand. Everything France did turned to gold and they made a sensational comeback, finishing as shock winners. I have always felt, since witnessing that game, that if you get in New Zealands faces and get on top of them, they are vulnerable.

In the other Semi Final, South Africa versus Australia I was wearing my union jack outfit when a South African dressed as a Zulu joined me for some pictures. As we stood and posed, he inadvertently turned towards me and poked me in my eye with his spear, to the amusement of the fans around us. A steward took compassion on me and escorted me around the pitch to get my eye attended to in the first aid room. Once I was patched up he escorted me back the same way. I remember the feeling of excitement as I walked pitch side, it was another precursor of good things to come! Incidentally, not only was I lucky enough to attend both semi finals of the rugby world cup in 1999, I also travelled up to the final at the Millenium Stadium in Cardiff and in the same year, I dressed in my Union Jack gear when I attended both the World Cup Cricket Semi Finals and the Final at Lords.

Prior to the Final, my mate Dave Williams and I believe the Semi Final we witnessed between South Africa and Australia was the greatest game of cricket either of us had ever seen. Shane Warne bowled one sensational over to swing the match in Australia's favour and was rightly nominated man of the match, what a player. At the end of a mesmerising, fascinating battle between two of the greatest teams ever, the scores were tied, both teams having been bowled out for 213. Australia progressed to the final because they had finished higher than South Africa in the super six table, due only to a superior net run rate, incredible! For the record Australia beat Pakistan handsomely in the final, the game was a bit of an anti climax.

I had been wearing my Great Britain uniform unofficially at every opportunity for years, attending as many international sporting fixtures as I possibly could, home and away. Now I was wearing my Mr England suit regularly to the rugby, the impact was even greater. People loved the St George's Cross design and were noticing me more than ever.

It was at an away international in Rome in 2000 that I first met Keith Webster, Twickenham's Head of Security, who would have a big impact on my progression as a mascot. I had learnt from Lawrence Dallaglio's dad, Vincenzo, (more about the D'allaglios later) who was acting as the official interpreter for the English party, that the English RFU council members, were staying at the Hotel Bellini in Rome. It was England's first ever Six Nations match against the Italians and as it happened our hotel was located not far from the Bellini.

That evening Pam and I, Jack and his wife Mary decided to go out for a couple of drinks at the Hotel Bellini. Soon after arriving, we met Sarah Swaby the RFU Press Officer and her husband Chris. We all got on really well together. The four of us then went for a meal at a nearby restaurant, before deciding we would like to go back to the Bellini. I guess we were hoping to bump into more of the England dignataries. We were stood at the bar when the chairman of the rugby union Brian Baister, a retired senior police officer came up to me and said, 'you're making a really good impression.' He continued, 'the Touchline magazine, (a quarterly publication at that time) has just done an article on you. Have you seen it?' As it happened I had, Brian was very positive towards me as we all chatted, everything was beginning to gel together really nicely.

Later in the evening we met Keith, who was a former Chief Inspector in the Metropolitan police, at the bar. I mentioned that I had been in the force in Devon and we discussed what Keith was up to on the trip. Keith explained his role. He was on a mission to reassure the Italian police that an English rugby fan was not necessarily from the same mould as an English football supporter. The Italian police were undoubtedly concerned by some of the minority stereotypical English football fans that had previously visited Rome and given English football supporters such a bad name.

Keith was cock a hoop that night, it was obvious his meetings with the Italian police and authorities had gone really well and we had a brilliant drink with him. I sensed as the night wore on that Keith understood me and didn't doubt my motives for dressing up and following the team. I believe he recognised that I was a decent man and I was just a totally dedicated supporter of the English nation and in particular any English sporting team. Some time later Keith, told me that for him to get me permission to walk around the stadium at Twickenham was quite a task. He had to be so sure that I was a legitimate supporter and that I was not a paedophile or someone who may pose a problem in any way.

The next day, Jack and I were walking down the road to the stadium and the bus carrying all the council members drove past us. We looked up and there they all were, waving at us! Little things like that night in Rome helped establish my reputation. I'd put myself about, mixed freely and generally had a great time.

Meanwhile, Richard Prescott the Director of Communications for the RFU, had been staying with the players at the team hotel the night before. Jack and I arrived in the stadium and made our way to our seats on the far side of the pitch. From the other side of the stadium we noticed Richard waving to us, trying to attract our attention. Richard walked all the way around the perimeter to greet us and I'll never forget what he said, 'When you get back, write to me, send me an email.' Wow, now I was excited, I had a good idea what Richard was thinking, but I didn't know for sure, I would have to wait and see.

I recall that after the Italian game in 2000 I was in the process of designing the livery for a Jaguar XJS I had bought. My intention was to have a Union Jack emblazoned on it, Austin Powers style! Pam would not have been impressed. To this day, she had no idea of my plan. While formalising the design I received a phone call from the Twickenham press officer Sarah Swaby, asking would I like to be the first ever official mascot of England? As I was speaking to Sarah I was thinking, yes, yes, yes! I exclaimed, 'of course I would be honoured to be England's mascot,' and the conversation continued, 'would you like to come to a briefing meeting at Twickenham?' Little did she know that I'd packed and was setting off as we spoke!

A few weeks later when I arrived at Twickenham I was met by Sarah and taken into a meeting with Richard Prescott (Director of Communications) and Keith Webster, (Head of Security at Twickenham). I'd spent days thinking about what the role should encompass, replaying in my mind over and over what I would say.

I confidently started the conversation by saying, 'I am really proud and honoured to be given this opportunity, I think I know exactly what you would like me to do. Initially, if you would allow me to explain what my plans are and what I believe will be right for the role, that would be great, if it's not what you are looking for we can fine tune it.'

I knew Richard Prescott had been a big supporter of mine and had been very keen on me becoming the official mascot for a while, it was the security aspect that had been his big concern. My impromptu night in Rome with Keith had hopefully answered any questions they might have had about me and my motives. I explained my plans, they all listened intently and I was delighted when they all agreed in principle with my initial suggestions.

My original proposal went something like this. Dressed in my full Mr England uniform I would greet the players as they disembarked off the team coach at Twickenham, welcoming them by enthusiastically waving the cross of St George flag as the team coach pulled up. Later, in the stadium as both teams sprinted onto the pitch from the tunnel I would be on the pitch welcoming them again proudly waving my England supporters flag. I would then stand directly facing the English players as the national anthems were sung just before the kick off. I also suggested I could provide a link between the players and supporters by walking around the stadium waving and chatting to the fans before the game and at half time.

The meeting went like a dream and I felt sure the committee would sanction my plans. I believe they had all decided that I had the right personality to be able to carry it off. I was destined to be Mr England, England's first ever official rugby union mascot!

Incredibly, during that meeting Keith asked me, 'Peter, have you got anywhere to park when you come to Twickenham? You could always use my parking space because I don't need it!' What a top bloke. Sarah approached me afterwards and said, 'Pete, you must have really impressed Keith because we've never known him to be so enthusiastic about someone getting an opportunity at Twickenham, he even offered you his parking spot!' I'm sure it had nothing to do with our quiet night in Rome!

When I had been in Rome for the six nations game against Italy, not only had I had a brilliant time with Keith Webster and others, I had also had the pleasure of Gareth Chilcotts company. I had suggested politely to Gareth that he was commonly described as one of dirtiest, hardest bastards that had ever played rugby. We got talking about hard men in rugby and during our conversation I said to Gareth that as far as I was concerned the hardest player I had ever played with was John Baxter when we'd both played for Exeter. It was in the days when players did used to punch each other in the scrums and at line outs, it was pretty lethal stuff but John had no problem at all with that, he was a real hard bastard too!

In my last season playing for Exeter I had played alongside John's younger brother Paul who was a prop forward and had skippered Exeter. Although Paul was shorter in stature than his brother he was another really hard man with a big reputation. Paul had propped against England Internationals when we played teams like Gloucester and also the All Blacks when he had represented the South West. I've heard it said many times those opponents really rated him and fellow front row team mates say he was renowned as one of the hardest and most difficult props to scrummage against.

Another old Exeter playing colleague of mine, Steve Williams, rang me one day when Rob Baxter the current Chiefs and one time England forwards coach, was still captain of the Exeter side that played at the old County Ground. Steve asked, 'would I like to do a speech at the Exeter players' annual dinner?' 'Of course' I quickly answered, it was an honour to be invited and I happily accepted his invitation.

When I was considering what I could include in my speech, I found myself thinking about the time I had spent with Gareth in Rome and it gave me some ideas for my speech. I decided to speak about a lot of the old characters of Exeter rugby that I'd known and in particular, the Baxter family. What a family the Baxters are, a Wigan family, hards as nails.

Originally, John's dad Teddy had bought a farm outside Exeter and brought all the family down to Devon. Teddy was a big north country man, a larger than life character, who turned out to be possibly one of Exeter's biggest supporters ever. Teddy had one of those voices that no matter how many people were watching a game, you could always hear him clearly above them all. Teddy was always shouting encouragement and supporting all the lads. He was an ever present supporter in those days, home or away. He would sit in the stand, or stand on the touchline, bellowing instructions to John and the team. Being on the wing I was close to the supporters and when a high ball went up I would prepare myself to catch it or suffer the consequences. Rugby fans can be the harshest critics. If an Exeter player dared to fumble the ball or cocked up, my god, Teddy would bellow out and let it be known!

When I played with John, although I was on the wing and he was in the second row, I was never in doubt about how tough a player he was. John was without doubt the scariest player I played with, I was pleased he was on my side. There was one incident I will always remember. Exeter were playing away at Newton Abbot and as always Teddy was there. Someone, a Newton Abbot supporter I guess, shouted out to John, 'Baxter you dirty bastard, send him off ref!' with that Teddy who was stood behind this poor soul whacked him with his umbrella! Saying, 'that's my boy you are talking about, he's not dirty!'

John's son and Teddy's grandson is Rob Baxter the highly successful Exeter Chiefs coach. Rob had been a popular first team captain of Exeter for a number of years and after retiring he was appointed by Pete Drewett as his forwards coach. Everyone was surprised when Pete was suddenly relieved of his post and the Board immediately appointed Rob as head coach. Pete had left an excellent club infrastructure, upon which Rob has built superbly, guiding them in his first full season to promotion to the Premiership. Rob has done a tremendous job with the Chiefs and surely repaid their faith in him. Improving the clubs standings and profile yearly in the Premiership and securing European rugby. Rob was rewarded for his outstanding coaching ability when in 2013 he was selected as a forward's coach in the England set up for the tour to Argentina. In 2014 Exeter Chiefs secured their first ever major domestic trophy, the Anglo-Welsh Cup.

I always felt that when Exeter played in the Championship that Rob's brother Richard was capable of making the step up to the Premiership and I am sure he had offers. I am also confident that Richard would have turned down any such opportunities because of his loyalty to Exeter. As it happened Exeter were promoted anyway and before retiring at the end of the 2012/13 season Richard had enjoyed two very successful seasons playing in the Premiership, regularly being voted his team's, 'man of the match.' Could he have played for England if he had played in the Premiership earlier? We will never know, but my call is that he could have. I was proud to be asked to support him during his testimonial year and cherished dressing in my outfit to wave the teams onto the pitch for his testimonial fixture.

John meanwhile was actively involved in the senior management at Exeter when they made the move to Sandy Park and embraced professionalism. When I'm at Sandy Park watching a game these days I often see John and his wife Bobby in the stands and it makes me laugh to hear John's voice bellowing out just like Teddy's all those years ago, he also makes his thoughts known! Rob, Richard, John, Paul and Teddy have all contributed so much, on and off the pitch since I played for the club in the sixties. Hopefully, my speech at that year's annual players' dinner illustrated what an unbelievably important family the Baxter's are in Exeter's rugby history.

Exeter Chiefs played their last competitive match against Coventry at the County Ground at the end of the 2005/6 season. Before the match kicked off I was invited to be on the pitch as some of the legendary surviving ex-

Exeter's last game

Back row, left to right: *Pete Cross, John Stark, Paul Baxter, Jon Jenkins, Andy Cole, Tony Hoppers brother David, Dick Manley, Richard Baxter, Rob Baxter, Jack Harrison, Trevor Harris, Ladies rep., Colin Paul, David Hartland.* Middle row: *Derek Atkins, Tim Woodrow, Graham Bess, Steve Donovan.* Front row: *Simon Day, Nick Bodnar, Bob Staddon, Roy Pikes grandson, Barry Carless, John Lockyer, Andy Maunder.*

captains of Exeter took a bow in front of the club's supporters. The oldest captain, who came onto the pitch first that day, was a guy called Jack Harrison. Jack, eighty odd by now, headed straight over to me and we shook hands. I knew Jack as he had been on the committee when I played for Exeter. Jack had set the precedent, all the other captains then came straight over to me and shook my hand and formed a line behind me. It was brilliant because I knew all of them!

In fact the only ex-captain who didn't come over and shake my hand was John Lockyer, who looked at me from about ten yards away and went off at a tangent. He opted to go straight to the end of the parade. I was surprised because John was the one I knew best of all. I asked him afterwards, 'why didn't you come and shake my hand?' John replied, 'because I had tears in my eyes already, if I had of come and shaken your

hand I would have just broken down.' That summed up the emotion of the day with all of those past Exeter captains all reunited on the pitch together. Incidently, I played with John Lockyer at Teignmouth and Exeter. John was and still is a ducker and diver, a guy who loves his rugby, Exeter and England. John played for the South West against the mighty All Blacks and to this day commentates on Exeter rugby and is a good man who is really into his rugby. John is known within Exeter Rugby circles as Mr Exeter, a fitting accolade. Unbeknown to me, the President of the Rugby Union Bob Rogers was present at the County Ground, as it was such a momentous occasion. I met so many ex-friends, players and RFU dignitaries, on the day, the whole stadium was full of a real rugby fraternity.

At the start of the following season, the club again invited me along to welcome the teams onto the pitch at the new Sandy Park stadium. Exeter had previously sold the County ground to property developers. This occurred at a time when a relative newcomer to the club management, Tony Rowe, had become involved. Tony had the foresight, vision and financial wherewithal to plan the future of the now Exeter Chiefs. Tony was ably supported by trustees, management, ex-players and supporters. Since professionalism, a number of top clubs, having sold their grounds have regressed and are no longer in the top flight. Tony Rowe oversaw the move from the County Ground and planned the development of Sandy Park with outstanding success. Having chatted with Tony during this period, I know that from day one, he has meticulously planned the ongoing development of the facilities and commercial revenues.

I was delighted and honoured to be present at the beginning of a whole new era for Exeter rugby and 'The Chiefs' as they were now christened. Ironically, Coventry were the opposition again, the stadium looked magnificent and you could tell that the whole set up was made for professional rugby. The atmosphere was electric and I could feel that there was a real buzz and sense of excitement around the club, trying to imagine what the future held. Tony Rowe joined me on the pitch for the ceremony and as we walked off I asked Tony, 'where should I sit?' Although I had my England gear on I hadn't actually arrived at the game with a ticket, I'd put my stuff in the office of the coach Pete Drewett before the game and just taken my place pitch side. Tony replied, 'come and sit at the top of the stand with us', so I ended up sitting with Tony and Bob Rogers, who was present again and their wives, brilliant!

In May 2010 Exeter had to play Bristol over two legs in the Championship play off final to reach the Premiership and I was privileged to be at both those fixtures. Rob Baxter, in my opinion did an incredible job that season, coaching the team he had inherited from Pete Drewett and managing the players appearances to keep them fresh for the play offs. Having already beaten Bedford in the semi final, home and away, the Chiefs managed to take a slender three point advantage from their home tie, to the 2nd leg at the Memorial Stadium in Bristol. It looked ominous for Exeter, most neutral observers and myself felt Bristol were unlucky to lose the 1st leg on the night.

Having been let down at the last minute, I managed to get tickets for the Bristol game courtesy of Tony Rowe. I travelled up on the management coach with Tony and others and was delighted to be invited into the pre match reception as a guest of Tony's. Matt Salter, the ex Bristol captain and important part of the Bristol coaching set up, a man I really like and rate did a presentation to the assembled guests, who apart from our table were all Bristol supporters. His speech left me feeling confident about the match ahead, Matt said things like, we know our weaknesses and we are aware we were outplayed in this department last week . . . For me Matt's speech wasn't inspiring and I commentated to the guy next to me that I had a gut feeling we would win.

As it happened Exeter won the game convincingly and we all jumped on the coach back to Sandy Park to celebrate the momentous occasion in the history of Exeter Rugby. When we got back to the club at about one in the morning it was bursting with hundreds of Exeter supporters who were determined to celebrate long and hard. When the team finally made an appearance, it was awesome, the atmosphere was magic, the players were mobbed and the supporters chanted their names. The party continued well into the night.

As a result of meeting Bob Rogers and his wife at the County Ground in Exeter at the Chiefs opening Sandy Park fixture, some time later, I was invited to join him for lunch in the President's Suite at Twickenham. It was for the Six Nations game against France the following season. An incredible honour for me as many of the Council Members of the

RFU have never been invited into the President's Suite. Situated in the West Stand, immediately behind the Royal Box, the President's Suite is Twickenham's most prestigious facility. You can sense the history of the Stadium as you look around at all of the brilliant photographs of legendary players and officials adorning the walls. Many Royals and VIPs have been entertained in this historic Suite on match days. The view of the pitch from the Suite is simply stunning

When I received the invite I asked Maureen Brewer, the President's personal assistant (who I've got to know and love over my years as England's mascot), 'what time is the lunch Maureen, I would love to come'. Maureen queried, 'why Pete?' I explained that I had to meet the England and French teams when they arrived and their arrival may cut across lunch. Maureen was very understanding and arranged for someone to phone through to me when the England coach was imminent.

I will never forget, I was sat next to Francis Baron, the Chief Executive of the Rugby Union and on my other side was a French guy, Jean-Pierre Lux, who was the Independent Chairman of the ERC, President of the European game. England were playing France and in the match programme there was an article entitled Entente Cordiale.

Bob Rogers wrote, 'Rugby union is a fantastic sport combining tough physical contest with true mutual respect. Crowds are not segregated because there is a camaraderie between rugby supporters the world over, even when supporting their home nation and trading good natured banter in the stands.

The reception of the England team at Dublin's Croke Park was testament to rugby union's ethos. We are proud of our sporting values where everyone is welcome and all are equal. We love the game for its passion and its sportsmanship, for its high intensity and its friendships, for its dynamism and its discipline.' Alongside Bob's brilliant words was a picture of Jean Claude and me. I was so proud, so honoured to be considered worthy of those principles. The article ended with bullet points, Bob saying. 'Lets respect the opposition. Respect the referee. Respect the unique ethos and culture of the game.' For me, Bob had summed up rugby beautifully.

Jean Claude and I have a brilliant relationship. In all the time I have known Jean Claude regardless of whether England or France have won the game, I have never fallen out with him. We both have a mutual admiration and respect for each other. Indeed, when England fans sing swing low sweet chariot at Twickenham Jean Claude will always join in. Sometimes I confess I sing the Marseilles, the bits I know anyway!

Halfway through lunch the call came through to me saying I ought to make my way down to ground level because the team were about to arrive. I had just had my soup and the main course was due to be served, but my England duties came first. I made my apologies to Francis and Jean-Pierre, they knew how important it was for me to be there and I raced downstairs to meet the team coach. I waited and waited but the coach did not appear, the security guys who all have walkie talkies were questioning where the hell the coach was and finally it was revealed, the coach driver had got lost. By the time I got back to the lunch I had missed my rack of lamb and they had moved on to the pudding, heartbreaking!

Years later when John Owens was the President of the RFU, I was fortunate enough to have the honour of going to the President's Suite again and this time my wife Pam was invited. Pam unfortunately couldn't make that game, so I rang Maureen and asked if I could take a good friend of mine, ex-Teignmouth rugby club captain Pete Cockram. Maureen came back to me and said, 'no problem, Peter' I was delighted for Peter and I knew he would be over the moon. It was a champagne reception and as you know by now, I never want to drink too much before a game, so we got there early . . . !

When we arrived I went up to John Owens and said, 'John, I am really honoured to be invited for lunch with you,' John replied, 'Pete, we are really honoured to have you up here with us' and I introduced him to Pete Cockram who was tremendously proud to be there. I sat at the top table with John, while Pete sat on another table with some important council members. We both had a thoroughly enjoyable lunch and managed to stay sober! Whenever I see Bob Rogers or John Owens these days we always get on really well and have a nice chat together. I love meeting so many interesting, genuine people and forging lasting relationships.

ENTENTE CORDIALE

I first met Jean Claude, the French mascot, in February 1997, before I had been made official mascot, in the days when I wore my Union Jack Arabian outfit. My dad on his first trip to Twickenham was sat with me fairly near the tunnel with my son Simon who was also at Twickenham for the first time. Jean Claude was pitch side with the French team as

Dad

their official mascot, a role he's been doing for nearly 30 years now. As I looked on I saw Jean Claude being ushered into the middle of the pitch by three photographers. One of the snappers noticed me in my Union Jack outfit and beckoned me over and onto the playing surface to be photographed alongside Jean Claude. It seemed that within seconds of me posing with Jean Claude there were loads of photographers competing to get the perfect shot of the entente cordiale.

Jean Claude and I were having a ball and enjoying a

conversation in broken English amidst the swarms of photographers all clamouring to get the photo. Jean Claude pointed to his watch and said words to the effect of, 'Peter at two forty, me and you will walk round the pitch together, I exclaimed, 'really?' I took up a position near dad and Simon and excitedly related to them what had transpired, I was going to walk around the pitch with Jean Claude.

I was a bit concerned, Jean Claude had remained pitch side, to get to him I had to cross the tunnel area. Two forty came and I thought to myself, dare I walk across the hallowed turf in front of the players tunnel area to join up with Jean Claude? I took what felt like an enormous step and walked right across in front of the tunnel, nobody stopped me and I rejoined Jean Claude. He suggested we swap flags and he encouraged me to hold hands as we set off around the perimeter. The hairs on my neck were standing up, the crowd were standing up cheering and clapping us as we walked around the pitch. This kind of spectacle had never been seen before at Twickenham. As far as I was concerned, only Ken Baily, the old England football mascot had ever done anything like this before at Wembley Stadium. I had walked around Twickenham in front of 75,000 fans. Fans from both teams warmly applauded us, this was on another level to anything else I had done before, I was elated. At the time it felt like a once in a lifetime opportunity, my dad and Simon had seen me, I was massively proud and excited.

Ken Baily was an iconic figure in the sporting world when I was growing up, known to thousands of sporting enthusiasts and others across the world. During the 1966 football World Cup, dressed in his John Bull outfit of top hat, red tail coat and Union Jack waistcoat, Ken had become known as World Cup Willie. Even royalty became accustomed to Ken's presence. 'What are you doing here?' asked the Queen on spotting Ken among a crowd in a Sydney street. 'I'd go anywhere for you, Ma'am,' replied Baily. On another occasion, when Prince Charles attended his first trade union conference in Ken's hometown of Bournemouth, Baily was at the door presenting him with a carnation buttonhole. Ken was England's first self-appointed sporting cheerleader, someone I noticed, always got a mention on the television or radio coverage. In lots of ways, in hindsight, he was an inspiration, everybody loved Ken at the time.

With the Basque Band

Jean Claude had been friends with Ken up until his death in 1993, although I am not sure Jean Claude was present the day Ken famously came to the rescue of the infamous Erica Roe at Twickenham in 1982 by covering the streakers assets with his Union Jack. Ken was the only man to become both a freeman of Bournemouth and a Subbuteo figure!

On completing our lap of Twickenham, we turned to each other and triumphantly shook hands right in front of the tunnel area, I was so caught up in the moment that I really had no idea that this handshake was being broadcast to

Jean Claude and Ken Baily

Jean Claude's Club

At Andre's. Don't eat the oysters Jean Claude

Entente Cordial at The White Hart

millions by the BBC. I got back to my seat in the stand and commented to dad and Simon that I had never done anything like that before. They were understandably very proud. Little did I know that one day I would become as regular a fixture at Twickenham as the seat I was sitting in.

These days Jean Claude and me are the best of mates. Incredibly, we are the only two mascots in world rugby, Jean Claude has devoted himself to his role and is highly regarded in France. I've known Jean Claude now for approximately seventeen years and he has been the French mascot for thirty plus years. He knows all the current French players really well and of course he knows hundreds of the ex-French rugby players. As a bystander, you can sense the affection and high regard they all have for him. Almost without fail when a player old or new bumps into him in a restaurant, bar or avenue they greet him in typical French style and then they immerse themselves in deep conversation that I can never understand. What I do understand and recognise from their body language is the love and respect that so many people have for Jean Claude. Most of the non rugby following French general public are very familiar with him too, he's definitely become a French icon!

Before the 2012 International between our two countries, weeks before the French Presidential election, Jean Claude and I were approached by some promotional guys, who asked if we would mind posing alongside the then Presidential candidate and now President of France Francois Hollande. Jean Claude's eyes lit up and I was pretty flattered, I was surprised to find Monsieur Hollande was quite a small man when I stood next to him.

I find it quite amazing that without either of us being able to speak each other's language, we have become such good friends and we have continued to meet each other annually since 1997. It's always a great occasion when England meet France and the perfect opportunity for us to spend time together. When I travel from Devon to Twickenham to watch an International match I always stay at the same pub *The White Hart* in Whitton, with friends of mine and when the French team are in town Jean Claude always joins us with his entourage.

It's the same in Paris when we meet up and stay with Jean Claude and his friends. It's a brilliant traditional annual get together that we have adopted now for the England versus France fixtures over all those years since 1997. Jean Claude and his great mate Andre are now massive friends of mine and I'm pleased to say it's all thanks to the rugby, the wonderful players, the families and the hospitality.

Prior to the World Cup in 2003, England had three warm up games. One was against Wales in Cardiff, virtually a second team played and we slaughtered Wales. Then we played France at Twickenham and France again down in Marseilles. I'd never been down there before to watch rugby, so we made the most of it, Pam and me, Jack, Mary, Ian (blastor) Glendenning and his wife stayed at a local hotel for four or five days. It was magnifique! Jean Claude had been to every World Cup since its inception and had been using Gulliver's Travels for years and introduced me to John Hall who he knew really well. I was delighted to meet John, the ex Gloucester player and owner of Gulliver's down in Marseille.

Jean Claude comes from a typical French town Plan D'Orgon with it's own bull ring in the heart of Provence, fifty odd miles to the north of Marseille. On our second day in the south of France, I had a massive surprise. Jean Claude had arranged an official champagne reception in honour of me at the town hall with the mayor of the town and loads of other French dignitaries. Jean Claude insisted that we were dressed in our outfits for the occasion and informed me that I had to make a speech. One of Jean Claude's mates translated my hastily arranged speech to the large audience of French folk. Then the mayor of the town made a speech ending with him bestowing the honour of the freedom of the town on me! As yet, I haven't taken a herd of sheep over any of the towns bridges, but it was a brilliant honour. After the speeches we all enjoyed a magnificent banquet and Jean Claude duly presented me with a great big glass ornament with the words, 'To my great friend Peter Cross' engraved onto it.

I've shared some wonderful nights with Jean Claude in France and have some brilliant memories. When I finish my 'duties' at Twickenham I like to get into my normal casual gear to go out for the evening, but when I'm in France with Jean Claude he likes us both to stay in costume all night. As our Anglo-French posse travel from bar to bar sampling the delights, all the other revellers seem delighted to see us. Rugby mad folk clad in their berets and waving the tricolour proudly surround us wherever we go. I'll never forget one lunchtime in Paris when we were all sat in our favourite wine bar. The Baron Rouge is an old style Parisian bar, typical of the nineteen twenties and thirties. After enjoying a fantastic lunch, we were all about to say our goodbyes when I turned around to see Jean Claude with tears rolling down his face, his friend Andre explained to me it's because you are leaving!

Before an England game, aware of my responsibilities I tend not to have a drink, apart from when I'm in Paris where I'll have a couple of glasses of wine with Jean Claude. However, the night after a game is sometimes a little different. One night I was with Pam and a couple of my mates and their wives in a bar near the Eiffel Tower. We all thought the evening was drawing to a close at about 11.30pm when Jean Claude announced he and Andre would give me and Pam a lift home. The others would have to get a taxi back to the hotel as planned. As we headed off, I whispered to Pam, 'we're going the wrong way.' I don't know whether Pam was more surprised by my navigational skills or that the evening was to continue. It transpired that Jean Claude's driver was taking us to a little bar in the middle of nowhere. When we eventually pulled up there was the thud thud of music playing, I was still in my England gear and Jean Claude was still in his outfit.

Within two or three minutes of us entering the establishment the owner came over to us and presented us with glasses of champagne. I smiled and said, 'thankyou Monsieur,' in true Del Boy style. As I enjoyed a dance with Pam I remember commenting to her what a tiny, but character-ful place it was. I was still getting to grips with the environment when it slowly dawned on me that two of the guys dancing were the French props from that day's match, Sylvain Marconnet and Pieter de Villiers. They promptly acknowledged us and within minutes I was dancing with their beautiful wives! Since that meeting, whenever I have seen them at games, they have always shaken my hand and had a chat. Amongst others that evening, in had walked Philippe Sella the most capped French inter-national centre, quickly followed by Bernard Laporte, the French national coach.

I didn't really know Laporte at that stage. He had walked past me at least a dozen times at international matches and not said a word, not even looked at me. (Incidently, his understudy Jo Maso, French international centre and legend, who has been on the coaching staff for over twenty years, would always come over and shake my hand when the French team got off the coach.) Laporte had never glanced in my direction and I had always thought he was a bit of a boring bastard, a scholarly type. Looking across the room that night I saw a very different character stood holding court at the corner of the bar. He was having a wonderful time, drinking champagne, smoking and dancing, a totally different personality than I had envisaged.

On another occasion, a Friday night before an international, we went to a bar together in Paris near the Eiffel Tower, 'a rugby bar', with a few of Jean Claude's mates and compatriots. All the Basques had come up from the South West and the bar was alive, it was really buzzing. A full band, twenty strong suddenly struck up and they started playing a really quick song. Initially, Jean Claude and me had just been enjoying the craic, but before I knew it, Jean Claude started Jiving. It turned out that Jean Claude is a top Jiver, he's brilliant, I absolutely love a good party and joined in, the whole bar was rocking.

Two years later history repeated itself, this time we were outside the Stade de France stadium in Paris where there were the usual array of great big marquees and top champagne houses. Jean Claude, as ever, had managed to get some top quality tickets for Pam, my mates and me. There were loads of ex-international rugby players there and all the hospitality was free and as ever we were enjoying it. At 5pm in the afternoon, all of a sudden the Basque band came in playing tunes. In time they all formed a circle and Jean Claude and me were thrust into the middle, decked out in our nations colours, jiving away, everyone was going crazy. The French rugby fans certainly know how to have a good time!

Another memorable pre-match story involves us having a quick drink at the Baron Rouge wine bar before a game before heading back to Andre's house. Andre's wife had prepared some gorgeous food including oysters and scallops. We all thoroughly enjoyed the delicious feast. After refuelling, we headed to the railway station to catch the train to the ground for the game. All of a sudden it became apparent Jean Claude had disappeared, Andre was asking, 'where's Jean Claude gone?' and he was looking very concerned. The English contingent, not knowing the area, didn't have a clue, but we did our best to help locate him. Next minute, out of the blue, Jean Claude in all his finery went running past us like the road runner, two minutes later he ran back past us the other way, it seemed he couldn't find a toilet and he had a major problem.

Just before the train arrived Jean Claude reappeared and the English and French compatriots all got on the train together and climbed up onto the top deck of the double decker train. Originally, I was sat near to Jean Claude and I have to say the whole carriage was humming and I don't mean in a musical way. I quickly organised a re shuffle of the seating arrangements making sure there was some distance between Jean Claude and me. French supporters on the train delighted to see Jean Claude were coming over as usual and shaking his hand and embracing him before walking away looking slightly miffed.

We arrived at the stadium, as usual Jean Claude had arranged all the tickets and I.D. accreditation, so we entered the stadium relatively smoothly. Jean Claude didn't seem to want to spend as much time outside the stadium meeting the supporters as usual. I think the feeling was mutual, 'Jean Claude,' they exclaimed as they met their national hero. Then I watched their faces drop, he really was humming!

Once inside the stadium I had to laugh when a top French official raced across the pitch to greet Jean Claude, you could tell immediately from his

First meeting with Eileen, Ann Worsley and Vincenzo

With Eileen

reaction, that this was not the Jean Claude he knew and loved. As amusing as it was for my friends and me, I was finding it a little more difficult to appreciate the humour, I knew what I had coming. We always do our lap around the pitch and I knew I would be getting my comeuppance because tradition dictates Jean Claude holds my hand and we walk together, stride for stride, there was no way I could get out of it!

I first met Eileen D'allaglio when I was outside Twickenham stadium in the early days of me donning my England uniform before I had become the official England mascot. A well dressed, rather elegant lady came over and asked, 'could I have my photo' with you please?' I replied, 'yes, of course you can, not a problem.' Next minute Eileen's friends had all gathered around for a photo and I was in my element! Eileen continued, 'oh by the way, I'm Lawrence D'allaglios mum, the lady on the other side is Joe Worsley's mum and over there is Vincenzo. Come on Vincenzo, get in the picture', I remember Eileen imploring Vincenzo to come over, 'No, replied Vincenzo, just as forcibly.' After the photos had been taken Eileen kindly asked me, 'would you like me to send you a copy of the picture.' I said I would love a copy and gave Eileen my email address and that's how my wonderful relationship with Lawrence's parents started.

From that day onwards Eileen used to invite me over for a drink in the car park at Twickenham with the 'Wasps crowd.' Before every game

Juggler

over many years I would arrive early before the game and join Eileen, Vincenzo, Steve Hayes the Chief Executive of Wasps at the time, Joe Worsley's mum Ann, Joe's sister, Paul Sampsom's dad, Josh Lewsey's Welsh dad and a few more friends and supporters, a really nice crowd of people who always gathered before an England fixture for a picnic. Many of that group were also destined to become my comfort blanket in the after match receptions I attended once I had become the official mascot. I knew I could rely on these brilliant people to welcome me into their group as I familiarised myself with the whole England after match set up. Eileen was at the heart of all of this camaraderie, despite what she and Vincenzo had been through in their personal lives, Eileen was an unbelievably positive women.

Our's was a very special relationship, we shared so much in common, not least the devastating grief at losing someone close to you. Eileen was a tremendously strong character who fought tooth and nail with the authorities. Eileen told me how she had been left feeling devastated when she had gone to the first inquest eight months after her beloved daughter Francesca had died after the Marchioness disaster. Eileen and family members of the other victims believed they would hear the reasons why their loved ones had died on the Thames. Instead she found a small army of legal people representing everyone involved except the normal people who had lost sons and daughters in the tragedy. Eileen quickly decided she did not want the Coroner who oversaw that first meeting to proceed with the inquest, but it wasn't that easy for Eileen or the other families to force change. Eileen needed to know how, where and why Francesca had died and she didn't care how long it would take. She and six other families forced the inquest to be adjourned. Despite being put under pressure to allow the inquest to continue, Eileen refused.

Eileen would tell me of forthcoming meetings and describe how she would have to stand up and speak. Privately, I knew she was as nervous as hell, but she was determined to speak up for all the families.

Lawrence D'allaglio's autobiography, 'It's In The Blood,' describes his mum's tenacity brilliantly. Eileen had worked as an air stewardess and therefore understood that if anyone had survived the impact of the collision and managed to find a way off the boat they should have had a very good chance of surviving. She didn't understand how more people had died in the water, than on the boat, which had sunk in the middle of London on a clear summer night. She and the Marcioness Action Group fought a long and often bitter battle to find out the truth. The skipper of the dredger Bowbelle that had ploughed into the Marchioness was prosecuted twice, on both occasions the jury couldn't agree on a verdict. Incredibly, at one stage the Coroner suggested that the Marchioness Action Group were a small minority of people who were seeking publicity from the tragedy, describing Eileen and others as 'mentally unwell' and another Margaret Lockwood-Croft as 'unhinged.'

The families of the victims sought a judicial review and lost, the whole process was expensive and not all of the families could afford to continue. Eileen and Margaret applied for legal aid and were refused, twice. Eileen's solicitor warned her that she could lose her house, Eileen replied, 'What are houses when you're in search of peace and contentment.' Eileen's strength of character and courage led them to apply for legal aid a third time and they challenged the Coroners refusal to resume the inquest at the Court of Appeal.

The Court of Appeal case found that the Coroner had acted with 'an appearance of bias' against the victim's families and that he should be removed. A new Coroner decreed that the inquest should be resumed. Meanwhile, Eileen brought one share in Ready Mixed Concrete, owners of the Bowbelle, along with twenty friends from the Marchioness Action Group and protested at the Annual General Meeting. Eileen spoke passionately saying that as the company's vessel had caused the disaster the company should fund the families fight for justice. The chairman of the company said that the matter was in the hands of insurers. That didn't deter Eileen; she went back every year to the AGMs and made the same case.

The final inquest lasted five weeks, Michael Mansfield, the Queens Counsel representing the families of the victims, said to Eileen that the best she could expect was an open verdict. 'No,' replied Eileen, 'that's not the best we can expect. You and I both know that Francesca and the other fifty victims in this tragedy were unlawfully killed and we are here to convince the jury of that fact.' Eileen had gone through legal books, studied merchant shipping laws dating back to 1894 and understood what a prudent shipmaster should have done on a voyage on the river. Eileen spoke for 43 minutes on the witness stand, concentrating as much as she could on the many mistakes and sloppy standards that had led to the collision. She spoke too about the terrible grief she and others had suffered through the years, some of the avoidable emotional fall out caused by the tragedy, and also the unnecessary trauma caused by the behaviour of the Coroners office.

Finally, after six years of campaigning the jury gave its verdict, unanimous, all forty four were unlawfully killed. (seven victims had already been dealt with in the aborted earlier inquest) Eileen told me she and many others cried, they all knew that negligence was the cause of the collision and yet for years no one had been prepared to listen. The verdict meant some person or persons were responsible for the death of fifty one people on the Thames.

Getting the coroner stood down in the Court of Appeal made legal history and opened the door for others who disagree with a coroner's decision to have it judicially reviewed. Lord Justice Clark's inquiry findings in 2002 made wholesale recommendations for the improvement of safety standards on our rivers. Now there are new lifeboat stations on the Thames, and the RNLI have high speed boats that can be used to get to the scene of an accident very quickly. The old, huge dredgers have been removed and safety standards on pleasure boats are more carefully monitored. For 15 years after Francesca died, Eileen was consumed by the struggle.

Eileen and Vincenzo were massive supporters of everything Francesca and Lawrence did. She told me Francesca was a very talented ballet dancer and was destined to be very successful. Lawrence as a teenager was an excellent footballer and could have made it professionally as a centre half. Both parents worked to be able to afford to send them to the best schools. They sent Lawrence to Ampleforth College in North Yorkshire, (coincidently my mate Tony Welsh had been a pupil there). I could tell Eileen and Vincenzo were parents who would do absolutely anything to support their children.

Once Eileen and Vincenzo started watching Lawrence play for Wasps they were made to feel very welcome by everyone at that special rugby club. "Everyone at Wasps understood our situation and there was always someone to willing to listen, or someone to talk to" Eileen once told me. From the moment Lawrence joined Wasps as a teenager, his parents would watch every game possible. Eileen became extremely well known, not just amongst the home fans but at opposition grounds too. Make no mistake, she knew her rugby and let everyone know her views. A true rugby mum!

One of my favourite rugby memories with Eileen and Vincenzo was when England won the Grand Slam in Dublin in 2003. It was such an important win in England's history which I talk about elsewhere in the book.

As I stood on the touchline, following England's win over the Irish, all the players' families were waving, cheering and making a lot of noise from above in the stand and I was waving back to them. Eileen and Vincenzo came down and asked if I was going into the after match reception. I said I couldn't because I didn't have a pass. Eileen said I could have Vincenzo's! I enquired, 'but what about Vincenzo, Eileen said don't worry, he'll find a way.' So there we were under the stand at Landsdowne Road enjoying our cream buns and tea when we heard a commotion. It was Vincenzo at the entrance and the stewards wouldn't let him in! One steward was insisting, 'you can be Lawrence D'allaglio's dad, you can be whoever you want to be, but you aint coming in if you haven't got a ticket!' I explained the situation to the steward and eventually we sorted it all out. It was so funny. How I had managed to get in as Lawrence's father dressed in all my England gear, I will never know.

Prior to the 2003 World Cup, Eileen contacted me and said she and her friend Cindy were coming down to Bickleigh in Devon for a few days and we arranged to meet up. Pam and I travelled up and enjoyed a marvellous dinner next to the River Exe with Eileen and her companion. As usual with Eileen we talked masses of rugby and I found out a lot more about Lawrence and the scrapes he had gone into as a teenager and all about his sporting career. Listening to Eileen talk about Lawrence was fascinating; without doubt Lawrence was a big favourite of mine. When I first met Lawrence I was probably the most excited I have been when meeting an England player. His personality, charisma and frankly, good looks made him stand out in my opinion. Eileen was staying at a bed and breakfast that belonged to a big Wasps fan, part of the 'Wasps family'. We invited Eileen and Cindy to our house for a barbeque the next day. I arranged to meet Eileen in my car at the M5 motorway so she could follow me to our house and after the barbie my dad escorted them back to the motorway. It was a beautiful spring day, I'd invited a few friends over and we all enjoyed some Champagne and beautifully prepared food, a memorable day.

From the very first time I went to the rugby at Twickenham I almost always had my good mate Dave Williams with me, home and away. Dave, a Cornishman from Falmouth was an excellent club cricketer and a very good rugby player. We both joined Teignmouth Rugby Club in 1967 having got new jobs in the area at a similar time. I've travelled the world over with Dave, over the decades, he is one of my finest companions, a ladies man with a brilliant knowledge of the game and sport in general. When asked who the ugliest player I ever played with, or against, my immediate humorous reply is Dave Williams. Dave suffered at the hands of rugby, whether it was a boot or a fist, Dave's nose was always being put out of joint so to speak!

Dave's dad, Bunny Williams, was a well known figure in Cornish rugby and cricket circles, he was an absolute legend. Everybody in Cornwall knew Bunny. Bunny formed a rugby club in Falmouth called One and All, he formed a cricket club in Falmouth, he was just an absolute sports nut case. Right into his eighties Bunny would get on his moped and go to a local sporting fixture, even if it was just a schools match and he would compile a match report to put in the press. For many, many years on a Saturday night Bunny and his wife would have all the teams around Cornwall ring them up with the results and reports from the days matches and Bunny and his wife would collate them all ready for 'The Cornishman' paper. A couple of years after Bunny had passed away, I met the ex England winger Kenny Plummer at a Devon versus Cornwall rugby fixture. Kenny, a Falmouth man himself, told me that he always regretted not nominating Bunny for an honour for all the brilliant work he did in Cornwall for sport, I agreed, Bunny definitely deserved an honour. Having known Bunny, it is very easy to understand how my mate Dave is such a massive sports nut.

I met my good pal John Playford on the flight back from Dublin after a re arranged International England had to play, the original had been postponed due to the foot and mouth crisis. John, an ex Bath footballer, was with the West Hill boys, a group of fans from a wealthy area near to Exeter. John lived near to Sir John Evans, ex-Chief Constable Devon and Cornwall Police, and overall he was so well connected. Most of the West Hill boys could afford to travel to away Internationals. I would have loved John to have been my companion for many more years had he not had a stroke and passed away suddenly just before the 2007 World Cup in France. John had arranged all the tickets and accommodation for Pam and me and him and his wife Lynne. We were all devastated.

John worked for Rank Xerox as a young man alongside a young Clive

Woodward and Clive's wife Jane, who was a secretary for the company. John was a smashing bloke, he had always been a mad rugby fan, spending thousands of pounds on a Box at Bath and travelling watching England home and away. John was so reliable and such good company and he knew his rugby inside out.

Before John passed away we attended the benefit match for broken neck victim Matt Hampson in May 2006. Matt was a terrific Leicester Tigers prop forward who suffered the terrible injury while training with England's Under 21s under coach Pete Drewett, who went on to coach Exeter for a while. The testimonial was played at Leicester Tigers ground, Welford Road. I'd never been to the famous ground before and was delighted and honoured when Pete, who I'd got to know at Exeter, invited me to go up for the game. I travelled up with John and we stayed at a hotel near the ground the night before.

When I arrived at the pre-match reception I was gob smacked and delighted to see so many people from the rugby union there in support of Matt. Martyn Thomas, the chairman of the RFU, his personal assistant at the time, Sandy Le Good who has subsequently become a good friend of mine at Twickenham, Jon Callard, Andy Robinson, coaches of the England team and under 21 team, spinal injury specialists and Sarah Butterworth a personal assistant, to name just a few. It was awesome. I waved my flag as the players took to the field and it turned out to be a cracking game played out before a large knowledgeable crowd.

After the game I introduced John Playford to Jon Callard. John was delighted to meet one of his Bath favourites. The Rugby Football Union organised their own little bar, which was free, if you showed a ticket at the bar. Somehow, John and I ended up with more tickets than we started with! Matt was in the bar with all his mates, it was brilliant to see him being so positive, having a drink and a laugh. Matt is a truly inspirational figure in the game, he has gone on to create the Matt Hampson Foundation, which does terrific work, inspiring and supporting young people who have been seriously injured through sport.

When my good friends Tony and Barbara returned from a spell in the Middle East in 1994 they introduced me to an idea that would bring us so much pleasure over many years to come. Tony and Barbara are a really sociable couple, their generosity and willingness to 'party on' is remarkable. Whilst abroad they had joined a Hash running club and Tony suggested we form a club in the Dawlish area. There were hardly any existing clubs in Devon, although there was one in Plymouth. We all decided to travel down to Plymouth to get feel of it and give it a go. We were warmly welcomed and it was brilliant fun.

After the trial in Plymouth Pam and I were convinced. Tony and I advertised for members for the new Dawlish Hash, we christened ourselves the Teign Valley Hash House Harriers. Our daughter, Ali, who was always a fit young girl having played squash with me as a youngster and Simon quickly decided to join us. Lots of people who we didn't know responded to the ad' and friends of ours joined too. We had no idea just how big the Dawlish Hash would become. On one occasion Pam and I had set a run over Dartmoor finishing at the Old Inn, Widecombe in the Moor. Well over a hundred people turned up and the happy landlord subsequently reported to me he'd had the best Monday's takings ever.

What is Hash running all about I hear some of you asking. Hash clubs promote social running around a trail marked out in sawdust or flour by the hare. A designated member of the group sets the trail for the week and everyone is guaranteed a get together back at the pub after completing the course. Invariably, the trail starts from a pub and no one knows where they are heading at the outset. The hare marks the check points, which the runners have to find, to be able determine the correct route. The slower runners catch up with the leaders because they are busy finding the correct trail. Often the more accomplished runners complete the evening having run much further than those less capable.

The original objective of hash running was to promote physical fitness amongst its members, to get rid of weekend hangovers (that's why our runs were on Monday nights), to acquire a good thirst, satisfy it with beer and to persuade older members they are not as old as they feel.

It is not competitive yet it does encourage those involved to compete with the terrain and other hashers. We found it was a great way to explore Devon with people of similar persuasions and interests. The average hasher male or female isn't a very serious or intense person and a Hash club is made up from a variety of people from all walks of life. Indeed on our hash we had two regular runners who had represented Great Britain!

Eventually, you get christened with your hash name and that is what you are known by. In fact it's not uncommon that you find that hashers have no idea of other hashers real names. My hash name was 'Cockie', Pam's was 'Saint', Ali didn't have one, Simon's was 'Poseur', Tony's 'Wally' and Barbara's, 'Peaches'. Very few hashers are teetotal because it's about having a drink and a good laugh after the run. It's very much akin to a rugby club and what happens after the game.

Dawlish Annual Run

AN ENGLISHMAN'S HOME IS HIS CASTLE

I'd met Pam in the summer of 1964 just after I had moved to Topsham and was still working as a Policeman. I was a member of the Police tug of war team and once a week we would all get together to train at the Royal Marine barracks at Lympstone. One of the Marine physical training instructors would take us and it was bloody hard work. In a way it served as some extra pre-season training for Exeter Rugby Club. By the time the season with Exeter started, having done the rugby pre-season too, I was really fit.

One summer's day we finished our tug of war training and as usual we headed off to Exmouth seaside resort for a relaxing swim in the sea. Pam was on a break from work and was staying at her sisters house. One or two of the lads already knew Dot who was married to Dave Jones, a fellow Policeman. When we noticed the two of them sat together on the beach, we had no hesitation in deciding to introduce ourselves to Dots younger sister. A few of us went and had a chat with them. Once we had finished chatting, all the lads were saying, 'wow, what about Dots sister!' Pam was seventeen, had a really good figure, in fact she had everything. I definitely took a fancy to Pam and I thought to myself, I've got to get in quick here before I get gazumped! I asked Pam if she would like to come out with me for a drink and thankfully she said yes. We went out that night in Topsham, I took her home afterwards to Dot's house where Pam was staying, I got a kiss and that was it.

That evening I discovered that Pam was working in London, so we decided to keep in touch by regularly exchanging letters. Pam had managed to get a job in the war office. It was a top secret job, albeit she found it quite mundane. She used to handle files that she told me contained highly sensitive affairs of the State. Knowing that she witnessed some very confidential information regarding actors, politicians and high profile figures, I have often questioned her with regards to the details. To this day, Pam has never shared with me any of the information she was privy to, even though I've sometimes interrogated her after she has had a few drinks!

I'd obviously impressed Pam enough after meeting her on the beach because some weeks later she had moved back to Devon and had got herself a job working in the treasurer's department of the Devon County Council. Pam soon became a regular at The County Ground watching me play for the Exeter rugby team. I was fairly new to the club and Pam would sit alone in the grandstand in all types of weather lending me

Pam – Braunton Carnival Queen, aged 16

Simon's first day at work

When Simon was about eighteen and had completed his college studies he decided he wanted to come 'repping' with me, he became my partner. He was brilliant, perfect for the role, six foot four, smart, polite, handsome and always willing. We would often set off in the car early in the morning headed for Cornwall, with sandwiches packed laughing and joking as we went. Invariably, by the time we had reached Cornwall at about ten o'clock, Simon had eaten most of the packed lunch. I would have to buy us another lunch, we loved

our Cornish pasties and fresh fish and chips and we were both fit and active enough to burn the calories off back then. I'd always drive down in the morning and Simon would drive back home late afternoon, early evening, when his old man was tired. These were the good old days of English tourism and we made hay while the sun shone, or even if it didn't!

Simon and me worked together for a quite a few years, we had a great relationship. We went to trade shows together, attended sales meetings and we were quite

I love you 2

a team. He would confide in me about absolutely everything he was getting up to, we were more like brothers, than father and son. Simon was always a pleasure to be around, he always had a smile on his face and the time to talk to anyone. When Pam and me were out for an evening in Dawlish if we bumped into Simon or Ali we would always be welcome to join them and their mates. It was great fun.

Simon's mates were my mates, we all watched the footy at the pub together, eyed up the girls and had a great laugh. They were special times. I used to say to Simon, if you ever want to bring your mates back to the house you're more than welcome, feel free to help yourself to my wine and beers, you can always pay me back the next day or whatever. Sure enough, Pam and me would often arrive back to carnage, half drunk wine bottles and beer cans strewn around. Young local girls that I recognised from town would be leaving the house early in the morning after partying the night away.

As Simon grew older he was developing into a fine young man, more confident and outgoing than ever. He began to work more independently as a self employed agent for a few of his own companies. We would still visit places as a team, working together on occasions. However, more and more frequently Simon would work on his own.

Simon was aged twenty one, when in January 1990 he suddenly didn't feel very well; something wasn't right. Pam called the doctor, who quickly came to our house, checked him over and gave him the all clear. However, his condition soon deteriorated and within twenty-four hours he was taken into hospital. Within eight hours he was in intensive care on a ventilator and he had tubes everywhere. It was without doubt one of the worst phases of our lives. I can remember feeling numb and totally powerless, not able to sleep and constantly replaying awful scenarios over in my head. The doctors and nurses at the hospital could not give us any answers to the questions we continually raised. Simon was in a critical condition for a week and was permanently unconscious.

I remember just talking positively to him all the time as we sat with him day and night. I used to say, 'when you get over all of this we'll go and watch Man United play', I would stroke him and kiss him as he just lay there, motionless. The nurses were wonderful and would give Pam and me sleeping tablets to help us sleep as the days passed.

Top agents. Me and Simon, 2nd and 3rd right, front row

Simon and I had both been due to attend a trade show together in Birmingham that week. We loved the trade shows, every night was party night and we had been really looking forward to it. Rather than us joining all the guys and girls in Birmingham, suddenly they were ringing me constantly for updates on Simons health, it was horrific, such an unexpected turn of events.

One morning we went into the ward and the nurse tending Simon was smiling, she said, 'Simon has come round', it was like a miracle had happened, words can not express the relief we felt. The doctors explained to us that they had no idea what the virus was, but his body had beaten it and it was gone. Simon was soon back to himself and I clearly remember him remarking about me being at his bed side. Smiling, he said, 'Dad, yes I really want to go and watch Man United play, but I couldn't stand you kissing me and rubbing my hair!' Intensive care was quickly forgotten and before long he was working with me again, running with me in the evenings and playing squash, as if nothing had ever happened. Pam,

Dover en route to Africa

Ali and me were over the moon and we quickly resumed being a positive family unit.

Some time later, out of the blue, Simon informed us he didn't want to be a representative any more. He wanted to travel around the world. Although surprised at the sudden decision, Pam and I backed Simon one hundred per cent. Life was for living. He left London in a big army lorry for an overland adventure with a group of about twenty young adults. They travelled all the way down through Spain and Gilbraltar, across to Africa, down the west coast and travelled throughout

Simon in deepest Africa

Africa, taking in locations which included, Casablanca, Marrakesh, Western Sahara, Senegal, Mauritania, Mali, Ivory Coast, Ghana, Nigeria, Cameroon, Central African Republic, Zaire, Rwanda, Lake Victoria, Tanzania, Kenya and Mombassa. Wow! Simon was elated when he came home. He told us the group got on so well and had so such fun together for the whole six months. It was a brilliant experience for him, not many youngsters get that kind of opportunity in life.

Having experienced an adventure of that magnitude and rarity, Simon returned home a more rounded and wiser young man. We as parents were tremendously proud and happy to have him safely back home with us.

On returning, Simon slipped comfortably back into work with the family business. Ali had coincidently just returned back home from London where she had worked in the Cheltenham and Gloucester Building Society as an assistant Manager in the big lending department in the City of London. Pam and I had just acquired the freehold of a shop in our hometown of Dawlish, so we all came together as a family and got the shop up and running.

In 1997, Simon was suddenly taken poorly again. He was twenty eight by now. He had been over his previous problem for years and was living life to the full. Simon had just enjoyed a stag weekend in Newquay, Cornwall with lots of his mates and was having the time of his life. Out of nowhere, soon after returning home his spleen burst. We immediately called an ambulance and he was rushed to hospital. It was so traumatic and there was no apparent reason. I could have understood if he had been punched or kicked in the stomach playing rugby, or had been injured in a serious road accident. It was very strange and extremely worrying for Pam and me. Simon was in hospital for a week, they removed his spleen and once again before we knew it he was out of hospital and apparently all right again. In retrospect, Pam and I think that it all had a lot to do with the original virus and the effect it had had on his immune system.

A short while later I remember Pam coming up to me, looking really worried, she was very concerned. Simon had confided to his mum that he kept getting little freezes in his face, nothing serious he bravely told her, although he was clearly worried. Pam's motherly instinct told her we had got to get him to the doctors as soon as possible even though Simon wasn't keen to go. We took him to the doctors who advised us

Simon and Emma

that we should get him checked out at the hospital, they thought he was having little fits. On the outside as far as I was concerned he seemed okay, Simon had convinced me at least that he was fine in himself and I needn't worry.

We took Simon privately to a hospital in Exeter where he had a MRI scan, one of those all over tunnel scans. After about half an hour or so Simon came out looking worried and said, 'dad, they want me to go in the tunnel again', my heart sank, I didn't like the sound of this. Pam had continued up to North Devon to be with her mum and I rang her to tell her the news, in as positive a manner as I could muster. Despite my best efforts I knew immediately she feared the worst too. After the second scan, we were given the news all parents dread, Simon had a brain tumour.

We remained so positive and just supported him as best we could. In return, Simon was so gutsy, he went away for a month to Brazil, Bolivia and Machu Picchu in Peru as if there wasn't a problem, really gutsy, climbing mountains and getting stuck in. In November of that year Simon and me went to watch England play Italy at rugby in a World Cup qualifier in Huddersfield, which England comfortably won.

Nou Camp, Barcelona,
Man United v Bayern Munich, 1999

The following day, a typical cold, grey November day in Lancashire, I took Simon to my hometown in Oldham and showed him around my old haunts. I think he was pleased he'd been brought up in Devon. The next day was brighter as we were flying from Manchester airport to Barcelona. We had joined the Manchester United supporters club and we had tickets to see United play Barcelona in the group stages of the Champions League. It was a brilliant, breathtaking game, United were one goal down, then two-one up and three-two up before Barcelona equalised again to make it three all. Two spectacular goals from Rivaldo and one from Anderson for Barca and three exceptional goals via the excellent Cole and Yorke partnership ignited the massive Nou Camp crowd. Simon was absolutely fine and really enjoyed the match and brilliant atmosphere. Neither of us were drinking, which our mates from Dawlish found unusual, but you would never have guessed Simon was poorly

United eventually made the final of the Champions League the following May and I was determined to get tickets for Simon and me. As a positive person, I hadn't thought about Simon dying. I thought with the right tablets he would eventually be fine. Eight of us from Dawlish applied for tickets for the final and remarkably we managed to get eight tickets, at a cost of twenty pounds each, amazing. We were all jumping around, whooping and hollering!

The day before we set off on the ferry from Plymouth to Roscoff was Simon's thirtieth birthday and he had a fit. It was the fourth serious fit he had had. Pam really had a bad feeling about it all, her mothers instinct. I remained positive, unrealistic I guess, Simon had always bounced back.

I remember being so protective of Simon on the day we arrived in Barcelona with Pam and Simon's girlfriend Emma. We were back at the Nou Camp stadium for the final of the Champions League, Manchester United against the German giants Bayern Munich. It was impossible not to think about the Munich air tragedy that had decimated the Manchester team in 1958 and Simon's condition. Nevertheless, we were going to have a day to remember. On arrival, the girls went off shopping together, while we arranged for a taxi to pick us up from the train station to take us to the ground and pick us up afterwards.

The match turned out to be one of the most incredible matches ever seen in United's illustrious history. United were totally outplayed for the whole ninety minutes, before equalising and then scoring the winner in the last couple of minutes of injury time. I remember the incredible feeling of elation, shared amongst all of the fans stood behind Oliver Kahn's goal, as the goals went in right in front of where we were stood. At the final whistle the Munich players were on their knees, desolated at how United had literally stolen the victory. Manchester United had achieved an implausible, unprecedented treble. I felt sure fate had been on our side, someone was looking over us that night. I had never experienced such a surreal end to a game, the emotions took over and I was cuddling Simon and we were kissing each other. We knew Bayern had been much the better team throughout the match, somehow for us that made it even sweeter. It was a tremendously personal moment shared between Simon and me, I can remember saying to Simon, 'we can say for the rest of our lives that we were there.'

Shortly after that memorable evening Simon had a massive fit in our house, Pam and I were so scared. I was just laying on the floor beside him, mopping him down, horrible. It's at a time like that when you realise how you love someone, remarkably he was all right when he came around, but we were massively worried.

When we had arrived back from Barcelona, I had been invited to be on a television show on Westcountry Television to help celebrate St George's day. They asked me to dress up in my England gear and I appeared alongside some other guests. Included amongst them was Geoffrey Rowe who had played rugby for the Penzance Pirates, but is probably better known for being Jethro, the Cornish comedian. During his interview Jethro made it clear he was very anti Europe, he loved England and he loved Cornwall. The two of us got on like a house on fire, he is naturally a very funny man and brilliant character. One of the questions I remember them asking me was, would I support Wales, Scotland or Ireland if they were playing another nation apart from England? I replied, 'of course I would', perhaps I lied with regards to Wales! During a break in proceedings, Jethro asked me if I would like to take part in an anti Europe rally at his club in Lewdown, Okehampton. He informed me that lots of special guests would be attending and I said I would love to go along and do my bit.

I never went.

On the day that I was due to go to Jethro's club, Simon had to go into hospital to have his bone marrow checked. The drugs he had been taking were too strong and had messed up his bone marrow and his organs. Pam stayed all night with Simon, on what turned out to be his last night. The next morning, I went in to see Simon and he said to me, 'Dad, I don't want any more of those fits.' We lost him that day.

I have remained in contact and am still great mates with many of Simon's friends and girlfriends. I've seen a lot of them go on to get married and have children. I often bump into them in Dawlish and some still come to parties I throw at our house. One of Simon's best friends Lee Henderson got married a year or so after Simon died. Simon was going to be his best man, so instead Lee asked if I would be willing to be his best man. I was extremely proud and honoured to be asked, it was a brilliant day, although very, very emotional. I regularly invite some of Simon's old mates to come up to Twickenham with me to watch England play and we always have a cracking time!

My daughter Ali, had planned to get married in September 1999. The wedding had been pre arranged to take place only eight weeks to the day after Simon had passed away. Pam and me talked to Ali about it and she asked whether we should cancel the wedding because of what had happened. Having discussed it as a family we decided we should press on and have the wedding, we couldn't bring Simon back, it might be harder if we re arranged it for twelve months later.

We pushed ahead with the plans, we had arranged to have a party on our lawn after the ceremony. We booked a big marquee and a ten piece soul band, Joey the Lips, a fabulous local group that everybody loved. My mate Tony and me had already agreed that we wanted to do things properly and we'd organised that we would travel down to Champagne to a Vineyard I knew to collect the booze. I rang the Vineyard to order two hundred bottles of Champagne, but because it was the Millennium year they had had massive demand and they could only allocate us a hundred bottles. We travelled down to the middle of France and collected the Champagne in Tony's van. On the way back home we went into a Carrefour supermarket and bought loads of wine, we were going ahead with the wedding and we were definitely going to party on. It was so difficult, I had lost my son, but being positive helps in so many ways and we got through.

Ali and Andy's special day

116

Dad with Ali and Emma

Ali got married in a beautiful hotel on Dartmoor with the most fantastic views of the stunning Devonshire country-side. The hotel management allowed us to take some of the Champagne up and some finger food we had prepared. Two of my best mates Barry Knight and Jack Smith were at the hotel in dinner jackets and black tie waiting on everybody. It was a top quality day. Ali looked absolutely stunning in her beautiful wedding dress, Andy wore his kilt and Pam and me were two of the proudest parents in the world. We travelled back to our house in two coaches that we had hired. Two of my other mates, Pete Cockram and Jim Hickson, had remained at home, making sure the catering was in hand, the Champagne was chilled and everything was in order.

During the wedding ceremony there had been a massive localised thunderstorm. In our absence Pete and Jim had to contend with a tremendous downpour and the marquee was caving in through the weight of the water. Luckily Pete and Jim are really practical blokes and they had managed to clear the water as it bucketed down from above. By the time we had all arrived back from Dartmoor none of the guests were any the wiser as to the drama that had been going on while we were at the

Young Teignmouth fund raisers with Olympic torch

hotel. In the evening it seemed as if half of Dawlish descended upon us. It was a brilliant night, with some fantastic dancing, it rocked and it rolled. There was no doubt it had been a fantastic day and a sensational evening. However, for Pam and me it was just like going through the motions, it was surreal.

Being positive through massive adversity is what helps Pam and me and many others like ourselves get through our grief. Doing my Mr England thing and my cycle rides with my mates for charity has helped me massively. It gave me things to do and think about and diverted my mind from the tremendous grief. I think continuing with the wedding helped all of us as a family move on with our lives a tad further. During this time Pam and Ali were brilliantly supportive especially given we had a business to run, their love and encouragement was massive in ensuring I could continue my personal journey.

The wedding was the future and Ali and Andy have since started their own family, our grand children Ross and Alex bring Pam and me so much pleasure. Since attending the Olympics in Atlanta, I'd always had an ambition to go to the Paralympic games, watching the way those competitors have battled against their own particular adversities has always brought a tear to my eye. When Great Britain were awarded the 2013 Olympics I vowed that I would get tickets for both the Olympics and the Paralympics. What a brilliant opportunity to take my grandkids to a major sporting event in our own country. Indeed, Ross helped his Grandad on the computer to apply for the tickets. I was able to allocate two thousand pounds towards our attempt to secure tickets, Ross was mortified and said, 'Grandad, you can't spend that much.' I replied that we would be lucky to get half of what we wanted. As it turned out we didn't get any tickets for the Olympics, but we were lucky to get most of the tickets we wanted for the Paralympics.

I was a bit miffed with regards to the allocation for the Olympic tickets, because we were looking to buy children's tickets and for me it was all about the legacy. However, we had two wonderful days at the Olympic Park and witnessed many world records being broken in the wonderful stadium, which was full to capacity with genuine fans and not so many corporate clients. Ross and Alex thoroughly enjoyed a fantastic weekend and you could sense all the wonderful paralympians that competed had enjoyed the time of their lives.

My grandkids take over our front lawn in summer

FOR QUEEN AND COUNTRY

Since the Atlanta Olympics in 1996 I have been to every England rugby international at home and every away Six Nations game with the exception of the 2012 fixture in Italy. The only other internationals I've missed were during some of the summer tours which to be fair would have been too expensive and time consuming. In addition, I have been present at every World Cup since 1999.

Billy on guard

A typical routine for an England home fixture involves me and six to eight mates, (I try to take different friends on a kind of rota system!) leaving Dawlish in Devon on a Friday afternoon and travelling the three to four hour journey up to the White Hart pub in Whitton near Twickenham where we all stay. Ann and her son Steve, the landlords, Sean, Michael and all the staff have been superb hosts to us all over the years. It is a no nonsense pub which plays host to hundreds of sporting enthusiasts and revellers.

On arrival we unpack all of our cases, including my Mr England uniform, spare top hat, flags and Billy the bulldog as quickly and efficiently as possible so we can head straight back down to the bar and have a couple of drinks to relax. After a quick change of gear we then head into Twickenham to enjoy some more drinks and a meal at one of our favourite restaurants. Discussions are varied and spontaneous, who should play in the front row, what game plan should England adopt and did you see that? Wow! Invariably we move on to Richmond and the Sun Inn a fabulous rugby venue for a couple more drinks and a lot more rugby conversation interspersed with an occasional, wow! My intention at the beginning of the evening is to have an early night and not to drink too much, but . . .

In the morning we gather downstairs in the White Hart for breakfast at about nine a.m. and it is at this point, just after breakfast, as in my playing days, when I begin to feel nervous and get butterflies in my stomach. I get dressed slowly and meticulously making sure every pin badge on my jacket is positioned correctly, my Wooden Spoon bow tie is straight and I have all the tickets to hand. I feel extremely proud and honoured every time I put the uniform on. When I reappear downstairs in my uniform I notice people nudging each other as I walk through the bar, it's incredible I've been relatively anonymous until then.

We all walk the half a mile or so down to the stadium and the adrenaline is pumping as we pass scores of excited fans. We chat about the potential outcomes, team news and weather conditions, nothing can distract us, well I tell a lie, some things do attract the eye!

Nearing the magnificent Twickenham Stadium the atmosphere really begins to hot up, it's noticeable now how many people are clocking me, it's fun to witness them debating whether to approach for a photo. One of my pals, (they like to be called my wing men!) usually want to carry Billy the Bulldog for me and another will offer to carry my bag, while I'm stopped and asked for photos. My friends like to carry Billy in particular; they've told me it makes them feel part of the occasion.

Billy the bulldog has become an iconic figure at Twickenham, supporters love to have their photos taken with him inside and outside of the stadium. Billy was originally, just another Bulldog, but with a little imagination, a headband and English waistcoat he soon became a celebrity in the dog world. I used Billy as a prop in the early days. I guess it was nice to have some company and the England supporters really took to him. Some would argue Billy's more popular than me! I noticed that when I was walking around the stadium it seemed to make it easier for people, especially youngsters to stop me and have a chat. Not only would people be drawn to me, they would want to meet Billy. I used Billy as a crutch, he would help me answer some of the more difficult questions. If necessary, I could ask Billy his opinion which bought me some time to think of answers and it provided some humour, me and Billy chatting away.

In 2004, Billy was subject to an elaborate kidnapping plot which was headline news in my local press. I'm not sure it made the National headlines, which is probably just as well given the affection for Billy. At the time, I commented in the Herald Express newspaper that I was calling in a former top cop, Sir John Evans to help track down ' these evil people,' I continued, 'I've got a fair idea who is behind it – one of them, a scruffy chap, was spotted walking through Newton Abbot with Billy.' The 'gang of kidnappers,' had delivered a ransom note through my letterbox, it stated, 'We have got Billy' and went on to demand fifty pounds for a charity of my choice to get Billy back in one piece, or they would start cutting him into bits, culminating with them severing his head. I was left with no option but to meet their deadline and save Billy from harm, despite my grave reservations on giving in to dognappers demands. The Wooden Spoon charity benefited to the tune of £100 and I vowed that ex-Teignmouth rugby player Craig Greenwood and his gang should never be invited to Twickenham with me again. The truth is they are great blokes and have since been with me loads of times, I just make sure I keep my eyes on Billy!

On arriving at the stadium, I head as quickly as I can to the Spirit of Rugby where I deposit my gear and leave Billy to go about his business alone. All I need with me for the arrival of the coach is my flag. I like to stop and spend time with everyone who asks for a photograph as I go, it really is an honour and I have a permanent smile on my face, it's lovely. I have been asked if I act differently when I am in my uniform. The honest answer is, being dressed up doesn't change me one bit, I am totally myself, I speak to everyone exactly as I would if I met them down the pub or in the street. Fans love to direct comments at me and shout from afar, I'm pleased to hear everything they cry out, most fans are complimentary! I always check with the security guards what time they are expecting the team coaches as I need to ensure I am in position for their arrival.

At one game the England player's coach arrived early and passed me as I was strolling to the Stadium, it must have been funny for all the spectators to see Mr England sprinting alongside the coach trying to keep up! There was another occasion when I was picnicking with the Wasps crowd and the security guards phoned me saying, 'quick Pete, get your arse down here, the England team has arrived and they will be getting off the coach in seconds.' I sprinted down and appeared from behind the coach, just in time to greet the players. Lucky I had given the security guys my mobile in case of such an emergency.

It's interesting the people I see as I am walking around the perimeter and car parks before and after a game. Once I had gone to meet my mate Tony in the west stand car park, he pointed out to me that Deborah Meadon of Dragons Den fame was drinking with friends nearby. Tony knew that in my selling days I used to deal with Debbie when she ran a family company in Minehead, Somerset. He suggested that I went and said hello, but I didn't want to trouble her. Tony persisted, saying, 'she keeps looking towards you'. I went over and said 'hello', she replied, 'Peter Cross, what are you doing here?' With that her husband said, 'Pete's the England mascot, don't you remember we saw him at the World Cup in Australia?' It was intriguing that unlike the majority of supporters, Debbie remembered my face, rather than the Mr England image.

To the best of my memory, I've never refused a supporter a picture; I love the camaraderie and joy it brings to the England fans and me. When buried in a scrum of supporters all clutching their pints of ale and guinness it's inevitable that I kop an early shower from time to time. I'm sometimes under a bit of pressure just prior to kick off when I am conscious of being in position to carry out my role in time. If I am ever rushing, I find taking my top hat off does the trick, amazingly supporters don't spot me as readily without it perched on my head. I am so focused on being in the stadium and in my place for the National Anthem, I have genuinely had nightmares. I visualise Richard Prescott demanding, 'where's Pete Cross?'

After one International I was making my way to the Spirit of Rugby when I was asked by a very attractive young lady if she could have her picture taken with me. Immediately I was joined by another member of her group who wanted to have his picture taken too. As I looked up at him, he said, 'thanks Pete, much appreciated.' I instantly clocked him as being Prince Harry's best mate Marko who some ten years earlier had been the guy that had requested on behalf of Harry that I joined them while at a reception.

A moment that I consider as pivotal to my role and possibly the most important, is waving my flag to welcome the England team coach as it

arrives at Twickenham Stadium, England's home. The security guards form a huge cordon to allow the coaches to draw up and I am so lucky to be able to stand there amongst the television crews and photographers ready to greet the players. Each and every time I perform this role I am overwhelmed with emotion, the sense of pride I feel is impossible to explain. Some players may be making their debuts, some winning their fiftieth cap, regardless, this is the moment in

Greeting the team

time, on the day, when they first set eyes on the supporters outside the stadium and sample the atmosphere. They all walk right past me once they get off the coach and the first thing I am always blown away by, is how bloody big they are. I have a sense of how they are feeling from their expressions and the look of tension on their faces. They are all different, some wear earphones and avoid too much eye contact, others shake my hand because they know me. A couple of the England team's coaches tend to acknowledge me and shake my hand warmly. Still buzzing, I follow the whole squad into the Stadium, it's just awesome, what a privilege! As we enter the stadium out of sight of most of the crowd the team is greeted by a lovely old Irish lady called Mary who traditionally presents the England captain with a rose. Mary who now lives on the south coast of England once said to me with a glint in her eye, 'Peter, I love this job, how many ladies can say they get the chance to kiss all the England rugby captains!'

I always head back outside and greet the opposition team, clap them in and welcome them with a smile. I like to say to the Manager of our opponents, many who I have got to know over the years, 'Welcome to Twickenham,' and then shake their hand. I follow the two teams into the stadium where I retrieve Billy who is a little restless by now, straining at his leash to enter the coliseum. Taking Billy Bulldog around the pitch with me, meeting the youngsters and disabled supporters is always an absolute pleasure. They love having their photo taken with Billy. It's all about a universal love of sport and the people who enjoy it. Recalling the expressions and excitement of the people having their photos taken with me, is what I love about my role, I love it, it excites me, I'm giving something and I enjoy people seeing what I'm doing!

Before the match kicks off I always place Billy on the halfway line facing the direction England will be attacking and at half time I turn him to face the other way. I've noticed over the years that Billy is getting more and more attention and he has definitely grown into his role. Sometimes I notice a cameramen crouching down to Billy's level and showing the viewer at home the match from Billy's perspective! During the 2013 Lions tour the sky commentator inadvertently called the stuffed toy Lions mascot Billy, a slip of the tongue pointed out to me by many of my friends and family, Billy took it as a compliment.

On one occasion having left Billy on the halfway line as usual I was stunned to find he was absent without leave when I went to collect him after the match. I wondered had Billy taken himself off to the bar? No, never, Billy had been well trained and as much as he likes a pint, I knew he would never leave without me. I asked the stewards and the RFU tunnel staff if they had seen him pass, but no one had seen him, everybody was getting very concerned and asking, 'Where's Billy?' We were all still frantically tying to discover where he was, when, after about ten minutes, a lady steward emerged from the tunnel with Billy in her arms. It turned out that Tom Varndell, who had been making his debut that day, had inadvertently taken him to the dressing room. Tom had scored on his debut with his first touch of the ball and in his euphoria when leaving the field, thinking Billy was the teams mascot, grabbed Billy and took him to the changing rooms! Apparently Billy had been quite content sitting there amongst the England lads, but he was very happy to be re-united with his master.

Why was Billy christened Billy? Whisper it quietly, I named Billy after the England legend and former captain Bill Beaumont who has gone on to be a top administrator and Chairman of the RFU. When I first capped Billy I thought, well, I've got to give him a name, I just looked at him and thought, he looks a bit like Billy Beaumont to me! Former captain Beaumont is a massively patriotic Englishmen, I thought to myself, you don't get any more passionate than Bill Beaumont. I wanted my dog to be ranked among the best in the world, so I named him Billy!

During the build up to a match against Scotland I was posing for photos with Billy and some excited youngsters when a six foot something Jock bedecked in a kilt whipped off my treasured hat and made off with it up into the Twickenham stands. Billy and me ran after him as he sprinted away, but it was in vain as he disappeared about thirty rows up into the stadium. One of the stewards had witnessed the Scots cheek and said with a knowing look, 'leave it to me, I'll sort it.' Sure enough he was as good as his word and he'd got my hat back for me by the time I'd finished walking around the pitch. Later, still seething, I looked up into the stands scouring for where the Jock was sat, I spotted him, I pointed at him and made a simple hand gesture. The audacity of this guy had really annoyed me, but I have a responsibility to always act in the right manner and shouldn't really be getting involved in situations like that, I could incite trouble, but he was a wanker!

Conversely, Joe Worsley's wife Nicky, is really good looking and at about six foot tall, is welcome to my hat anytime! Nicky was always a good sport whenever we bumped into each other at games, always giving me a great big hug and invariably, because of her height, knocking my hat off my head. In time, I knew what to expect and as she hugged me, I would anticipate my hat falling and would always catch it. That was, until, outside the stadium in Perth at the 2003 World Cup just after beating South Africa I bumped into Nicky and Fran Gomersall (wife of Andy, the England scrum-half). We were on the outside concourse when Nicky noticed me, she came running over to greet me and as usual she knocked my hat off. This time I missed catching it and it flew over the barrier landing miles away on the concourse below. You can imagine how I felt, my mate Dave Williams and me raced down the steps to retrieve it as quickly as we possibly could. Luckily Dave spotted a guy running away with it and managed to grab him and retrieve it.

Without my hat I would be knackered, it's such a big part of the make up of being Mr England. Both ladies were relieved to see the hat back on my head where it belonged, and I'll never forget Fran saying there and then, 'Pete you're a legend in world rugby', that meant a lot from a players wife.

People often ask me if I am recognised as Mr England when I am not in my outfit. No, is the simple answer. In and around my hometown of Dawlish a lot people do know me and have become accustomed to what I do over the years. Yet, after so many years of being pictured at Twickenham it's remarkable that I am still quite anonymous out of my uniform and I don't get recognised anywhere else in the Country. Many England players and opposition players have begun to clock me over the years, but it's amazing, without my top hat most still wouldn't know me.

I was talking to the television pundit Nick Mullins and commentator Myles Harrison at Twickenham, when Nick said, 'tell me Pete, when you are not in your uniform do you get noticed?' I replied, 'No.' Nick continued, 'Millions of people around the world know you, I find it amazing, but I can understand it.' On another occasion I was at a black tie do at Twickenham after a game against Ireland. On our table were, Mike

Ford, the defence coach, John Wells, the forward's coach, Brian Smith, the attacking coach, and one or two others. Brian didn't have a clue who I was, even though he had always said hello to me when I was wearing my Mr England gear over many years. The other coaches were laughing and saying, 'you must know him!' Brian just could not recognise me. It was hilarious; the other guys were taking the piss out of him and eventually they had to tell him who I was. Most people only see the image I convey, they recognise the suit and the hat and that's all. Interestingly, I have noticed that ladies are much more observant and they are more likely to recognise me when I am dressed in my normal clothes!

Do I like to be recognised? Yes, I do to be quite honest. The truth is I'm very proud of what I do. Ultimately though, it is all about the sport. I am extremely honoured to be the official England mascot, to represent my Country and support my Country in such a highly visible way. I try not to flaunt it, I just want to be me. The truth is I am a naturally positive person and I love to socialise. In the early days it was fantastic to be seen on television, it felt really good and it was lovely to return home and have people say, 'hey Crossy, I saw you on the box the other day.'

I'm genuinely surprised at how my uniform and in particular my hat transforms the way in which people perceive me. My notoriety transcends sports in just the way I wanted it too when I first started dressing up patriotically in Atlanta. Some years ago, I treated my grandchildren Ross and Alex and my nephew Simon and his son James to an international football match, a world cup qualifier at Wembley. We arrived at Wembley early and parked the car. In the car park, I donned my full Mr England uniform and gave Alex and Ross their own mini Mr England top hats! As we wandered around looking for a place to eat, we all noticed the positive reaction of the footy fans. We managed to find a suitable pub for some pre match refreshments, it was packed to the rafters with die hard English football fans and their reaction to me was immense! I was inundated with requests for photos and the amount of times the supporters cried 'legend' was incredible, we were all stunned at the welcome I was given. As we entered the new Wembley stadium and found our seats, the loyal football supporters engulfed us once again. I am genuinely so proud and honoured to be supported by such passionate English people.

As a result I am fortunate to be approached by supporters of all sports asking really interesting questions on all manner of subjects. One of the most common questions I am asked about, by not just rugby fans, from all over the world is about the famous Kiwi Ha Ka, it's such an iconic moment before a game. Generally I am asked what it's like to be so close to the Ha Ka as it's being performed. I can only answer it is a stunning spectacle, different on every occasion and it sends shivers down my spine. New Zealanders enquire, do I think the English fans are disrespecting the Ha Ka by singing Swing Low? My reply is that I personally don't think the English fans are being disrespectful, I genuinely believe the England supporters love it and are just responding to the challenge. What are my thoughts as I stand on the edge of the pitch and watch it being performed? In my experience it is marvelous, I love it and I treasure it, I think it's wonderful for the New Zealanders to perform it before a game, the sense of theatre it brings is awesome. In my opinion when the English players respond and the fans react that is us taking up the challenge.

I'll always remember the famous match at Twickenham when at the end of the Ha Ka the Kiwis gesticulated as if to slit their throats! The atmosphere that day was the best I have ever known, it was electric and so emotional. The English fans immediately reacted to that gesture and suddenly the whole stadium was alive as the crowd responded by singing 'Swing Low Sweet Chariot' at top volume. As I walked back to take my seat for the game I was shaking, the hairs on the back of my neck were standing up, it was magnificent. The game lived up to the pre-match entertainment and hype and England played really well, pushing New Zealand all the way, eventually losing by just three points. I was in the tunnel afterwards stood by the changing rooms and unusually the New Zealand team waited by the English changing room rather than going straight into their changing room and warmly shook hands and congratulated the English team on a great performance. It was a massive show of respect for the opposition players.

For a brief moment on a Twickenham match day the whole stadium comes to a standstill as the massed ranks of English supporters ready themselves in the cathedral that is England's home to sing the national anthem. I am stood directly opposite the England players and I look straight into the players eyes as, to a man, they sing God Save the Queen with intense passion and patriotism. I suspect they are picking out their relatives in the

stand behind me in what has to be one of the proudest moments imaginable for a patriotic Englishman. It's a moment in time for them to cherish, a chance to puff their chests out and reflect on the glory of representing their country. Sometimes, I catch a glance from a player looking straight back at me, I feel so privileged to share in the pride and honour they will treasure forever with their family. Emotions run high, for a few minutes, my family and my son Simon are uppermost in my thoughts. It is a very poignant time.

In 2003 I came very close to missing a match at Twickenham that turned out to be one of the most emotional days of my life. Jason Leonard was to earn his 100th cap, I had planned a bespoke banner made in his honour and I was really looking forward to the day. I had arranged to travel up the night before to meet Dan Luger's dad Darko at the pub he owned in West London. I had first met Dan Luger's parents Darko and his wife Nane, (who had represented her country at Athletics) at a European Cup final at the Madejeski Stadium in Reading, when Harlequins beat Narbonne. I was dressed in my Union Jack gear at the time and got on with them both really well. I later bumped into Darko in Brisbane in 2001 when I was following the Lions and we became good friends.

I couldn't believe it when I woke on the Friday I was feeling poorly. I was also due to meet Jean Claude (the French Mascot) and all his mates who were staying at the White Hart pub with me. I phoned Darko and told him the bad news, I couldn't make it, I felt like I was making an excuse, then I contacted my mates, to let them know. It was a disaster!

All my friends travelled up on the Friday, I went back to bed, setting my alarm for early Saturday morning in case I felt anything like half decent when I awoke. I woke up in the morning, took a few painkillers and thought to myself, yes I think I can drive up now, I'll be ok. I was driving up the M3 when I heard that one of England's rugby players, the exceptionally talented Harlequins scrum half Nick Duncombe had died aged twenty one. At twenty years and eleven days and with only four senior club matches under his belt, Nick had recently become England's youngest number nine. Astonishing considering he had broken his neck only two years earlier. The Harlequins scrum half had won two English caps and had been warm weather training in Lanzorote the newsreader announced as I listened to the car radio. I arrived at Twickenham feeling numb and yet I knew I had to follow my usual routine, eventually greeting the team coach.

As I entered the tunnel area, a television cameraman asked me if I had brought a banner for Jason, similar to the one I had done before. I did have a banner, so the television crew told me where I should stand to enable them and the photographers to get the best shots. The England squad were clearly aware of the tragic situation, I decided that I would still hold aloft my banner for Jason, reasoning that everybody should still be positive as the game was going to go ahead as planned.

When the National Anthems were played I was facing the squad including three of Nick's Harlequins team mates and his England com-patriots. It was so emotional as we sang the Anthem that day, you could see how much the players were suffering and there was absolute silence from the crowd as they honoured Nicks memory. Jason's 100th cap paled into insignificance as the country mourned the death of a very talented young man who had a brilliant career in front of him.

My seat at Twickenham is just behind the England replacements bench so I am in a really privileged position. Often sitting in the row of seats in front of me are some of the injured Afghanistan and Iraq war veterans who are being rehabilitated at Headley Court. They have all suffered from serious loss of limbs and other traumatic war injuries. Before a game I would often see Lympstone marine Bob Toomey who always introduced them to me and I would have a photograph taken with them. For me it's always brilliant to see them enjoying themselves, having their pints of beer and soaking up the atmosphere. Sometimes they have their wives and girlfriends with them, it's great that the Rugby Union look after them so well.

I remember the RFU (through Richard Prescott) once arranged for me to meet with loads of Iraq war veterans in a suite overlooking the pitch before a game. I noticed the President of the Rugby Union and other committee members were present as we gathered high up in the stadium and mingled. Lots of the guys asked for a photo with me, it was a real privilege and so humbling. I looked into the eyes of some of the veterans that outwardly seemed so normal and I could tell from the way they reacted how traumatised they were, some were still clearly in shock and had blank expressions on their faces. It really shook me up, some of the injuries sustained by these big athletic men were horrific to see, leaving me in no doubt of the terrible times these brave guys had been through. I went down to my seat at pitch side and I had tears in my eyes, it really was awful seeing the haunted look on those heroes' faces. After the game, all the England players spent time with the veterans, signing shirts, having photos taken and chatting to them, phew, what an emotional day. It was brilliant how the Rugby Football Union had accommodated them all.

Ever since I started attending Twickenham I've known Getty Images' photographer Dave Rogers. These days, I class Dave as a good mate. Before every international we bump into each other pitch side, waiting for the teams to come out and we discuss our predictions for the match, which as it happens are usually wrong! At half time we might share just a fleeting glance or look if we are busy, or we might get a chance to discuss the game, Dave is a really passionate rugby man, a Northampton Saints supporter. After the games are finished, Dave can still be seen, scurrying around, looking for that perfect photo, one telescopic lens pointing at a player and another hanging from his shoulder.

At one game, when England were being captained by Steve Borthwick,

I was present when unfortunately England were beaten. Steve is a really good guy who I always got on with and supported. The team was going through a period of inconsistency and I was stood in the vicinity of the England player's circle as they had their post match de brief huddle. As ever I waved my flag with my usual enthusiasm, win or lose I see it as my role to always be positive, regardless of the result. Indeed, for me it is more important to be positive in support of the team when they have suffered adversity. England rugby council members and supporters had regularly commented over the years how pleased they were to see me sending out such a positive message from the pitch especially when the lads had suffered a defeat and their heads were down.

Ed Dawes the head of the England supporters club approached me before a fixture soon after the match in question and said, 'Pete, I've been asked to speak to you, can I ask you to temper your flag waving if England lose a game, today or in the future.' I've got to admit I was gob smacked, I am a positive supporter of England, win or lose, it's how I was brought up and I was going to find it very, very hard to not be positive, even if we had lost. I dampened down my flag waving after the games finished for a little while, especially if we were defeated. I think about it to this day, but, win or lose, you can rest assured, I am positive inside still.

Had great fun with Blowers (Henry Blofeld) and his lovely wife

Matthew helping convert Harry Brydon, son of comedian Rob

Meeting the England fans with Lol

Miss England

*Mr England image on a
pillar at HQ offices*

138

Proud Grandad

Singing anthems with unsung heroes

Singing voice of sport, Martin Toal and you know who

With young Junior Teignmouth players

WE FEW, WE HAPPY FEW,
WE BAND OF BROTHERS

One day, we were on our way back from Twickenham, having watched England play in the 1999 World Cup, when my mate Jim said, 'I've got this idea of a big challenge, why don't we do a bike ride in Spain?, I'd love to do it and we could do it for a charity associated with Simon.'

Doing the bike rides has given me a focus, although the intention is to do the ride on behalf of others, you are actually helping yourself, it's a massive part of moving on. It's a challenge, all your energy is dedicated to achieving a personal goal, yet the support of your mates and enjoying their camaraderie is what makes it really special.

For our first bike challenge, six of us (Tony Welsh, Pete Cockram, Jim Hickson, Martin Richie, Bob Board and myself) flew to Spain. We cycled five hundred and three miles over seven days, going from Rios on the Mediteranean coast near Barcelona to Santander, on the Atlantic coast crossing through the heart of Spain and over mountain ranges that were pretty high.

Our plan was to use as many minor roads as possible for safety reasons and to try and ensure we got the real flavour of Spain. We were virgin mountain bikers, it was so exciting, we took survival blankets on our first ride as we didn't know what to expect or how far we would travel on any given day. Every day was a mystery. In time, we discovered that wherever we got to by the end of the day we could always find somewhere to stay, even in the smallest of villages and we always found a way to enjoy loads

Finished. Done over 500 miles

The challenge ahead

Taking the flat route from Polperro to Fowey

of booze! On average we were doing between seventy and a hundred miles a day in the Spanish sunshine. We also learnt to our cost that the Spanish villages we ended up at were nearly always at the top of a great big hill with a church at the top. We invariably had uphill slogs to do in the late afternoon when it was really hot and we were knackered.

It was less than 12 months since we had lost Simon and I found a few times I'd be biking on my own with tears in my eyes. At those times it was just me in the wilderness with my thoughts, it was very emotional. On the last day of our first trip we cycled 103 miles in scorching heat over the Picos Europa mountain range, quite an achievement on mountain bikes. We were carrying all our luggage packed in panniers on our bikes and at the end of a gruelling five hundred odd mile journey we were pretty exhausted. Finally, when we had reached the peak of the mountains we found ourselves facing due north towards Santander. Looking down from high above the clouds it felt like we were on top of the world. I looked across at Jim and he had tears running down his face, we had conquered the climb and reached our goal, it was so emotional and we all knew we had done it for Simon.

We'd sweated our nuts off when reaching the summit because of the extent of the climb and the searing heat. However, when we started to descend and passed back down through the clouds, suddenly we all felt freezing cold, it was incredible. I guess we weren't expending any energy,

First ride. Proud and happy

but still, I could not believe how cold I was. That evening I told all of my mates that it would have been Simon's 31st birthday, all the emotions came pouring out once again. The support I had from all of my rugby and cycling pals was massive in getting me through that terrible time.

A year on from our first cycle ride, I was at Lords on a lovely summers day watching England play in a Test match and sat in front of me I noticed Nigel Starmer Smith, the commentator of Rugby Special fame. I'd read in the Telegraph weeks before about Nigel losing his nineteen year old son Julian to a variant of T cell Lymphoma cancer. Before that he'd lost his sixteen old daughter Charlotte to an unrelated cancer, I couldn't even read it at first because of my tears, I've still got the article at home.

What Nigel, his wife Ros and their other son Charlie had been through was impossible to comprehend, they had three beautiful children and they'd lost two to cancer. I was wearing my England gear and felt I could approach Nigel, so I went down to see him and explained I'd read his heart rending article in the Daily Telegraph. I said to Nigel that I was terribly sorry to hear about Julian, Jules as he preferred to be known and we chatted for a while.

Nepal Annapurna with porter Sital and sister at her B&B

Sister Mag and Pam walking in the Lake District

The family at Grimspound Bronze Age Village, Dartmoor

When I next met with the cycling boys I suggested we arrange the second bike ride for the benefit of Nigel's favoured charity T cell lymphoma, a really rare cancer. When I mentioned it to my mates, they quickly all agreed, their attitude was incredibly positive and they said, 'fantastic, lets go for it', I got back in touch with Nigel and told him what we were going to do and that's what we did.

Our 25th anniversary

We flew to Madrid Airport, where we had to re-assemble our bikes, we'd stripped them down at one of the boy's houses and boxed them up in England so they didn't get damaged in the aircraft's hold. When I say, we stripped down the bikes and re-assembled our bikes, it's a team effort . . . Pete, Jim and co sort the bikes, while I offer to make the coffees! I'm lucky to have such good and practical mates. Four hundred miles and six days later we ended up in Santander.

Ultimately, having raised the money I managed to get permission for my mates to go onto the pitch at Twickenham and present the cheque for £10,600 to Nigel prior to an international versus South Africa. Nigel couldn't believe how much money we had raised and my mates were delighted to get onto the pitch to make the presentation.

Our third bike trip for charity started at Alicante Airport, from there, we cycled up into the mountains and down through Grenada. We all hated cycling through big cities, but sometimes you have got to do it. Getting into a city is usually easy because everything is well signposted, but getting out of a city isn't as straightforward. As we departed Grenada it was a nightmare, the traffic was awful and funnily enough there were no signs for the little roads we had planned to use. We were stopped on the side off the road looking lost and a local cyclist pulled up and stopped to chat to us. He said in broken English, 'I'm meeting my mates in about 15 minutes, if you hang on, we will see if we can get you out of town.' They were brilliant, they knew exactly where we needed to go and they escorted us in the right direction, otherwise I think we'd still be there! We finished the trip in Malaga and flew back to Exeter.

For the fourth journey we took the ferry to Santander, cycled up the Picos Europa, did a loop around the top of the mountains and came back down into Santander again.

Over many years, Pam and I have done a lot of back packing together, having enjoyed a wonderful experience in Nepal where we climbed the Annapurna circuit. Since then we have walked in New Zealand, across the Cumbrain Way, coast to coast across the Lake District and many routes across Dartmoor. One of our ambitions over the years has been to walk the Santiago De Compostela Pilgimage route across Northern Spain. This gave me the inspiration for an exiting new challenge for the boys on our fifth cycle. I figured we could maintain our love of cycling in Spain,

Great mate Jim and daughter Vicky

Great mate Pete and daughter Anna

Presenting cheque to Nigel Starmer Smith

Team support Doctor, Nigel and Ali

while completing roughly the reverse journey the pilgrims take. We would cycle as far as we could until we reached the Picos Europa mountain range and then head back to Santander. We managed to complete the route and once again as a team we managed to raise over £10,000 for Wooden Spoon. Overall, we had organised and participated in five bike rides in aid of Simon's charity Epilepsy Bereaved, Nigel's charity and the Wooden Spoon raising over £80,000.

We do it for ourselves really because we enjoy each other's company and we love the challenges that present themselves. We all decided to do one more ride in 2012 without asking for donations, we felt we had been asking the same people to sponsor us for year after year. We knew the recession was hitting everybody hard, so we just did it to keep fit and for the fun. Most importantly, Pam was finding the rides were too emotional, although she understood the reason we did the rides, for her it was just too painful a reminder that we had lost Simon.

Martin Johnson lost his mum, Hilary in 2002 and in 2011 his lovely Kiwi wife Kay and Charlotte Thompson helped organise the Rampant Rugby Ball Run – named after the Leicester clothing company and event sponsors, Lions Rampant. The runners pounded their way to Twickenham from Paignton Zoo, while passing a rugby ball between them, prior to an international game against France. Along the way they

made bucket collections and magician Chris Korn who had starred in the BBC magician show performed in bars and cafes.

Ian Coulter was the main driving force behind the run, Ian was a friend of mine from the Hash and like me had played rugby locally. Ian asked if I would run a leg. Unfortunately, by then my knees were knackered, but I did offer to start the run in my Mr England gear. Many people supported the event, including England international Lee Mears who went to school at Paignton Community College. Lee joined the run when it passed his home in Bath. Graham Dawe and some of his Plymouth Albion players, along with the then Plymouth Argyle manager and ex England football player Peter Reid ran the first leg of the run. Other notable runners included, Phil Vickery, Phil De Glanville and Danny Grewcock from rugby, former GB athlete Jack Buckner, model Emma Larvin, triple amputee Mark Ormrod who was injured in Afghanistan and adventurer Ed Stafford. When the final leg reached Twickenham on the Saturday they had another bucket collection and I met some of them on the pitch with Prince Harry and we all had our photograph taken.

For about the last seven or so years my hometown Dawlish has had an annual air show with famous aircraft like the Red Arrows, Vulcan and Lancaster bombers, Meteor, Typhoon, Tornado and Royal Navy Black

Cats flying in the Dawlish skies. Dawlish is only a small town of about fourteen thousand people, but the Dawlish committee that organise it, including my daughter Ali who is the secretary, put on a fantastic show every year. In 2013, I was invited by the committee to attend the air show and stand alongside 'Red 10' of the Red Arrows in my Mr England gear as he did the commentary, for the photo opportunity.

The 2013 Air Show attracted an estimated audience of one hundred thousand people, which is an absolutely brilliant achievement and a real boom for all the local businesses. I'd actually met the Red Arrow pilots and 'Red 10' at Twickenham before a game the previous year. The first thing Mike, Red 10 asked me when he saw me that day was 'have you still got the Red Arrows lapel badge that I gave you last year.' As it happened I had made sure I was wearing it that day, I tend to rotate the pin badges as I have been given so many over the years. Thankfully, I had prepared well and was able to show Mike the badge on my lapel.

The badges are massive, I realised when I was in Atlanta for the Olympics how popular they were and how many thousands of people collect them. My eyes were opened when I had learnt that some people would spend up to a thousand pounds for a special limited addition pin badge. The passion for the pin badges I witnessed in America inspired me to start collecting them in Atlanta, Kuala Lumpa two years later at the Commonwealth Games and in South Africa on the Lions tour.

Since then my collection has grown to include the official World Cup winning pin badge. I was delighted when I managed to obtain a streaker's pin badge from the streaker squad as it was quite a unique and original badge. For a short while there used to be a streaker squad at Twickenham, a group of about ten volunteers, fit young stewards who would patrol the perimeter of the pitch. They had been formed to combat anyone intending to be a Erica Roe copycat streaker and their job was to stop the streakers entering the pitch. I've often thought that if anyone resembling an Erica Roe streaker came onto the pitch while I was the England mascot would my hat fit!

My first opposition international pin badge was an Australian badge, that one of their players gave to me. I seem to remember Sir Clive was in charge of England for the first time. Over time I have collected dozens, often players give them to me, occasionally supporters give me a badge of their hometown club, it's brilliant. Once a chap gave me a badge and it was the official Norfolk referees pin, coincidently the guys surname is Cross. Every time Mr Cross sees me at Twickenham, often in the after match reception, as I guess he's quite high up in the hierarchy, he and his wife check my lapels and scan all my badges to see if I'm still wearing his, sometimes I'm not and I get a telling off!

In the mid to late 1990's a local family Dave and Jo Cridge and their friend Mervyn, launched a charity and named it The Special Peoples Fund. This supported local children in the south Devon area with serious or debilitating illnesses, by sending them on trips and providing specialist equipment. All the Cridge's children helped to raise money and support functions. In total, they raised locally over, £100,000.

Sadly, one of their children Richard, when just 14 years old, was diagnosed with Ewings Sarcoma, a rare form of cancer. Richard was a very likeable lad, who played rugby for Teignmouth and was well known in the scouting movement. A friend of the Cridge's and mine, Jim Hill, broke the news to me. Both of us could not believe how a family who had given so much to help others could have this happen. We pledged to ourselves that we must do something for Richard.

Jimmy and I arranged for Richard and his dad to accompany me to see an England game at Twickenham. A number of local businessman clubbed together and Jimmy organised for Richard and his dad to be taken in a limousine to Exeter St David's railway station where they boarded a first class carriage and travelled up to Twickenham where I met them. We were playing South Africa on the day and it was a special, special day. I arranged for Richard and his dad to sit with me at the front of the stadium directly behind the England substitutes bench. Prior to the game we had our pictures taken on the pitch. Unfortunately, England lost the game, but Richard commented, 'he couldn't care less, everyone was so friendly.' After the game we all had a fish and chip dinner. Richard and Dave got another first class train back to Exeter and a taxi back to Dawlish.

Richard was a really lovely lad and he actually sent me one of the pictures of us together on the pitch, he'd had it all framed up and he'd written on it, 'Pete, one of the best days of my life'. I am so lucky and feel very honoured to be able to use my position to support such wonderful people as Richard and his family.

Exeter Rugby Club also supported the family and Richard. On one special occasion, Jimmy organised via a friend who is a helicopter pilot a very special surprise for Richard. Richard was told that a helicopter would land at a garden party the family were having and take him on a little trip. I had organised with Tony Rowe of Exeter Rugby Club and his Deputy Chief Executive, Keiron Northcott, for us to land the helicopter on Exeter's pitch at Sandy Park, it had never been done before and up until now, it has not been done since.

The plan was, Richard, Jimmy Hill, Richard's dad Dave and me would then go into Tony Rowe (the Chief Executive's) box for lunch. The day went like a dream, Richard was sat in the garden enjoying the party when the helicopter appeared from the back of Dawlish and landed in the garden. The pilot got out and said 'Are you Richard? I'm taking you for a little ride, have you got your coat?'

To Richard's surprise he took Richard on an amazing journey, all the way down the coastline to Dartmouth and on the way back they came along the River Exe and landed at Sandy Park with me waving my flag and dressed up on the pitch. During Richard's illness a few of Exeter's senior players supported him and the family, even joining them for dinner

Richard pitchside

Richard's helicopter surprise

With South African fan

at their house. Very sadly, a year or so after the memorable helicopter journey Richard died, aged only seventeen years old.

As was Richard's request to his parents, after his passing, Jo and Dave formed a new charity, naming it Richard's Wish. The goal was to support children with terminal conditions and in particular those being cared for in the Bramble Ward at Exeter Hospital.

I regularly get asked to support Richard's Wish childrens parties. I dress in my Mr England attire, greet the children and have my photo taken with them. Seeing the smiling faces of the children, the parents and siblings is an absolute pleasure.

The people I meet at these events make me feel so proud and lucky to do what I do. I've met some wonderful characters over the years, I was so pleased to meet an ex-hooker of Plymouth Albion and Exeter, a real hard nut Bruce Priday at a Wooden Spoon function in 2002. It was during the World Cup in 2003, when I really got to know Bruce, along with Roger Haywood, another brilliant guy and owner of the Passage House Hotel in Kingsteignton, Newton Abbot. I've since gone on to meet Bruce and

Roger at both the French and New Zealand World Cup's, boy have we had some fun.

Despite his reputation in rugby, it turned out Bruce is a wonderful, caring, thoughtful man. Along with Roger and a few others Bruce launched the Devon branch of the national charity Wooden Spoon, a rugby based charity. Originally Bruce and more recently Roger have led Devon Wooden Spoon, to be one of the most prolific fund raising regions in the country. Every pound raised in Devon, remains in Devon to support all the noble causes identified by Spoon. One of the main fund raisers in the Devon branch is Paul Jewells from North Devon. Paul has raised massive amounts of money, organising numerous events in North Devon, which are always great fun for all the people attending. Dave Trick, ex Bath and England winger who originates from Tavistock, regularly entertains and hosts the fundraisers, delighting audiences with his brilliant humour and yarns.

It was at the 2003 World Cup in Australia that Bruce encouraged me to attend more of the charity events, he gently said, 'come along to our do's, we'd love to have you there', without pressurising me. Bruce once asked me, 'Pete, why are you like you are? Personality-wise I mean,

Combe Pafford

158

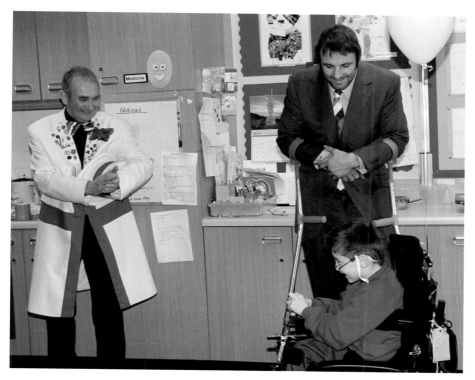

Vranch House, Exeter

With Spoony, aka Trudy

159

Danny Grewcock officially opened an Exeter playpark for Wooden Spoon

why are you always smiling, always happy, going for it and having a laugh? Is it because you lost Simon, are you trying to compensate?' I replied, 'I am the same personality now Bruce, as I was before.' It's true I am exactly the same person, just heartbroken.

With the support and encouragement of Bruce I was soon lending my services to the cause when I could. One of my first opportunities to help was when I went to the Calvert Trust riding school for disabled children on Exmoor. HRH The Princess Royal

Wooden Spoon in Dartmouth with Freddie Woodward

Where's Wally!

Nigel Redman and the Jewell twins

was officially opening the school on behalf of the Wooden Spoon charity. Jason Leonard was present too and we were all introduced to Princess Anne. In the evening the officers at the Royal Marine base in Lympstone put on a do. Andy Salmon, the Commandant was present and Pam and me were invited. It turned out to be a fabulous evening. I was wearing my Wooden

Night fever

162

If the hat fits

Tricky at his brilliant best auctioning for Wooden Spoon

Topsham RFC guest speaker, Craig Dowd

Tony Richards, Jason, Bruce Priday and Pete Drewett

Spoon tie and in conversation one of the officers said, 'why don't you wear your wooden spoon tie as part of your uniform, we could all have a bet on who will be first to see you wearing it.' As a result of that conversation I've worn my Wooden Spoon bow tie at Twickenham, instead of my original red bow tie ever since. I'm pleased that officer convinced me to wear it at Twickenham, I think it's a smarter tie anyway. When Dave Rogers of Getty images noticed me wearing it at Twickenham, as a supporter of Wooden Spoon himself, he wanted a photo straight away. I have since worn the Wooden Spoon tie at every international.

Ever since I became involved, Peter Scott (whose from Pinner, North London and a big Wasps supporter) has come down to Devon with his lovely wife Sheila to attend and support all the Wooden Spoon do's. Peter and Sheila show a tremendous commitment to the cause and are brilliant company. Peter is one of the original founding members of the Wooden Spoon Nationwide Charity and has been a leading light in moving the charity onwards and upwards.

HRH Princess Anne is the patron of the national charity along with the English, Welsh, Scottish and Irish RFUs. Many current and ex international players including, BBC rugby correspondent, Ian Robertson support mentally and physically disabled children through Wooden Spoon. The charity organises their own fund raising initiatives, raising money and spending it where it is most needed. Donations have contributed to capital projects such as medical treatment and recovery centres, sports and activity areas, sensory rooms and gardens, playgrounds and hydrotherapy pools and include out reach programmes for young people in their communities. All the money raised in Devon specifically helps poorly children from Devon.

A year after the World Cup victory in 2003, England centre Mike Catt had a testimonial season. My big rugby mate John Playford who was a massive Bath supporter wanted to organise a testimonial dinner for Mike. John asked if I'd be on the organising committee with the ex-Devon and Cornwall Police Chief Constable Sir John Evans and BBC Devon presenter David Fitzgerald. We organised the event at Woodbury Golf Club, on the outskirts of Exeter, which at the time was owned by Sir Nigel Mansell.

It was a fantastic evening with over a couple hundred guests including

Catty's Testimonial

Richard Hill's Testimonial, Woodbury Park Golf Club

Danny Grewcock, Phil Vickery, Trevor Woodman, Martin Haag and Ollie Barclay. Before proceedings started we had a champagne reception and Nigel Mansell showed a small group of us around his museum, which was brilliant. Nigel pointed out all the cars he'd had victories in and all the trophies he'd ever won at Grand Prix. He explained that he had insisted in his contracts that he should be allowed to keep the trophies rather than giving them back, as was the norm. He'd also contracted to keep the cars he won the Grand Prix in and they were also all on show.

Before the dinner Mike Catt and me waited in the wings as John Playford introduced all the special guest players individually to the audience, with a little speech including how many tests they had each played. Finally, it was just Mike and me waiting in the wings to take our bow. I could not believe how nervous Mike was, I was thinking to myself, god they're human! It was such a brilliant night, we had arranged a couple of surprises and all the guests had a great time. We managed to organise for the World Cup to be with us on display and the singer who performed the national anthem before the World Cup Final was present too. Mike graciously gave a good percentage of the money he had raised to the Wooden Spoon charity.

The next season I was in the tunnel at Twickenham when wing forward Richard Hill came over to me and said, 'could I have a private word with you Pete?' Richard said, 'Catty has told me what a brilliant night you organised for him down in Devon, it's my testimonial this year, do you think you could organise a dinner for me?' John Playford, supported by Sir John Evans did most of the organising and we had another fabulous evening for Richard and subsequently Richard has become a great friend. The evening was hosted by Ian Robertson with Andy Robinson and Tom Shanklin in attendance too. Richard generously donated a substantial amount of his fee to Wooden Spoon.

Mark 'Ronnie' Regan the England hooker soon wanted a piece of the action too. Unfortunately, my pal John who took care of most of the arrangements had died of a stroke. Instead, I agreed with Mark in conjunction with Bruce at Wooden Spoon that we should have a dinner on his behalf at Exeter Rugby Club's fantastic new conferencing facilities and share the proceeds between Mark and Wooden Spoon. Mark brought quite a few Bristol first team players along with Victor Ubugo and Kiwis

Good pals, Pete Drewett and Andy Robinson

Mark Regan's Testimonial at Sandy Park

Harry Langley, Danny, Dave Trick, Jason, Mark Regan and Gareth Chilcott

Help for Heroes. Presenting cheque to Coldstream Guard Colour Sergeant,
Adam Swift, with his proud father Mike, who is holding the flag

Andrew Blowers and Neil Brew amongst others. It was yet another brilliant function.

I've always tried use my notoriety to do a little bit to help charities. Originally, it started with the local Rotary Club asking me to speak at Teignmouth Rugby Club for a good cause. My initial reaction was to say, 'look, I don't really like to do talks, because I might come across as big headed, it's all me, me, me.' They retorted, that's what people want to hear about. So, I agreed to do a speech and told some behind the scenes stories.

Talking of Teignmouth Rugby Club, in 2001 I found myself at an emergency meeting in the clubhouse which was packed full with over a hundred people many like myself ex-players. Most were reeling from the shock of learning that the Club had gone into receivership. £30,000 was urgently needed to pay off an outstanding VAT bill and other tax and utility bills. Bob Freshwater who had taken over as the chairman of the club and discovered the mess he had inherited described the accounts as a shambles. The debts eventually turned out to be closer to £90,000.

During the evening I stood up and suggested that a finance committee was set up to mastermind the raising of the money. The members present agreed that my friends Dave Williams (ex skipper of the club and retired bank manager), Geoff Webber, Steve Dale (the Chairman), Mark Tibbs, myself and Chris Ovens the newly installed treasurer would become trustees of the fund.

Dave spoke about the need to win the confidence of the members, business people in the town and sponsors before we had the chance of moving forward and promised an outside enquiry to discover what had happened and find out why the finances were in such a mess. Dave believed before looking to move forward we should be able to give assurances that a similar situation couldn't happen again. Bob stressed that everything was now computerised and if the club survived it would be run on a proper business footing in the future.

We all agreed to launch a rescue package to 'buy' back the club, which was facing extinction after 127 years, from the liquidator. The receiver was bound to consider all offers for the club and we were all shocked to learn that another bid had been mounted by a local businessman and property developer who headed a consortium that was meeting the Liquidator in London on the following Friday. The Receiver made it clear that time was of the essence and we were in danger of being closed within weeks.

We asked all of the clubs members to contribute to the rescue fund and past players, businesses and sponsors were approached for help. We promised everyone who supported us that if the target amount was not reached we would refund all donations. We targeted everybody who had an interest in the club, going back as far as we could remember. We wrote to them, we emailed them, we phoned them and we generally made nuisances of ourselves!

Geoff was in charge of collecting the donations and his details, phone number and address were published in the local press. With three weeks to come up with the money, according to the local press we had raised £24,000 in two weeks after a magnificent effort by everybody. Donations ranged from £3 to £1,000 the response was incredible. A 92 year old lady, who had read of our predicament, but had nothing to do with the club called at Geoff's house with £100, incredible.

Teignmouth RFC had a thriving youth section with 100 plus members and the youngsters all backed our campaign, even featuring in the press with a 'Save our Club' banner, some offered their pocket money to help the cause. 'It was a nice gesture, but we didn't feel we could take their money.' I was quoted as saying. 'We are a community club used by all ages, from kids to pensioners and it would be a tragedy for the town if the club folds,' I insisted.

The wonderful boys and girls with their families support, still contrived to do their bit to help the club. Teignmouth RFC mini and youth teams strode out across Shaldon Bridge on a cold and wet Sunday, earning sponsorship for every completed lap. This initiative alone brought in several hundred pounds for the fighting fund.

Exeter Chiefs, then of National Division One, donated £250 and gave 20 free tickets for the fixture against Waterloo for the club to sell. They also handed over the proceeds of a draw made during the match, along with an offer to play a pre-season game at Bitton Park, Teignmouth's home. Chiefs Director at the time Steve Williams said, 'We have had good relations with Teignmouth for many years and are very grateful for the services of all the players who have turned out for us after starting their careers at Teignmouth', brilliant!

'The crisis had surprised many in the sporting world because Teignmouth had a busy bar and a full diary of bookings for its clubhouse from outside organisations and has always had a healthy turnover of cash', it was reported locally at the time.

Meanwhile, the club was on the open market, the local businessman and his consortium repeated their assurance that they wanted rugby to continue, 'but under commercial management.'

Ultimately, the magnificent response to saving Teignmouth RFC from extinction or falling into the hands of the consortium was so 'over-whelming' the target figure was doubled. The cash flowed in and Dave Williams revealed at the time that we had realised the target was going to be exceeded. Dave kept it quiet to wrong foot the commercial consortia who were trying to acquire the popular and profitable clubhouse and bar. The extra cash would clear the VAT, tax and trade debts in full. It also meant an agreed overdraft could also be paid off, saving the Club £1,500 a year in interest. Dave emphasised that the total liabilities were nearly £90,000 and paying the balance would be a priority.

Our biggest creditor, at this stage was a big, well known brewery. They would not agree to accept a percentage of their debt, as most if not all of our other creditors had.

We used to have a Trustees meeting every month after finally sorting things out and at one such meeting a year or so later I came up with an idea to pay the brewery off with our own personal money, so we could say, stuff the brewery. This would allow us to become a Free House and start making generous margins on booze sales. I approached sixteen people and they all quickly agreed to lend the club £1000 each interest free for two years. We did offer to pay interest at the going rate but no one took up the offer. Because of the much more preferential margins on our booze sales, we were able to pay everyone back in full within 12 months.

For me it was not just about the history of the club, it was about the future. The hundreds of kids who would benefit from playing rugby in their home town, rather than having to travel or not playing at all.

CRY GOD FOR HARRY,
FOR KING AND FOR ST GEORGE

Right from day one as the official England mascot, for the game against Australia, the RFU allowed me to go into the tunnel area. I was soon in the habit of following the teams, once they had disembarked from the coach, straight into the inner sanctum. The players headed into the changing rooms to get ready for the match and I deposited my gear into the nearby interview room. Conveniently for me the interview room remained vacant until after the game. Once the final whistle had blown I could go to exactly where I wished to be, in the heart of the stadium, perfectly positioned to be able to hang around and get to know all of the Twickenham officials, players and staff in that area. It was always a tremendous, unique, privilege to be in the tunnel, to be able to get close to the players and hear some of the 'behind the scenes' stories and get a true insight into the minds of elite sportsmen.

In 2002, we played South Africa who at that time were renowned for being a really hard, aggresive side to play. It was the infamous fixture when their second row forward, Labuschagne, was sent off quite early in the game for an outrageously late tackle on Jonny Wilkinson. Typically, a battered and beaten Jonny played the full eighty minutes as England hammered the Boks. In the tunnel afterwards, Phil Larder came out and started talking to me, he said, 'that game was the dirtiest game I have ever seen in my life, they were animals.' I was thinking to myself, this guy has played Rugby League, coached the Great Britain team and he is saying this, wow! Corne Krige was South Africa's captain on the day, a really hard wing forward and an absolute animal on the pitch. However, off the pitch I found Corne to be a really nice courteous man, chatting to him many a time at after match receptions.

I remember an occasion when Iain Balshaw was the player who the television and radio journalists wanted to interview after the match. Iain was having the time off his life on the rugby field, he really was on fire. Iain came out of the changing room in readiness and sat down on a bench next to me and started chatting about the game. I remember thinking, what an honour this is for me! Another time Lawrence D'allaglio came out of the changing room and walked straight up to me, shook my hand and said, 'all right Pete'. For me little moments like those were priceless.

A terrific memory of mine is being stood outside the changing room after the game in which Graham Rowntree had won his fiftieth cap. I asked Graham to sign his autograph on the match day programme, which featured his photo on the front cover. I will never forget that moment, we had lost the game and although Graham had reached an outstanding personal milestone, I could tell he was absolutely devastated at the loss. It was then that I realised what a competitive animal Graham was, he was ferociously committed to the cause and absolutely hated losing. It's been no surprise to me whatsoever to see Graham going on to have tremendous success at coaching the English and Great Britain and Irish Lions forwards.

From a supporters point of view I felt as if I had been part of the campaign that saw the 2003 victorious squad eventually bring the Webb Ellis trophy to England. Being an ever present supporter was memorable, watching the team win game after game you could see their confidence growing by the day. I had spent a lot of time with the players around the changing rooms and got to know them and their families really well at some of the after match functions.

To be in the company of all these English heroes for so much time during this period and witness at close hand their triumphs was truly inspiring. To be able to share with their families in their personal heartbreaks and euphoria in equal measure was sometimes harrowing but always a privilege.

During the three or four years leading up to the finals in Australia, one man, Martin Johnson was so focused on achieving his goal of captaining

England to world cup victory. Martin would never look at me, let alone speak with me, before or after a match even at the after match receptions. I understood that, as captain, Jonno had extra responsibilities to the media et al and that he was concentrating on the business in hand. Jonno was unbelievably driven. I knew he recognised me, but he would always walk straight past me as if I was not there. I was not bothered one bit. I had so much respect and admiration for the man.

Shortly after the successful World Cup Campaign I had just watched England play and was hanging around the changing rooms, chilling out. I planned to try and get a World Cup shirt signed by all the players for myself. Over the years, I had managed to get players' autographs on various memorabilia for good causes. I enlisted the support of Richard Prescott, who was always so supportive. I had already secured the signatures of many of the all conquering squad, when Richard queried, 'Peter have you got Jonno's signature yet?' Jonno had retired immediately after the World Cup and I hadn't seen him around Twickenham. Richard told me, 'He's out the back in the gym.' I started walking to the gym and bumped into Sir Clive Woodward who happily signed my shirt. As I entered the gym I saw Lawrence Dallaglio who was writing his Sunday newspaper column with a journalist and he also willingly signed. I could see the legend Martin Johnson out of the corner of my eye talking with friends. I walked across the gym and sensing the conversation he was having was casual, I seized my opportunity. Excuse me Martin, would you mind signing my shirt?, it's my own personal momento of the World Cup, I tentatively enquired. Jonno looked at me right in the eye, bearing in mind he had hardly spoken to me for three or four years, prodded me directly on the shoulder and said . . . 'You are a top bloke and it's my pleasure!'

I'll come back to the victorious England World Cup winning team later in the book, firstly let me tell you about more of the things I have experienced and witnessed behind the scenes whilst enjoying my role.

In 2005, when England were going through a transitional period I remember a cracking victory against a very strong South African team. Martin Corry was immense in leading England to victory, the whole pack had performed brilliantly and we played really well. After the game I was sitting outside the changing rooms when a South African television crew came out of the interview room after interviewing some players and asked me, would I like to do an interview. Although slightly shocked and surprised they wished to interview me I felt honoured to be asked to do an interview for South African television. The guy who interviewed me, Kobus Wiese, was a massive man who'd played second row for South Africa when they had won the world cup in South Africa in 1995. He asked me all the usual questions, including, asking me to sum up the game, which for me was good, as we'd won. It went really well at the end of the interview Kobus asked me, 'what does it take to be the England mascot?' I instantly replied, 'well, one, you have got to be passionate about your country, two, you have got to be passionate about your rugby and three, you have got to be good looking!' All the crew were pissing themselves laughing!

Once, I was chatting with Ali Mitchell (the New Zealand second row forward who later played for Toulon) outside the changing room when Dan Carter, for me the best player in the world, came out walked straight over to me, offered his hand and said, 'Dan Carter, really pleased to meet you!' Yes, I thought to myself!

A moment that I will never forget and I know English fans will enjoy in equal measure, is when I was in the tunnel at Twickenham and I suddenly noticed David Campese. I was surprised to see him, but it was an honour in a way to meet him and shake his hand. I was curious because although I knew he lived in Durban in South Africa, I wondered what he was doing at an England versus South Africa fixture and how he'd got into the tunnel area. I enquired with David and he responded that he was looking for Francoise Steyn the young centre, as he was his mentor. I knew he shouldn't have been allowed into the changing room area, he must have bull shitted his way past the initial security. Happily, for all real England rugby fans I can report that an alert security guard noticed he was there and cornered him. Campese was giving it the big I am, he's quite a gobby character, but to no avail, Campo had had his collar felt and I had a quiet chuckle to myself as I witnessed him being frogmarched away!

I'm often asked, 'do you ever get any stick off the players as they run past you onto the pitch at Twickenham before a match or at any other time?' I believe I am relatively invisible as far as the players are concerned as they steam onto the pitch. It's the moment when the player's adrenaline is flowing at it's maximum, it's the highlight of their careers, they are so focused and I'm convinced they don't notice me. I must have a small place in the player's minds though because I remember a time when Jason Leonard the legendary prop was with me at a Wooden Spoon charity event we were attending along with Danny Grewcock. As I was in the middle of getting changed, Jason turned to Danny and said, referring to my position on the pitch at Twickenham, 'fucking Crossy, he gets in the way, I'm gonna have that fucker, I'm gonna knock him arse over tit!'

I developed a great rapport with the South African centre Jean De Villiers due to a close shave we had as Jean ran onto the pitch, I nearly blinded him with my flag. Jean had to take last minute evasive action as I jumped up and down waving my England supporters flag with my usual excitement and enthusiasm. After that incident, in following fixtures against South Africa, at half time and full time, as Jean ran off the pitch, he performed an exaggerated ducking motion as he ran past me, with a glint in his eye. I particularly looked forward to greeting the Boks team coach after that hilarious incident. I always greeted Jean with a massive smile, he in turn pointed at my flag and looked at me, as if to say behave or you will get it!

I'm reminded of a match where another massive Springbok made a lasting impression on me. As I watched from my customary position just behind the replacements bench, I heard a voice bellow out from the crowd behind me, 'sit down, I'm trying to watch the game!' The replacement blocking this guys view was Andre Venter the South African flanker, who was renowned for being one of the hardest men in rugby turned 180 degrees and glowered 'and what if I don't.' It was a memorable moment, Venter had a look that could kill! Bill McLaren the legendary Scottish commentator once said, 'Look at Venter, he's no oil painting, but look at him working the blind side like a pop up toaster.' Sadly shortly after retiring, Venter was confined to a wheelchair after contracting a degenerative syndrome, transverse myelitis a condition that affects the spine.

As the years passed, I noticed that there were not as many legendary players like Fran Cotton present in the tunnel area after matches. The familiar Twickenham staff were around me, but apart from television crews etc, the area was becoming more and more 'sanitised'. After about eight years of being in the tunnel, a tremendously privileged position,

Keeping Jean De Villiers away from my flag

The Beast

I received an email saying they were trying to 'tidy up the area around the changing rooms by only having operational staff there.' I had seen it coming for a long time and although I didn't want to relinquish the massive privilege, I understood the reasons. I did try and fight it a little bit, I spoke to Richard Prescott and said what about Billy and all my gear, but Richard responded by saying it was the operational staff's call. We reached a compromise whereby I could be escorted into the area and leave my gear and then after the game be escorted in again to retrieve it, but after a few games I decided it was better for everyone if I found an alternative arrangement.

Ultimately, it turned out to be a positive move for me, I always find a positive in everything! There is no doubt I had really loved that hour or so after a game mingling with the players and staff, it gave me a real sense of belonging. However, my new routine meant that before kick off I would leave my gear in the Spirit of Rugby and after the game I would head straight back there, pick up my gear and go to the member's bar, prior to the official reception. It was then that I found I started to meet loads of the Rugby Union Council members and developed some fantastic relationships with these true heroes of county rugby. I found it really enlightening; these people were not at all like the stereotypical image that had been portrayed in the media. The Will Carling old farts stigma had stuck for some time, but I quickly discovered that things had changed, massively. Yes, the guys I met were all dressed up in suit and ties, but they were genuine people, many of them had played rugby at grass roots level and had given up their own time to coach junior sections, man the bars and generally help run small rugby clubs all over the country.

The first time I ever went into a reception after a game as the official England mascot was after my second match against Argentina. Before the game I was stood near the Royal Box and I got talking to Phil Keith Roach who was the England front row coach. We were chatting away and Phil asked where I was from, and I replied Devon. Phil responded that he'd been to St Luke's College, so it transpired that we must have played against each other years ago. I asked Phil, 'what happens after the game then, what do you all do?' Phil told me, 'we all go upstairs for a reception' I enquired, 'how do you get into that?' Phil replied, 'you need a ticket.' With that he put his hand in his pocket and produced a ticket!

Mixing with the Old Farts!

Enjoying post match reception with Richard Hornblow

So, once I'd done my bit pitch side after the game I went down to the tunnel area (I still could at that time) and mixed. Eventually, I found my way into the Spirit of Rugby section of the stadium to be greeted by a smartly dressed concierge. I waited in a group of about ten people for the concierge to open the doors to allow us access to the reception. Amongst those waiting was a guy who I have to say looked a bit like Wild Billy Hickok, I also clocked Grizz Wylie the famous All Black number eight who had previously coached Argentina. I learnt after a quick chat with Grizz that he didn't have a ticket to get in. I can remember trying to explain to the concierge that this guy next to me was Grizz Wylie, the famous Kiwi number eight and a man who had been the Pumas coach. I'm glad to say they eventually allowed him in.

I'd asked Phil Keith Roach, would he mind if I went and talked to him, once I was in the reception, as I possibly wouldn't know anybody. Phil had said, 'of course, no problem, wherever I am just come over and join us', which is exactly what I did. As the England players filed in, I noticed how all the front row boys came over to speak to Phil, who was their mentor. As I stood there taking things in, I couldn't help looking at this guy I'd clocked earlier looking like wild Billy Hickok and thinking to myself, I know your face. He was standing really close to me, eventually it came to me, that's Martin White, I used to work with him in the police force. I remembered Martin as being a really fit guy and here he was thirty plus years later stood next to me at a rugby union reception in Twickenham.

I was bemused as to why Martin was there, puzzled at what capacity he was attending the function. I said to him, 'You're Martin White, I used to work with you.' He replied 'Pete Cross, how are you, I didn't like to say anything earlier.' I went on, ' what are you doing in here?' He said, 'oh, my son plays for England', I was stunned, then it came to me, I enquired, 'what, Julian?' Martin replied, 'yes, that's my boy.' He continued, 'he's over here, I will introduce you', we went over to Julian and Martin said to his son, 'tell Peter who I am.' Yet Julian responded with a classic, he looked at his dad and said, 'I haven't got a clue who you are!'

Incredibly, as we reminisced it transpired Martin and me had been in the same life saving club together and we'd played rugby and tug of war in the same teams. At about eight o'clock Martin piped up, that he'd got to go, I asked, 'where are you going?' Martin answered, 'I've got to get the train back to Devon.' Astonished, as the night was still young, I turned to Julian and asked, 'why's your dad catching the train back all the way to Devon at this time of night,' Julian responded, ''cos he's a dick!'

Later that night, I suggested to Julian that his dad should stay with us at the White Hart pub, figuring in the future he could stay and enjoy the full benefits of the hospitality, after all his son was an England International. Sure enough, in time Martin regularly joined us at the White Hart, which turned out to be a good move for us both as it happened. Martin was entitled to a couple of tickets for the after match receptions which enabled me to take along a friend of my own. I would describe it as a win, win situation! So soon after getting to know Julian and being re acquainted with Martin, I was sometimes able to use a spare ticket for my mate John Playford.

While chatting with Julian at another England reception, we discussed how tough Phil Larder was. I remember thinking that Julian was renowned for being the hardest man in the England team in those days and he could eat like a horse. I will never forget at an after match dinner some time later, there was some extra food on offer. Julian put his hand up and claimed it in an instant. I cheekily announced that, 'I will have half of that mate!' 'Does Crossy realise who he's taking food off?' An astonished Pat Sanderson, the Sale flanker asked from across the table. Julian's dad, Martin quickly piped up that Julian knew Pete and he could relax.

Also on our table that evening, were the Sale boys, including Charlie Hodgson and Andrew Sheridan. It had been Andy's first outing for the England team and we'd all been having a lot of fun. Andy is such a big man and he was delighted when he was invited onto the stage to be presented with his first cap. As he walked back to the table, this mountain of a man, with a tiny England cap perched on his oversized head, I couldn't resist. Andy sat down about four places away from me and I said, 'Andy, that hat looks stupid on your head, it would fit me better than it fits you!' I was very relaxed in everybody's company, having a fine time and enjoying my dinner when all of a sudden, whoosh, I felt a massive thud on top of my head, 'fits you better than me' Andy laughed! I always got on ever so well with Andy, a really nice guy. Interestingly, the prop forwards are virtually always the quieter types, although Jason Leonard is larger than life, so perhaps an exception to the rule!

John Playford was often with me in the early days, we were getting to know more and more people but it wasn't always plain sailing for John and me. After one match we went into the reception only to find that we didn't have table settings for two of us. We looked around and could see that there were spaces on the table adjacent to us. It just so happened that the Bath centre Mike Tindall and his new girlfriend Zara Phillips were sitting there chatting away. I said to John, 'why don't I sit here and let's ask Mike if you could join them on their table,' knowing John was a massive Bath supporter. We asked Mike and Zara if they minded John joining them and they were fine, John ended up sitting next to Zara and he got on famously with the pair of them. During the evening I went over and joined in the conversations on a couple of occasions, you could tell that Mike and Zara were for real. They were besotted with each other, so comfortable in each others company, laughing and joking all the time and gazing into each others eyes.

Mike Tindall broke into the England team at a similar time to me becoming the England mascot. I have always enjoyed Mike's company and enthusiasm for the game of rugby, he always had a smile on his face and a get on and do it attitude. At one stage Mike had quite a serious back injury and was out of the game for a long while. Bath reached the Premiership final at Twickenham during his absence and I was stood in the tunnel area before the game when I noticed Mike running about with water buckets and throwing himself into the Bath team ethic. Later, as I stood waiting for the players to appear onto the pitch I suddenly felt my hat being tipped over my eyes, I turned around quickly, I can get quite protective over my hat and there was Mike grinning like a Cheshire cat!

During his career, just before he was due to marry Zara, I noticed in the newspaper that a Mr Peter Cross had been invited to the royal wedding. I knew it wasn't me, but I thought I would have some fun. There were a crowd of us at a reception and I cheekily asked, 'When am I getting my invite to the wedding Mike?' In an instant, with a big smile on his face, Mike retorted, 'I've known you for a long time since I got in the England team . . . now fuck off! When Mike eventually played in his last game for England against the Baa Baas, as he sprinted onto the pitch, he veered off at a right angle and came over and shook my hand, awesome!

In the early days of attending the receptions I used to spend a lot of my time with the Wasps crowd and their families. Those early receptions were real, 'family affairs', it really was lovely to see all the players and their wives, girlfriends and children having so much fun together. These days I still adore the receptions although they have become more formal and traditional. When Lawrence D'allaglio had his young son Enzo with him once, I remember Lawrence's wife Alice bringing Enzo into the room, putting him up on a table and changing his nappy there and then.

I will never forget the evening that I was enjoying a post match reception when I felt a giant hand on my shoulder and turned around not knowing what to expect. A grinning Lawrence looked at me and said, ' So, how is Mr England today?' It turned out the England boys had christened me, Mr England. For me this was the ultimate accolade. Thrilled, I couldn't wait to tell Pam and anyone else who would listen. When I arrived home in Devon the next day, I excitedly greeted Pam and asked her, 'Pam, guess what the England players call me?' Pam had a few ideas of her own, (one being, The Prat with the Hat!) totally ignoring her flippant comment, I excitedly replied, 'they call me Mr England!'

Since that moment the England players, Twickenham staff and rugby supporters worldwide, have gone on to call me Mr England.

I got friendly with Joe Worsley's mum through Lawrence Dallaglio's family and the Wasps crowd. One evening I was with Joe's wife Nicky and mum Ann in the reception waiting for the players to come up after the game when Ann said to me, 'you know what Peter? Joe's body is shattered', she said, 'he has never had a rest period since he was about sixteen because he has always been going on tours to keep himself in the respective teams, his body is shattered.' Ann continued, 'after games it takes days for him to recover, he can hardly walk.' That evening Joe came up to the reception from the changing rooms and came over to us and said, 'I've got to sit down, I'm shattered.' I thought to myself, wow, what a commitment these boys put in, they get a hell of a pummelling to their bodies and they can't recuperate in the Summer because they've got to go on tour. Whether it's the under sixteen's or eighteens or whatever, once you are identified as a player with the potential to be part of the England set up you are on the incessant treadmill. Yet I had never seen Joe Worsley shirk or miss a tackle, he is one the most phenomenal tacklers I have ever saw in English Rugby.

My appointment as Mr England seemed to coincide with Prince Harry starting to support the team. On one occasion, whilst having an after game drink, Prince Harry approached and started talking to me. He mentioned how he saw me on the pitch at every game and he enquired how I had become Mr England. We had a great chat and appeared to enjoy each other's company. He introduced me to a couple of his mates who joined us. At a later match Harry's best friend Marko approached me at Harry's request, saying he would like me to join them. On this occasion he had up to a dozen of his friends, to whom he introduced me. I got on brilliantly with them all and had a good laugh. I've always found Prince Harry to be completely natural and I always look forward to seeing him.

On another after match occasion, I got into conversation with a lady I didn't recognise. She said to me,' I am not a massive rugby fan, but every time I come to Twickenham, the first person I look out for is you, for me you are Mr Twickenham.' I was delighted, whether it was Mr Twickenham, or Mr England, in those early days people were identifying with me. Later that evening, whilst chatting to Clive Woodward, I asked him if he knew who the lady was. He replied, 'that's Francis Baron's wife.'

What a fine pair. Jim Grewcock and Billy!

I felt incredibly proud of what she had said, bearing in mind her husband was the Chief Executive of the RFU. It was at a time when I was just starting to feel more comfortable in my role, Roz's words helped reinforce those feelings.

Often, I am chuffed to find the players families are incredibly down to earth and really interesting characters. At one after match dinner I was seated on the same table as Danny Grewcock's mum and dad. They didn't realise I knew who they were. Over time, at many a function, I had spotted people and worked out the relationships from a distance. I sat down next to Danny's dad and turned to him, saying, 'cor, you've got to be Danny Grewcock's dad haven't you?' Surprised, he replied, 'how did you know that?' I countered, 'Danny's one of the best looking blokes in the rugby team, all the women fancy him, I just looked at you and I could see you were his dad!' That's how I introduced myself and it turned out we got on really well, I loved their company. Jim and me proceeded to

Dear Pete,

Photo enclosed as requested.

Don't you make a fine pair!
Sadly we shan't see you this
Saturday as Dan is not playing
but we'll be watching out for Jan
on the television.

Fingers crossed we might
catch up with you for the second
game against South Africa if
Dan gets a chance to play.

Best Wishes
Jim & Jennifer Grewcock.

187

have quite a lot to drink. Sadly, Jim has MS which is quite debilitating, but it didn't stop us having a brilliant evening. Jennifer and Jim were really good company that evening and by the end of the night Jim had probably drunk a bit more than he was used to.

Jennifer was showing some concern at how she was going to get Jim back to their car, which was parked behind the North stand in Tescos car park. They had quite a long journey home to the Dorset coast to negotiate but the immediate concern was escorting Jim to their car. I offered to help escort Jim back, not thinking that I had Billy Bulldog to carry, my flag and my bags with my change of gear. We made it down from the upper floors via the lift, went out into the cold night air and all of a sudden Jim was gone in his electric chair. An exasperated Jenny was saying, 'we can't let him go off on his own like this, he's been drinking!' I raced after him with Billy in tow. Fortunately, Jim somehow managed to stay on the path and we caught up with him before he crashed. We all roared with laughter together as we made our way to their car and I chuckled as I waved them off. Billy and me then had to walk the mile or so back to the White Hart, luckily Billy kept me on the right path!

I once met a Welsh guy at a reception and he said to me, ' I must be the only Welshman that supports England', I was surprised to say the least. I looked at him and jokingly said something like, what are you doing in here? He answered, 'My mate is Nick Easter', we chatted away for a while and he continued, 'I genuinely support England, I like Wales as well of course.' In conversation he asked if I knew that Nick's dad used to be one of the best squash players in England, I had met Nick Easter's mum at one of the do's previously but not his dad.

Driving home to Devon the next day I was thinking about the name John Easter. Then it occurred to me, it must be the John Easter who used to be a professional squash player in Plymouth when I was playing squash. I remembered how John used to come and do demonstration games at our club in Dawlish. At that stage he had been the number one squash player in England and he would have been the number one in Britain if it hadn't have been for Jonah Barrington. I met John in the council bar at one of the subsequent England games and we reminisced together. We talked about how in the old days John came up to Dawlish quite regularly, coached the kids and put on demonstrations. Indeed, John explained to me how him and a pal had very nearly bought the Dawlish squash club. I found John to be top bloke, another who is sadly suffering from MS these days.

I love mixing with the England players and their families after the International matches at Twickenham. I'm so lucky to have been involved for so long now that it feels like I am part the scene. I adore the 'club feel' the special atmosphere you only find in rugby clubhouses. In all my years attending after match receptions I have never witnessed anyone being ill, fighting, bad etiquette, poor manners or bad attitude from England players or the opposition, that for me is testament to the ethos and spirit of rugby and why I love it. As an example, Jason Leonard, without fail, would always be stood at the little cubby hole bar with the opposition props sharing a beer prior to sitting down for dinner. Jason is the most likeable of all the players I have encountered, great fun, easy company, you just can not fail but to like him.

I have had the pleasure of meeting some terrific characters. People like Frank Cueto. Frank was a real Cumbrian man with lots to say for himself and strong opinions. He and his wife Anne were always great company. I got to know Lewis Moody's mum and dad, Heather and Lewis Senior really well, especially during the 2011 World Cup when Pam and me went out for dinner with them regularly. Peter Jones, Chris' dad was another favourite of mine. I shared a lot in common with Peter. Like myself, he was in the gift trade, we always had plenty to talk about. One of the downsides of making friends with so many of the families is when all of a sudden their boy is no longer in the England squad that is often the end of our friendship.

When Joe Worsley was playing, pre game his mum Ann would often lay on food and drink from her own car in the Twickenham car park. Ann gave me an open invitation to take along any of my friends who had travelled up from Devon with me. Another proud parent I got to know and really liked was Martin Johnson's dad, David. Like me, he originates from Lancashire, I found him to have a fantastic knowledge of not only rugby union, but rugby league also. I understand Martin inherited his father's encyclopaedic knowledge of sport.

England played Samoa in 2011, we all sat down to eat our meals at the

post match reception, having had a couple of drinks in the President's bar, with the usual mixture of officials, players and their families. As the evening went on the Samoans were sat round at their dinner tables and one or two had guitars. They started singing traditional Samoan songs, one or two even stripped to their waists and were dancing in front of the England President's wife.

It was absolutely brilliant, my nephew Simon, my guest on the day, was as enthralled as me. Simon remarked, 'this is just like any rugby club in the country, the captains making a speech, thanking the opposition for coming and cracking jokes about incidents that occurred during the game. International players, pop star girlfriends, (Ben Foden was with his Pussycat Doll) interacting with each other so naturally, so soon after knocking seven bells out of each other on the pitch.' It was true the England team and Samoans were all so charming and friendly with everyone.

To be at Twickenham after a game and sat at one of the round tables is such an honour for me. Maureen Brewer, the RFU Presidents personal assistant, Sandy Le Good and all the staff do such a fantastic job at organising the hospitality. The tables are arranged in such a manner that it is easy to socialise, all the RFU dignataries and the players and their girlfriends are dotted around the room and

With my good friend Maureen Brewer

191

everyone mixes so well, particularly as the beer and wines flow! Most, if not all opposition teams are always friendly and sociable to be honest. The Kiwis are especially humble, I guess they are from small communities and are used to playing in front of their own friends and families, they're just brought up that way.

In the early days of attending receptions at Twickenham I had the pleasure of meeting an all time hero of mine, rugby union legend Jonah Lomu. I was amazed to see queues and queues of supporters, many of them children waiting to get an autograph or a photograph with Jonah. A member of the New Zealand management team confided in me that it was the only time in their history when they had a minder deployed to look after the team and another specifically assigned to look after Jonah, everybody wanted his time and Jonah obliged. He explained they needed this extra minder with Jonah to remind him to get his ass in gear as invariably the team coach would be waiting to leave and all the other players and staff would be waiting for Jonah to appear!

Jonah was a really humble and friendly man, I had quite a few conversations with him during his career and he was always polite and great fun, a lovely bloke. The last time I bumped into him, he was recovering from his kidney problems and he organised a team to play a team led by Martin Johnson. Jonah, despite all his medical problems, played in the game. Afterwards, I managed to get Jonah and Martin to sign the programme in which they were photographed facing each other on the front cover.

Richard Prescott sometimes asked me to do him a favour at the after match reception to help with the many charities the RFU support. In 2001 he asked me to get three or four Lions shirts signed by certain players, he gave me a list of the players needed and set me to work. Invariably the signed shirts are needed for a players' testimonial, or a charitable organisation. That day, I knew that Martin Johnson would be difficult to catch. Experience told me that straight after the match Martin would always be tied up with a million and one media commitments and other obligations that an England captain has. I remember him exclaiming when he saw me approaching, ' I can't, I've got to go!' I understood, he was such a busy guy, I saw him another three or four times that evening and every time he saw me coming he said, 'I'll catch you later.' Eventually, he told me to meet him down in the relative solitude of the changing rooms, where I caught up with him and he signed every shirt without any hesitation. It was one of the only times Martin had spoken to me at that point. I have never been nervous about meeting or talking to any of the England players or management I have encountered and I have met some truly intimidating characters. Of all the players I have met, Martin filed me with the most trepidation, I think I was slightly in awe of him, he was the ultimate.

During one Autumn home series, Richard Prescott gave me some shirts and asked me to get the opposition teams to sign them on behalf of the famous Leicester ABC club, the internationally renowned front row unit of Darren Garforth, Richard Cotterill and Graham Rowntree to support their testimonial. To be honest I saw this as a brilliant opportunity to meet the Australian, New Zealand and South African players I'd not met before and enjoy some banter with them. Without exception all the international players I met during that series were brilliant, there were no Billy big boots. I loved it!

At a following six nations game in the Spring at Twickenham, Richard asked me could I get a Welsh rugby shirt signed after the match to again raise money on behalf of the Leicester ABC club. England had absolutely stuffed Wales that day and the Welsh players hadn't come into the after match reception which is very unusual. Suddenly, someone said they had noticed that the Welsh team were all getting on their team coach outside. It's a fair way down to the car park and I hurriedly ran down the stairs, still in my full Mr England gear, desperate to get the shirt signed before they disappeared. In fairness, players of all nationalities would always sign something when requested, regardless of the score on the day. I was just going to climb the steps into the coach when the doors went whoosh and closed! I think the Welsh were feeling so humiliated after their thrashing that they just wanted to get away. I am sure if they had known what it was about and who it was in aid of they would have signed.

It's quite normal that members of public who are enjoying an after match reception for perhaps the first time will walk around the tables approaching players from both sides asking for shirts or programmes to be signed. I've learnt over the years that you have to respect the players time and space, especially when they are eating, but I don't always get it right! Once I had a chap with me called Marcus Webb who was a friend of my good mate Sean Nicks. Marcus had played first team rugby for Exeter in his day. He wanted to get Chris Robshaw's autograph, so I said, 'no problem, we'll go over and see Chris now.'

We approached Chris, who was with a lady, I thought they were just having a casual chat, it didn't look too personal so I asked Chris, would he mind signing for Marcus. Unfortunately, Chris was quite abrupt. It was the first time I'd actually spoken to him and I'd messed up! Chris moved away and before I knew it, a security guy who I'd never seen before came over and said, 'You shouldn't be disturbing players while they are having their meal', I immediately apologised and said, 'I am terribly sorry' and that was it. I felt really bad. It was the first time it had ever happened to me and I felt really uncomfortable for the rest of the night. Marcus did manage to get Chris' autograph later in the evening, but it had really affected me because I don't like impinging on players. I was trying to help a friend, but my judgement was wrong. That was the first time I'd spoken to Chris, not the best of starts! I have met Chris on many occasions since then and I'm pleased to say he has been as good as gold with me and nothing has been said about the incident since.

Another time, my mates Willie and Wayne accompanied me into the reception for an England versus Baas Baas game and they were really excited. They were reluctantly going about getting some autographs, while feeling a touch awkward, it can be a bit nerve wracking for some people. I spotted Jonny Wilkinson and pointed him out to them and they went over to where Jonny was stood chatting away and managed to get his autograph and were really pleased. While they'd been away, I'd been joined by the then England captain Phil Vickery and we were having a relaxed chat when Willie and Wayne settled in alongside us. One of them questioned Phil, 'dont you get pissed off signing autographs all the time', Phil answered, 'no, it comes with the territory, anyway you don't mind chatting with your mate Pete and he's a legend in world rugby!'

Memorably for me after one Baa Baas game I went for dinner at the players' reception with my mates Pete Cockram and Jim Hickson. As we were walking in to the room, George Smith the legendary Australian flanker, beckoned my pals and me over and said sit down, come and have dinner with us. As far as I am concerned, George Smith is an absolute legend and I couldn't believe it! I had got to know George previously having chatted to him after games. The memory of having an Aussie legend invite my mates and me to eat with him and his pals is priceless. It just serves as another reminder of the absolute pleasure and joy my role brings me and re affirms the passion I have for the game of rugby.

I always prioritise watching the annual England versus Baa Baas game. In the age of professionalism it is a throwback to how international rugby used to be played. Players of both sides enter into the spirit and it is great to see both sides interacting and having a drink together. I've noticed that all the players massively respect and enjoy the company of the Barbarians main man for generations, Micky Steele Bodger. I too find him to be great company and fun to be around, his boundless energy, enthusiasm and commitment to the Baa Baas is for all to see. Mickey's wife, Muff, is charming and great to talk to and supports Mickey wholeheartedly. I love both of them.

It was at one of the after match dinners that John Owens announced during his speech that Francis Baron was to retire. John made a brilliant speech highlighting all Francis' achievements since becoming Chief Executive of the RFU. He had turned around a loss making organisation, overseen the development of the stadium and most importantly England had won the World Cup, all during his tenure. For me, I felt a warm glow hearing what the RFU had achieved in Francis' time. I was gutted, as I had got to know and like Francis and his wife Roz. I'd sat next to him at dinner or lunch on three occasions and had many chats with him and his family. Francis had supported me wholeheartedly in my role as Mr England, he saw me as a link between the supporters and the team.

ENGLAND EXPECTS THAT EVERY MAN WILL DO HIS DUTY

The Millenium Stadium in Cardiff is unquestionably one of the best venues in the world and Cardiff is an absolutely electric place to be on match days. It is full to bursting point of proud Welsh men and women, many of whom have come down from the valleys, regardless of whether they have tickets or not. Most are on the pop all day and if I'm honest it can be a bit of a nightmare.

Spanish Steps, Rome preparing for the Chariot

I'll never forget one particular incident when England came to Wales in great form and were overwhelming favourites. Iain Balshaw had come into the team and was on fire, scoring wonderful tries and using his electric pace to rip teams to shreds.

Before the match, Dave Williams and I had a coffee near the stadium, as we left the shop we were surrounded by about ten Welsh fans being aggressive towards us, one of them flicked my hat off. I picked it up and immediately went to react, forgetting how many of them there were. For a moment or two there was a stand off and I don't mind admitting I would rather have been anywhere else than Cardiff at that point. Luckily, sense prevailed and I said to them don't be so stupid, or words to that effect and we managed to walk away and we got to the game safely.

England, as expected, slaughtered Wales by sixty plus points and played some phenomenal rugby. During the match Richard Prescott, Director of Communications, came up to me and asked me if I was all right, I explained to him that I had had a tough day, I'd had my hat knocked off and had been cornered by a group of people wanting a fight.

On the Monday after the game I took a call from Sarah at the press office in Twickenham asking how I was and I said it was nothing and I had dealt with it. She then described how hundreds of Welsh supporters had been spitting at Martin Johnson and other players as they had boarded the team coach. They had needed extra police protection, when they had left the stadium to go back to their hotel. The same thing happened on their return to the stadium for the after match reception. For me, it was a sad day for rugby and a great rugby nation, the country had been let down by a minority of idiots.

I'm sorry to say Wales is the only country that I don't wear my suit now until entering the stadium. A lot of the problems are caused by the Millenium stadium being in the heart of the city, enabling fans with or without tickets to get bladdered. Overall, wherever you watch a game of rugby, the majority of fans can usually handle their drink and enjoy the brilliant, unique atmosphere. On an international weekend in Cardiff, many non rugby people, have a big day out and sadly some can become involved in, or cause trouble.

In contrast on the Friday before that game in Cardiff I'd been to Pontypridd to watch the England versus Wales A teams. In fact, Rob

Andrew had sat next to me during the game and had asked to borrow my programme. Rob is possibly the most intelligent player I have come across and I enjoyed his company. (He never gave back my programme by the way!) At Pontypridd, both before the match and when I went in the bar afterwards in all my gear all the supporters were brilliant, the atmosphere was great and many of the old boys came up to me for a chat and commented on what a great job they thought I did.

If England lose a game I am a realist, if the better side has beaten us, fair enough, tomorrow is another day. I am not one who contemplates suicide, or is morose for the rest of the weekend, I go straight to the bar and get pissed, win or lose! I understand England are a transient team who are always developing, striving to be the best and that simply is what I want, for us to be the best in the world. If anything, I am more anxious and sleepless the night before a game with the anticipation of the match whirling through my mind than I am the evening after, whatever the consequences of the result.

The pilgrimage to Scotland is always one I look forward to immensely. The Stadium itself is a couple of miles out of the City and as a result the atmosphere is usually a lot more jovial and relaxed, only the true rugby fan is present in and around Murrayfield as kick off approaches. On the down side Murrayfield is always bitterly cold, it's always pissing down with rain and the stadium signs are so bad that I always get lost when I am leaving!

I remember one year we lost the game to the Scots when we were massive red hot favourites. Lawrence D'allaglio had scored a try really early in the game and I had thought to myself, here we go! It wasn't to be and having lost the game, we left straight after the final whistle to beat the crowds and get back to our digs quickly. We came out of Murrayfield, thinking we were in a good position to beat the rush. One wrong turn, meant we quickly had to re trace our steps, only to find we had been engulfed by thousands of Jocks. The wind was whistling around our ears, the Jocks were in my ears and in my face and the rain continued to pour down.

There was only one way to lift the gloom, a cracking night in Edinburgh was called for. After sampling many of the City's delights, we came out of a bar and immediately recognised Sir Ian McGeechan, the Lions legend. We greeted Sir Ian enthusiastically and I mumbled, 'Ian, Ian, I love you, I love you, but not when you are planning our downfall!'

Scottish trips are always memorable for me. However, not all of my family share my enthusiasm for England. There was an occasion when my son in law, who is a massively patriotic Scotsman, was out with pals dressed in his full Scottish paraphernalia, kilt, sporran, haggis etc, readying himself for a big six nations game. Highlights of previous encounters between the auld enemies were being shown on the pubs big screen. All of a sudden my image appeared on the screen and the whole bar reacted, hundreds of die hard jocks erupted in a chorus of boos and jeering. Andy just looked at all his mates, put his hands to his head and cried, 'Fucking hell, that's my father in law!'

Wherever I go during the six nations I am regularly besieged by fans wanting to have their photos taken with me, for some reason when I'm in Rome the clamour is incredible, the Romans cant get enough of me. I can't move anywhere without hundreds of Italians surrounding me and queuing to have their photo with me. I always say to my travelling companions, you go and get the beers and I'll join you later, it's fantastic!

It was on a trip to Rome that I met Wendy, the retail manager of the RFU shop at Twickenham and the main buyer Jane. Me and my mates had all jumped into a taxi to go from the airport to the stadium when the two ladies asked if they could jump in with us. The journey was memorable, me and my mates started to sing rugby songs and without any hesitation the two girls joined in, it was great fun. It was only during conversation the ladies discovered that I was Mr England. Years later, I came into contact with Wendy Pocock and Jane Barron again when they approached me and asked if I would mind if the RFU produced a Teddy Bear dressed as Mr England! 'Of course not', I replied, 'I would be delighted and honoured!'

Around the same time I was invited up to Twickenham to feature in a DVD the England Rugby Supporters Club were producing to celebrate the major redevelopment of Twickenham stadium. I was invited along with Josh Lewsey, (who had the main input) and Andy Robinson, (the coach at the time) to provide some insight on what Twickenham meant to us. The completed DVD was given away in the official programme on a international match weekend and in national newspaper supplements.

Ready Teddy Go

Andy Robinson succeeded Clive Woodward as coach; it was a posinous chalice in many ways. I remember Andy a wonderful family man took some fearful stick off the media at the time. After one game, Sam, Andy's wife came down to where I was sitting in the tunnel breathing fire, she was livid with the press and supported her husband ferociously. On a later occasion when I was queuing to get a flight up to Scotland to watch England play against Scotland, coached then by Andy Robinson, I bumped into Sam, who was surprised I recognised her. She said to me, 'Pete, Andy and me really miss the England set up, that said everything to me about the man and the family.

On the day of filming, before I went inside the stadium at Twickenham to be interviewed, I went to the retail office where the ladies showed me a proof of the Teddy and asked me what I thought of it. I said it was excellent, but there was no cross on Mr England teddies hat! The girls said they would get that sorted and arranged for a photographer to join me at the stadium to take my photo to use on the swing ticket of the soon to be produced teddies. When the finished article eventually arrived in the shop it turned out to be a best seller for a while!

Another trip to Rome provided a particularly funny memory. My mates and I decided to hire a horse drawn chariot to take us to the stadium. It was Blasters idea, the rest of us said, 'no, we can't do that, it's too expensive.' Undeterred, Blaster negotiated a deal with the vendor and before long we had mounted our chariot. I was in my full England gear with my flag, Jack had his outrageous Union Jack outfit on, Blaster and Dave held a flag each and we were off! We were carried through the centre of Rome like conquerors. As we went through the piazzas the English fans were cheering. At one piazza there were a group of Torquay rugby boys who bellowed out their support. Some of the more 'normal' English followers couldn't believe it as we all went past like Diocles on his chariot! It was reminiscent of a scene out of the 'Italian Job.' The Italians were bemused as they witnessed hundreds of English supporters hailing an all conquering chariot journeying through the heart of Rome bringing traffic to a standstill.

In 2003 in Dublin, before the World Cup we decided we had had so much fun in Rome we would re enact the scenes in Dublin ahead of the six nations decider. Pam had a ticket for the game, we'd heard they were changing hands for a thousand pounds on the black market. Despite this, Pam on learning John Playford didn't have a ticket offered her's to John. Pam said she would much prefer to go shopping and set off alone. Unbeknown to me, Pam then proceeded to get on an open top bus to do a tour of Dublin. As we were on our way to the Landsdowne Road stadium, our chariot was given right of way at a roundabout. I later learnt from Pam that at the same time her tour bus had stopped to let a chariot go through and the driver/tour guide had said, 'look at this, it's fantastic.' Pam laughed and thought to herself, that's my bloody husband.

The Irish are really welcoming too, I love them! Win or lose they are always good fun with a great sense of humour. They come up and greet me, many of them dressed as leprechauns and have their photo taken with me, it's a great craic.

Croke Park is a really interesting venue; the location of some tragic historical events between our two countries. In the lead up to the very first game between Ireland and England to be played there in 2007, the media were warning there could be repercussions because of the dreadful atrocities that had happened in years gone by. The worries before the match stemmed from the political situation behind Ireland playing England at the home of the Gaelic Athletic Association

Pam had read all the coverage in the papers and she was really worried about me going to the stadium in my England gear. Pam thought I could be a prime target for Irish extremists. She hoped that I wouldn't dress up at all, as she really feared I could be murdered. Pam was adamant she did not want me to wear my outfit on the way to the stadium as she felt the security outside Croke Park might not be adequate.

As usual, I listened to her advice, thought about it long and hard and then I ignored her! Well nearly, as a concession to Pam, I put my jacket and my hat in my bag as I do in Cardiff and walked to the stadium as a normal supporter. The bond between the Irish and English fans borne out of England's willingness to travel to Ireland during the 'troubles' of the early 1970s was so strong that any concerns that we may have had were brushed aside.

I got to the ticket area and I handed my tickets in. Then I changed into my gear on and the reaction I got was immediate and unbelievable. Within seconds, stewards and Irish fans were stopping me and asking if they could have their pictures taken with me. I could hardly make any progress towards my allocated seat. Eventually, I did make it down to the front row to take up my position for the match. I was taken aback to see just how many police were on duty. Yet the police were very welcoming too, coming over to me and exclaiming in their beautiful Irish accents, 'brilliant, well done, great to see you here', it was absolutely wonderful, the welcome so genuine, I have never felt safer.

Just before the anthems were played you could sense in the air that the anticipation ahead of the match was different. There had been an awful amount of concern in the press, speculation that the English anthem, God Save the Queen, may be disrespected or interrupted. They needn't have worried, there wasn't one voice of discord amongst the tens of thousands of Irish folk present, it was awesome. Ninety thousand people were in the stadium and when the English anthem was played you could have heard a pin drop, it was brilliant and brought tears to my eyes. The Irish people had shown so much respect for the English.

That is what I love about sport, it can do that, unite people, bring nations together. It speaks volumes for rugby and sport fans and what we

specially made and Jack was wearing his Union Jack bits and pieces. We were queuing up to get our steaks and got talking to these Aussie guys, we got on with them really well, in spite of them labelling us Poms! We joined them for the remainder of the evening and it transpired that one of them was the father of Nick Stiles who would be making his debut for the Wallabies that weekend. The guys were both from Brisbane and we really enjoyed their company and local knowledge. Later in the evening we were explaining that we only had two tickets for the match and how we had come about those, Nicks dad said, 'don't worry, I'll get you another couple of tickets.' On the day of the match, Nick's dad turned up at our hotel at a pre-ordained time and gave us two tickets for the girls, brilliant!

It wasn't always all good news on tour. When we had arrived in Brisbane, we found our accommodation at the Holiday Inn, (which the England team subsequently stayed at during the 2003 World Cup), was not exactly as it had said on the tin. We had been given a big suite with two double beds, we complained 'we are not having that' and put the management under real pressure. They responded saying, 'we are really sorry, but all these Brits keep turning up'. So many people were booking hotels independently, as we had, all of Brisbane's hotels were totally overwhelmed by the numbers of British supporters. They offered us an alternative hotel, located down on the Gold Coast, but we decided we would rather stay where we were as the proximity to the City was perfect. As it happened, the four of us had a very cosy stay!

The first Test in Brisbane was awesome, we all walked from the City to the famous Gabba Stadium and as we strolled along, we realised there were Lions shirts everywhere it was amazing. Jack and I had donned our Union Jack uniforms as we had done so successfully in South Africa and went to greet the Lions team coach as it arrived at the stadium. As the players disembarked one by one they were all acknowledging us and giving us the thumbs up. The English lads knew me, but players like Scott Quinell were brilliant too. Graham Henry who was usually quite a quiet character, not known for being demonstrative interacted with us smiled and shook our hands, it seemed their confidence was oozing.

Once inside, we had never seen anything like it, the whole stadium was full of red shirts, there were thousands and thousands of us in the stadium.

The Australians may not have wanted me on the pitch, but instead, what they got was thousands of Lions supporters, it really knocked the Aussies back.

The Lions played sensational rugby, Jason Robinson skinned Chris Latham the Aussie full back to score. Later, Brian O'Driscoll scored a stunning try when he waltzed through the Wallabies defence, the Lion's were on fire. It was one of the most stunning games of rugby I had ever been to, we destroyed them and beat them all ends up.

We went back to our Hotel to celebrate with our new friend, Alan Phillips, and his group. Days earlier I had befriended Alan, the current Welsh Team manager, in the hotel gymnasium. Alan was staying at the Holiday Inn with his brother and a large group of touring Welsh fans. Alan was the tour leader and was at the centre of everything. The party of Lions fans became our drinking mates, we got on famously with them. Alan was working for Gullivers Travels. He was a really likeable guy, an ideal candidate to look after the touring Brits. It was hard to believe that as a player Alan had been a real hard case.

As the night wore on word reached us from the bar that they would be calling last orders soon and would not grant an extension. Alan turned to me and suggested we have a whip round. Immediately, my wallet was drawn and the notes came out, everyone quickly followed and we brought as many drinks as our money allowed, you couldn't move for drinks! We were not going to curtail our victory celebrations for anyone!

Talking of Welsh rugby legends and heavy drinking. I will never forget the time I sat next to Phil Bennett, legendary fly half of Wales and the British and Irish Lions at Topsham Rugby Club. Phil had a pint in his hand, as he made a fantastic speech, regaling us all with stories of Welsh rugby and the Lions, it was brilliant. Not once did Phil need to look down at his notes, the whole speech came from the heart. During the evening, Phil explained to me that he had a driver. Foolishly I asked why? Phil replied, 'because I like a drink boyo!' As you know by now, I like a pint, but I have never seen a man drink pints like Phil Bennett, astonishing!

Back in Australia, we were feeling slightly the worse for wear when we bumped into my pal Dave Rogers of Getty images by chance at the airport the day after our night with the Welsh boys. He implored, 'Pete, you couldn't look after my equipment while I go and have a pee could you? Dave continued, 'on my way here, I was on the beach and I went to the loo and all my gear was nicked, I had to replace the whole lot'. Before I knew it I was guardian of all of Dave's camera equipment, a big responsibility if you think of the fantastic images he has been responsible for over the years. It's not all glamour for these unsung characters, we aren't always aware of the travelling and carrying of equipment that a professional like Dave has to do in order for a brilliant sports photo to be published. Dave is a big mate of mine and definitely not a paparazzi.

Melbourne was the next City due to feel the presence of the mighty Lions contingent and not surprisingly they were equally unprepared for the size of our army of followers. On arriving at our hotel we were flabbergasted to find that we only had one room, this time with two single beds, for the four of us. Although we had adapted well to sharing a room in Brisbane, our relationships remained good, but not that good! Yet again we complained, the hotel again assured us they had Jack and Mary's booking confirmation and yet we were told a similar story as we'd heard in Brisbane, Melbourne was apparently full. Finally, the Manager agreed that we could stay in separate rooms if we transferred to their sister hotel, we had no choice but to accept this 'offer', as it was so chaotic in Melbourne.

The alternative hotel was down a little side street and our first impressions were not very positive. As we were being led up to our bedrooms we exchanged knowing glances as we had all totted up the number of female figures in the vicinity who had a 'lady of the night' look about them. It hadn't taken us too long too work out we were in a brothel area, it was ridiculous, but by now we had moved hotel, we were tired and we felt as if we had no choice but to stay. We heard many more similar stories as we met with other supporters, who like us, because of the potential financial savings, booked their hotel rooms independently rather than through official tour parties.

The Australian press and authorities were determined that their yellow colours would be much more prominent inside the stadium for the second test. Outside the Colonial Stadium Melbourne the main sponsors were capitalising on the interest generated by the Lions huge following and reaction to the sea of red in Brisbane by handing out yellow hats and bits to the Aussie supporters and red hats and stuff for the Brits. For me it was an excellent commercial ploy and it was just good common sense.

When we arrived at the turnstiles, the guys manning them were obviously under instructions not to allow any Lions supporter into the match with any of the 'extra' free merchandise. This caused severe delays and there was intense frustration as the irate British fans argued the toss with the turnstile operators, it was farcical. The Aussie supporters were just as incredulous; there was just no need for such pettiness, they were embarrassed and frankly doing their nuts, saying this is just not sport. The arguments were to no avail, all the freebies were confiscated.

When we eventually took our seat inside the stadium, the picture that greeted us was the exact opposite of the week before. A sea of yellow had been manufactured, to compete with the Lions' spontaneous support of the week before. The Australian authorities and fans had been so over-whelmed in Brisbane that they had done everything in their power to restore home advantage.

Having stuffed the Australians in the First Test, we started the Second Test really well, to my mind in the first half it really felt as if we were going to win the game. Crucially, Richard Hill was struck in the face by Australian centre Nathan Grey's elbow and broke his cheek bone. This proved to be one of the major turning points of the whole tour. Richard was a massive key player for England and the Lions and we just didn't recover from his loss. I remember just before half time, Jonny Wilkinson threw a long pass that was intercepted and Joe Roff went on to score in the corner. Suddenly, we were under pressure. We had lost the Test and the tide had turned. Not to worry, we had some wine to taste!

We headed to Adelaide for some rest and relaxation and were welcolmed by Pam's uncle Dick at the Yalumba Vineyards in the Barossa valley. Dick was really friendly with a chap called John Auld who was Yalumbas world marketing man. John personally took us on an escorted tour of the vineyards and afterwards the company treated us to wine and a meal.

A day or two later, we were welcomed by a friend of Jack's son-in-law's family, Brian McWilliams. Brian and his family owned the McWilliams vineyard, the biggest independent vineyard in the whole of Australia. We stayed with Brian who was responsible for sales and marketing throughout the world. We went out for some wonderful nights with Brian and he would always choose the most delightful wines to eat with our meal. When it was time to bid Brian farewell he presented both Mary and Jack and Pam and me with a pudding wine he said would be the finest drop of wine we had ever sampled. I was really looking forward to tasting the wine, incredibly, we didn't drink it the next evening. Instead we carried the bottle of wine with us throughout the remainder of the tour.

After a delightful few days in Adelaide we had flown to Sydney and I'm delighted to report our accommodation was, as we had booked. It was fantastic. We were ideally situated on McMahon's Point on the quay opposite Darling Harbour overlooking the waterfront with the Sydney Opera House and Sydney Harbour Bridge all adjacent to us. Sydney Rugby Club had been recommended to us by friends and it proved to be a great watering hole. Each time we visited the club, it was full of ex rugby internationals. The walls were decorated with loads of classic memorabilia, we loved it, it was a brilliant venue.

The third and final Test was upon us, the Wallabies had the momentum and although we played well, it didn't look like we were going to pull off a famous victory at any stage of the match. However, in the last minute we managed to get a lineout right on the Australians' line, a perfect opportunity for us to find Jonno and get the try we needed to nick the victory and win the series. The Australian second row read our call and nicked the ball, the series had been stolen from our grasp, devastating.

I found out in subsequent years that the players had been trained to the point of exhaustion, they had been beasted by the coaches. It's all about opinions. As an example I'm inclined to believe that Iain Balshaw who was one of the most talented, naturally gifted of rugby players had been asked by Graham Henry and his coaching staff, which included Andy Robinson, to play in channels. Graham had a system and Iain had to adapt his game, which was based on imagination, flair, speed and elusive running, to fit into the team pattern. I reckon Balshaw remained affected by the loss of confidence he suffered during that tour for some time afterwards and for me he was never quite the same player again.

When we eventually landed at Heathrow weeks later we still had the special bottle of wine safely in our possession. Having taken great care of the valuable wine for weeks we were really looking forward to enjoying it when we finally arrived back in Devon. Pam carefully hung the bag carrying the priceless cargo over the luggage trolley handle. As we went through arrivals en route to customs, crash, the pudding wine hit the floor, smash, the pudding wine slowly seeped everywhere. Disaster!

THIS WAS THEIR FINEST HOUR

When I first started out as a mascot for the England team Jack Rowell was the England coach, but Jack was not around for long before, (the now), Sir Clive Woodward became the head coach. At the time, Clive did not have an awful lot of experience really. He'd coached at Bath and London Irish and he had done some media work. Yet Clive immediately had his own ideas and set his own agenda. I personally liked him a lot, because he was very approachable, he would talk to people, he would listen to people and he was always very confident. Clive was appointed in 1997 and he said from the outset, 'judge me on results.' The 1999 Rugby World Cup, hosted in England, Wales and France was a bridge too far for England and we were knocked out in the Quarter Finals in Paris. Clive studied the preperation of the squad, analysed England's performance and set about building a completely different mentality.

For my mind, Clive put together a fantastic coaching team, a coaching team that was world beating. Clive was revolutionary in building his coaching teams. For example, an Israeli, Yehuda Shinar a graphologist and life coach was enlisted to help Clive analyse and evaluate specific roles within the coaches and team. Time management in a sporting context was an example of something Clive picked up on. Yehuda had a phrase called, 'correctly thinking under pressure' which Clive soon translated into the phrase T-Cup – 'Thinking Correctly Under Pressure!' Players and coaches were given high performance behaviours, benchmarks for the coaches and players to aspire to which helped them to understand and perform their roles within the team.

Clive brought in Phil Larder from Rugby League, (who incidentally was from Oldham, the same as me) Phil had an illustrious career as both a player and coach, culminating in him coaching the Great Britain rugby league team. Phil had also played Rugby Union when he was at Loughborough College, so he was familiar with both codes. Bringing Larder into the England set up as a defensive coach was a masterstroke from Woodward. Larder was a real tough cookie, he ensured the England team had tremendous organisation, was extremely disciplined and well drilled in defensive strategies. Phil Larder was an incredibly hard man. I remember Julian White, himself acknowledged as the hard man of English rugby telling me one night, 'Pete, I was scared of him'. Those were his exact words.

The Royal Marines based at Lympstone in Devon were enlisted to test leadership capabilities within the squad, sharpen the team's proficiency in decision making under pressure and enhance communication and team-work skills.

Clive also utilised Brian Ashton's strengths by appointing him as his three quarters coach. Brian came from a background of long term success and experience at Bath. He was widely acknowledged as someone who was always thinking ahead of the time and studying attacking formations and tactics. Brian was brilliant in the attacking coach's role and he got the players playing superb attacking rugby. Phil Keith Roach was Clive's scrummaging coach, he'd played at a really good level with St Lukes College and Rosslyn Park and was acknowledged as the best front row coach in England.

On top of that Clive brought in Sherylle Calder, a South African girl who had worked previously for the All Blacks developing hand eye co-ordination skills. Sherylle became an integral part of Clive's background staff . She was responsible for some revolutionary hand eye co ordination drills and was widely recognised as one of the top people in the world in her field. After Sherylle helped England to lift the World Cup in 2003, she went on to perform the same role for the victorious South African team in France 2007.

Incidently, having got to know her pretty well when she was working with England. I rang Sherylle during the 2007 World Cup to ask how things were going and have a chat. Sherylle invited us over to the South

African team hotel for a coffee. Unfortunately, I had to decline Sherylle's offer as logistically it was too far for us to travel. Perhaps I had missed out on a chance to do some espionage on behalf of the England team!

Some years later, when the South African team played England at Twickenham, I greeted their team coach when it arrived at Twickenham. I saw Sherylle getting off the coach and smiled cheerily, while saying, 'welcome back Sherylle.' Later in the day, I was in the tunnel and Sherylle came over to me and said, 'Thanks for your welcome Pete you really made my day. I was feeling very tense and nervous about coming back to Twickenham and seeing all the people I used to work for. As soon as you welcomed me, you really made me feel at ease.'

Continuing with Clive's coaching team, Dave Alred was assigned the role of coaching the likes of Jonny Wilkinson in their kicking duties. Dave was a master of honing their skills and ensuring they had a routine to follow and were mentally 100%. Dave Alred was in a class of his own and instrumental in helping England win the World Cup. His work in terms of personal preparation and psychology were ahead of the game at the time and as Wilkinson's kicking coach Dave was an invaluable asset.

Dave Reddin, the fitness coach, was another smashing guy I enjoyed meeting. Dave is currently employed by the England football team who I am sure will benefit from his expertise. Every facet of the game was covered, all members of the team seemed to have their own coach, including Simon Hardy the line out specialist. Clive was also brilliantly supported by a great support staff, the likes of Tony Biscombe, (Video Analyst), Dr Simon Kemp (The Team Doctor), Nathan Martin, (Head of Performance Services), Phil Pask (Physio), Dave Tennison, (Bag Man) and Louise Ramsay, (The England Team Manager). Clive even had the foresight to enlist Steve Lander as an advisor on refereeing matters.

I chatted recently with Keith Kent, Keith is the head grounds man at Twickenham and has been since 2002. Clive in his quest for every little advantage to make 'Team England' function better, visited a number of English Premiership football clubs, with a view to improving Twickenham's playing surface. He quickly established that he wanted the head groundsman of Old Trafford to care for the Twickenham pitch and initiated the heirachy at the R.F.U. to 'head hunt' Keith. Together with his staff, Keith has transformed the hallowed turf into what is widely acknowledged as the best in world rugby. The way the surface is able to cope with the number of games played, for example, during the weekend of the annual England versus Baa Baas fixture is testament to this. The pitch remains as good for the last game of the weekend as it was for the first.

What Clive did so well in my opinion was to bring in the very best specialists for every position within the team and beyond. Clive also displayed immaculate timing and ultimately what he had in abundance was the right ammunition and quality to work with, quality players and proven winners. At the outset of his reign, Clive had looked at what the Southern Hemisphere teams were doing and said, 'right, we've got to do that, but better.' I agreed.

In the games at Twickenham that led up to England winning the World Cup I can always remember Clive's passion and enthusiasm. We were playing some cracking rugby at that time, when England scored a try the music would blare out around the stadium and I would be jumping up and down celebrating. It was such an exhilarating time. Often, I would turn around to see an equally excited Clive jumping up and down like a mad thing too, brilliant! For me, enthusiasm breeds enthusiasm.

I had first hand experience of Clive on a personal level. When I'd greeted the England team on the first occasion, I had been made the official mascot versus Australia, I was stood next to some people in wheelchairs by the players' entrance to Twickenham. Clive got off the coach and walked over and shook me warmly by the hand and said 'Well done, I'm really pleased for you.' I realised then that the bosses at Twickenham must had told Clive what was happening and Clive must have sanctioned it. Clive had a load of England pin badges that he used to give to people, he gave me a handful and said, 'you might like to give these out as you go about your duties.' I had seen Clive play for England and followed his career in management, I could tell he was an excellent man manager and I was convinced we now had a winner guiding us.

After that game when we'd beaten Australia in the last seconds of a pulsating match, I greeted Clive in the tunnel and said, 'Well done Clive,' he tapped me on the shoulder and said, 'come and meet the boys.' He promptly led me into the changing room and urged me to , 'meet and mix,' I needed no second invitation, so as the players were getting changed and having their showers I chatted with Lawrence Dallaglio, Jonny Wilkinson, Martin Johnson and generally mingled. That was the only time I have been around the showers in the changing room at Twickenham. When I got back to the White Hart that evening and told everyone I'd been in the changing rooms, one girl on hearing of a certain players physique asked, 'did he have a big willy!' I replied I daren't look. Since then I have been asked by people, jokingly I guess, whose the longest in the shower! To be honest, there is a code of conduct in rugby that you don't disclose such information, anyway, I just looked at their faces. Listening to the players banter was quite funny, some of the players hadn't even bothered to watch the conversion of England's last minute try. I think it was Iain Balshaw who said something like, 'did you kick the conversion Jonny?' Iain did not even wait around for the answer, he was so confident Jonny would have, even though the kick had been from right on the touchline!

Prince Harry, who was only about sixteen at the time used to watch England a lot in those days. Clives wife, Jayne, had taken Prince Harry under her wing. In fact the day Clive took me in the changing rooms, Jayne brought Prince Harry down into the changing rooms to mingle with the players. I noticed in the games that followed that Jayne would really look after Harry, even though he was quite capable of looking after himself to be honest. A larger than life character!

England had not won a Grand Slam in a long while, but with Clive's positive influence and man management skills, by 2001 we were playing some fantastic rugby. Memorably, we went up to Cardiff and won by about fifty points. For me, it was the start of the World Cup winning team being created. Our last game of the season was due to be in Ireland, but it was postponed because of the outbreak of foot and mouth. The game was re arranged to be played the following year and we lost. Had we had played it at the scheduled time, I am sure we would have won, we would have probably have stuffed them. We'd missed out on the Grand Slam in 2001, two years later, however, we found ourselves in the same position. We had to beat Ireland in Dublin in the last game of the season to win the Grand Slam, I wasn't going to miss it for the world.

I'd got a good vantage point for the match just off centre of the half way line near the front of the stand with the help of some friendly stewards who I'd got to know over the years. Ireland were a very good side and it was an extremely intense physical match. I think it was one of the best games of rugby an England team has ever played. At half time it was really cut and thrust, I believe we were just in the lead, but it was anyone's game.

In the second half, we cut loose and scored some fantastic tries and we won the match and the Slam. I was in the tunnel area at the final whistle and I saw all the England team on the pitch with the management team celebrating. Clive came over to me shook my hand smiled and walked down the tunnel into the changing room leaving all the players and his staff to take the adulation. Clive, I suspected was already focussing on his next target and was immediately planning the next step, the World Cup. I, meanwhile, was about to do my best Vincenzo D'allaglio impression and join the victory party!

After celebrating the six nations victory in style, I was soon thinking about organising the trip to go to the World Cup in Australia. I was on a massive high and feeling more positive than ever about Clive's England team. This was going to be a big trip spanning six weeks so I needed to get it right. My good mate Dave Williams and I were soon planning all the fine details together. We wanted to go to every game, but we eventually agreed to miss the first game, which was against Georgia and save ourselves a lot of money.

Clive is on record as saying the toughest decision he had to make when choosing the World Cup squad was not selecting Graham Rowntree. I agree. In my opinion, the other notable absentee from the original squad was Simon Shaw, who had been outstanding in the games leading to the selection. As it happened, Danny Grewcock got injured in the first game of the tour and the unlucky Simon Shaw was recalled.

Dave and I flew to Australia, full of anticipation for the next five weeks, believing that this was England's moment, our time to shine, the time to deliver the World Cup to the Northern Hemisphere for the first time in its history. Talking of history, I was carrying a sign with me to commemorate Jason Leonard passing the world record for the most Test caps in the world. My personal show of respect for the great man. I had previously had the signs specially made to commemorate when Jason had become the most capped England player ever when he surpassed Rory Underwood's

Dad and Pam enjoying a boat trip on the River Exe (shortly before Dad passed away)

previous record and when he had become the first England player to reach the milestone of one hundred caps. I had marked both these special occasions, by holding up a banner as Jason ran past me onto the pitch at Twickenham. Being very proud of the photos of those times, I was hoping to be in the right place, at the right time again if and when Jason broke the world record.

Our first game was the group game against South Africa, the biggy. England were seeded and were the favourites for the group. We watched the game unfold and we were pleased with the victory, a good result, but it was only a group game, we must not get carried away we thought to ourselves.

It was becoming much more noticeable to me in Australia how many young English fans would approach me and ask for a photo and say that I was a legend. I had got used to being asked to pose for photos by now, but I was amazed at the amount of times, I was hailed as a legend. I suppose that the players, the real legends are detached from the ordinary supporter and therefore I was performing a role that I had always aspired to, a link between the fans and the players. This excited me, the RFU had created a role for me specifically to act as a link and I could see all of our efforts coming to fruition. Paul Baxter, the ex-Exeter Captain, summed it up perfectly when he said to me recently that the RFU maybe subconsciously enlisted my services because they saw an image that they could use for marketing purposes, planting a seed to create an England brand and identity that supporters could relate to. Namely, the

219

Dave Williams and Roger Hayward

The Dallaglios, Australia 2003

Bruce, Sydney 2003

Sydney 2003, with Serge Blanco

Thierry Lacroix

wearing of the white England shirt with the English Rose or St George's flag.

After the South African victory, the next day Dave and I agreed we would hire a couple of cycles and go and watch the cricket at the WACA. We watched Western Australia play against another Australian provincial team, enjoying the beautiful warm sunshine and the lovely hospitality that was flowing. This was what being on tour was all about.

I will never forget what happened next as we headed back to our accommodation. We were cycling up a steep hill and my phone rang, it was my wife Pam, who told me my dad had passed away. I was totally shocked as dad was healthy as far as I was concerned. He had been the last person I'd spoken to before leaving the UK. He was totally hale and hearty and the news came completely out of the blue.

I needed to get home to England. Dave and I decided to go into a bar, which coincidently was opposite the England teams hotel, to digest the sad news. We had a couple of beers and chatted about our options. I knew I had to get back as soon as possible to pay my respects. We discussed how I could get home and what arrangements we could make for Dave to continue the journey, with just Billy the bulldog for company. The next morning, we spoke to Trailfinders in Perth to organise the flights home and back.

Catching a plane to Melbourne to watch the England match versus Samoa had been our only priority. We were due to take the plane the next day. All of a sudden, even the England rugby team paled into insignificance. I made the arrangements to fly back to London, leaving Dave to look after Billy and some of my gear – including Jason Leonard's commemorative banner. I flew back to London and travelled back down to Devon to be with my family. My sister Joan who lived near dad in Bournemouth was on hand to make the funeral arrangements, which took a lot of pressure off me. I spent time carefully working on my Eulogy for my dad. I wanted to make sure I gave him a fitting tribute.

It was Saturday by now and I was back home at a mates house watching England play Samoa in Melbourne. It was surreal. Days earlier I had been in Australia watching the games, supporting the boys and now I was at home, without a dad.

In the midweek we travelled up to Bournemouth for dad's funeral. I read the Eulogy for dad which was terribly painful. I went through every imaginable emotion. Then I travelled from Bournemouth back down to Devon with my Pam and Ali. The following day I caught the train back up to Heathrow to fly back out to Brisbane to be at the next England game.

As I made my way back to Heathrow my phone rang and it was Eileen D'allaglio, she enthusiastically said, 'Pete, me and Vincenzo are flying to Australia and we would like to meet you out there.' Eileen understandably didn't have a clue that I was in England as we spoke and that my dad had passed away. As far as Eileen believed I was in Australia having a ball, after all she had seen me at the South African match on the television coverage. I said 'Eileen, I am on the way to the airport now.' I explained the whole tragic situation and that I would be flying back to Brisbane. Unfortunately, for me fate hadn't meant we were booked on the same flight, but we knew we'd meet soon in Australia.

Only two weeks previously, I'd flown to Australia in a Business Class seat with Emirates and here I was back at the Heathrow terminal ready to fly again. When I appeared at the check in again, one of the ladies on the desk asked me, 'What are you doing here again, you left two weeks ago?' She'd recognised me, because I was in my Mr England gear.

I wear it when travelling so it doesn't get lost, it's just easier for me to wear it, carry it and keep it in my sight. I explained the circumstances with regards to my dad and she listened sympathetically. Just as I went to board the plane an attendant stopped me and said, 'Mr Cross, you're in First Class'. They had upgraded me all the way to Singapore, which was a brilliant gesture. I had never flown First Class before and when I re-boarded the plane again in Singapore, after our stop over, to fly on to Brisbane, I found out they had upgraded me again.

Having eventually arrived back in Brisbane and rejoined Dave and Billy, Eileen was soon in touch and explained, 'Pete, we are staying at the Versace Hotel'. Lawrence had booked them in to the really posh hotel. Eileen continued, 'come down and join us.' Dave and I were only too pleased to see them and headed immediately to the Versace and went straight up to their extremely plush room. It was brilliant evening, as usual with the Dallaglio's, we were all so positive about the upcoming fixtures and enjoyed great rugby banter.

Some years earlier, I had attended a match in which the Cornish Pirates were playing a game against Esher. The Pirates had to win to secure promotion to the Championship. A mate of mine, Keith Hall (now sadly departed), was sponsoring the game and he asked me if I would go down to Cornwall in my gear to support this game?

In a way, it had always been a principal of mine to only wear my gear when I was watching England, but Keith had been a good friend to me over the years and helped me out a lot. I'd stayed in his house when I'd been in Cornwall on business and he was a really good mate. So I decided I would do it, I had a Cornish flag and I went onto the pitch, supporting the Pirates. John Inverdale (a big fan of Esher) was there with the BBC who were covering the game, so there was a real sense of occasion.

Whilst I was at the match I was introduced to Dickie Evans, a staunch supporter and the main benefactor of the Pirates, who was actually born within 100 metres of Penzance's Mennaye Field ground. At that time Dickie was mostly living in Kenya and commuting regularly back to the

UK. We had a few minutes interesting chit chat and went our separate ways.

Back in Brisbane in 2003 at the World Cup as we sat and waited for the teams to come onto the pitch for the final group game, England versus Uruguay, I got a tap on the shoulder and this gentleman said, 'I bet you don't know who I am, do you?' I turned around to see this smiling face looking at me and I immediately replied, 'Dickie Evans.'

Dickie seemed surprised and said, 'how do you remember me?' I retorted, 'I always remember the people I meet'. In fairness, you don't forget characters like Dickie. Dickie asked, 'where are you off to after this game?' I replied, 'we'll be going to Sydney.' He took my mobile number and rang me when we he had arrived in Sydney. I had no hesitation whatsoever accepting his invite to join him, Martin Hudson and the rest of the Cornish crew. I knew he would be fantastic company and a great host. As it turned out, from then on, we met up regularly at Dickie's base, The Four Seasons Hotel Sydney.

After the end of the group matches, we had qualified for the Quarter final and were fortunate to be remaining in Brisbane where we would be meeting Wales. The Suncorp Oval in Brisbane is a magnificent stadium, with loads of bars and restaurants close to the ground. The venue is small but with a fantastic capacity to produce a brilliant atmosphere. On the day, thousands of Welsh and English fans were present and the atmosphere was electric, particularly as Wales had done so well in their pool match against New Zealand. Wales posed a massive threat and put England under tremendous pressure during the game.

Mike Catt a replacement for Mike Tindall managed to change the course of the game in England's favour with some clever tactical kicking before Jason Robinson's phenomenal break set up Will Greenwood for a try that clinched it for England. The truth was that we hadn't played that well, but at the time we just had a tremendous confidence, will and desire within the team and we knew we would win.

After the game we went to the Holiday Inn in Brisbane, where the England team were staying and met with quite a lot of the management and players. We just chilled out and mingled with them. I remember Phil Larder came up to me and said, 'Pete, let me introduce you to my son Dave, he's just flown out from the UK, he would love to meet you.'

225

Continuing our conversation, we discussed what a close game it had been and our performances in general. Phil said, 'Pete, the players have got to go out and get pissed, not only that, we have got to get pissed.' I found it really interesting coming from Phil, who was a driver of the pack. The England team were favourites for the tournament and the pressure was massive.

The next day we flew down to Melbourne, we'd covered our backs and bought flight tickets and match tickets for the Quarter Final that England would have played, if we'd qualified in second place in the group. It wasn't a bad decision! We watched South Africa play New Zealand and we had a great night in Melbourne before flying back to Brisbane.

Some days later we flew to Sydney, ready for the Semi Final meeting with the French. Of course, that meant a reunion with our good friend Jean Claude. One evening when we were dining at the Four Seasons, Serge Blanco the legendary French full back approached Jean Claude, who he already knew and asked if he could have a photo with us! I was delighted, Serge Blanco is an absolute legend.

The night before the Semi, Jean Claude enquired, 'would I meet him at Sydney Harbour?', as he was due to be doing a pre recorded interview for French T.V. that was to be broadcast 'as live' ten minutes before the kick off of the Semi Final. I was delighted to be invited and Dave and I went down to the harbour to meet Jean Claude. We were escorted up to the studio facilities where the interview was to be conducted. The backdrop to the interview was the Sydney Opera House and Bridge, the interviewer was the Ex-French and Saracens fly half, Thierry Lacroix. The production crew advised me, 'Peter, we are going to conduct our interview with Jean Claude, you will be sat next to him and we would like you to say these words in French when we prompt you, will that be ok?' I asked , 'what do the words mean?' They wouldn't tell me, I didn't have a clue what I would be saying, they just smiled and told me not to worry!

Dave was in a room next door to the studio watching the interview on a big screen with the French television production crew as it was being recorded. He told me that he too had no idea what I had said in French. Whatever it was, it had gone down really well with the French audience, apparently they were in hysterics! Butch White a good mate of mine was watching with his French girlfriend Natalie in France on the day of the game and said it had come across really well.

By now, I'd got to know John Hall, the ex-Gloucester player and owner of Gullivers Travels really well. He has always been very enthusiastic about Jean Claude and me being in our uniforms and has often invited us both to numerous functions he has arranged. John understands that we are genuine rugby fans as well as the standard bearers for our respective countries.

We'd bumped into John in Sydney and John asked where we were going to be sitting to watch the Semi Final. I informed John that we were not together and that we had seats in different parts of the stadium. John was clearly dismayed and said, 'we've got to get you going around the pitch together as you do in Paris or Twickenham, it would be the perfect build up to the big match.' Both Jean Claude and I agreed, of course we would like to walk around the pitch together. We were into that big time.

John is very well connected within the game and I believed he would arrange for us to do it without any problems. Frustratingly, a very disappointed John came back to us having spoken to the Rugby World Cup committee and said, 'they wont allow it because of the security risk'. It seemed to all of us a bit petty as Jean Claude and I were universally well known in rugby circles all around the world. John managed to compensate us for our disappointment by organising seats for Jean Claude and myself to sit next to him in the front row of the stadium, top man!

The Semi Final against France was always going to be a tricky encounter because you never know which French team will turn up on the day. England were definitely bolstered by the return of Richard Hill who had been out since the first game of the tournament. For me, Richard was a key player within the England squad. Although the French took an early lead when Serge Betson surged through after a mistake at the back of an England line out, England were full of confidence and always in charge. Jonny Wilkinson's kicking ensured we pulled away from the French in the end to win the game comfortably. I had to take a very despondent Jean Claude back to the Four Seasons hotel and cheer him up with a few nice bottles of wine. Jean Claude had been to every World Cup and was beginning to despair at ever seeing his beloved

French side win the tournament. Meanwhile, my hopes were rising by the minute.

Mike Catt had replaced Mike Tindall in the centre for England for the Semi Final, it was another big call for Clive. Although it was pretty clear that Catt should be involved, the choice of which player he should replace, Tindall or Greenwood was not so straightforward. After receiving the shattering news, that he was dropped, from Clive personally, Tindall later decided to spend an evening with Austin Healey who was over in Australia. The night Mike went out in Sydney was the night he met his wife, the Queens Grand Daughter, Zara Phillips. It turned out to be one of the best fortnights of Mike's life, he met his future wife, an heir to the throne and was recalled to the team for the Final.

I woke up on the day of the Final full of anticipation and nerves. I picked up the commemorative sign Dave and I had carried around Australia in anticipation of Jason Leonard winning his world record breaking cap. I had my tickets arranged for the 2003 World Cup Final, sitting alongside Ben Clarke, (the ex-Bath and England player) right down the front of the Sydney Olympic Stadium, again organised by John. As I surveyed the scene in the stadium my heart was lifted by the magnificent sight of the huge travelling army of English fans occupying at least 50% of the capacity. I belted out the National Anthem, my senses were overcome with the enormity of the occasion. I was so consumed in passion and pride and yet, clearly recall our anthem being sung the loudest. The Australian press had spent the whole week running England down and slagging off Jonny Wilkinson, saying he couldn't tackle and trying to expose any chink in England's armour. I knew we were the overwhelming favourites, we had stuffed the Aussies in June and they were actually lucky even to be in the final.

As it happened, England were by far and away the better team. Phil Vickery was slaughtering their prop but Andre Watson, the match referee just kept penalising him. Any neutral could see he was getting it wrong. Watson was keeping Australia in the game, when everybody could see they just didn't deserve it. As the game drifted into extra time, Clive Woodward substituted Phil Vickery and put Jason Leonard on. I was sat in my seat, powerless, save for offering more vocal encouragement to the lads, it was excruciating. Nevertheless, I had total belief and trusted Martin

Johnson and the players on the park to sort the situation themselves, that's all you can do. You also have to give credit to the Aussies who were typical Aussies they just never give in.

The first thing Jason did when he went onto the park was to look at the ref' and say something to the effect of, I wont be pushing or competing, I'm just going to make sure we win our own ball. Jason just did it in his own way, he is just a nice man, he spoke to the ref' in a friendly and courteous manner and the ref' just had to respect him. I am sure that is why we won the Cup, just as I knew we would. We could have won it in normal time had it not been for the referee. However, the players on the pitch sorted it out, England were the World Champions of rugby!

I was ecstatic, we had won the World Cup, with Jonny Wilkinson kicking the vital drop goal, I just sat in my seat, I was emotionally drained and fatigued, as if I had played myself! I'm sure it was the culmination of everything that had happened over the previous five weeks. After a few moments, I stood up ready to applaud both sets of players as the English team did a lap of honour and the Aussies thanked their own fans. I was quickly surrounded by loads of people, mainly girls, mainly English supporters, wanting to be photographed with me, or in my vicinity in case the cameras picked me out I guess. I was totally lifted by the amount of well wishers that gathered around me and I felt so proud and elated as I clapped our heroes. When the teams passed I saw Phil Vickery tap Jonny Wilkinson on the shoulder and point me out in the stand and they waved over to me and gave the thumbs up. The girls and I were full of smiles as we all waved back. Unfortunately, I was too far back to be able to get a picture taken with Jason and his commemorative sign.

Coincidently, at the Final in France in 2007, when England were defeated four years later, the team were walking around the stadium thanking the fans for their support, Phil and Jonny were together again as they passed my position and Phil saw me again, higher in the stadium this time. He pointed me out to Jonny again and they waved, which I thought was nice, two World Cup Finals in a row it had happened.

Once the victory celebrations were over and the players had left the field, Dave and I made our way very slowly back to the Four Seasons, still carrying Jasons commemorative sign that I'd not had chance to display. We eventually arrived back at two in the morning, due to the late night

World Cup arrives at Torquay RFC

Devon World Cup tour

kick off and the throngs of people leaving the stadium afterwards. Dickie had laid on bacon butties! Bloody lovely they were. Dave, myself, Dickie, his right hand man, Martin Hudson, and his entourage of Cornish rugby supporters were all ecstatic. We had a really good rugby evening amongst great rugby people, it was brilliant.

Back home in England, after winning the World Cup it felt as if the whole country was still celebrating England's success the wave of optimism the victory had brought was tangible. The Rugby Union contacted me to ask if I could attend the homecoming parade which would end in Trafalgar Square, I was overjoyed, 'yes, yes, it's an honour, I'd love to do that!' was my response. I was later informed that unfortunately there was no room for me on one of the buses that would transport the England players, their families and other officials along the route.

I was very disappointed, but there was still a chance that they could utilise me if I agreed. They hoped I would be allowed to walk in front of the buses carrying the England team and officials, waving my flag, leading the way, if I was interested. Wow, I thought, that would be awesome, 'yes please!' I replied. Unfortunately, the organisers came back to me and said because there would be a lot of mounted police around the coaches I couldn't do it because of the Health and Safety risks. Finally, it was agreed they could get me a pass for Trafalgar Square and as the horses dispersed in Trafalgar Square, I would take over from the police horses at the front of the entourage and act as a one man reception committee.

The RFU had commissioned a special commemorative England flag to be made for me especially for the occasion, but it was incredibly heavy and there was not much chance of me being able to wave it. The procession, which had travelled through the heart of the city, cheered on by masses of hysterical England supporters, culminated in Trafalgar Square. Proudly I greeted the two coaches as they pulled into the square and walked with the flag above my head, my adrenaline ensured I managed to wave it a little!

I stood beneath the two England coaches, waving my flag as best as I could and looking out at thousands and thousands of people as the England boys and the management waved from the open top buses. It was surreal, one of the proudest moments of my life.

As I stood there in glorious isolation between the players and the

231

Torquay Rugby Club Wooden Spoon members

We brought the trophy home

thousands of cheering fans, I received a text message on my phone. I quickly took a look at it and noticed it was from the wonderful Eileen. She was overlooking the parade from a hotel where she had been doing interviews for television and radio. I was delighted that she had taken time out to text and say she could see me. I was so, so, proud to be part of such a spectacle, it was the icing on top of the best cake you could ever have. I just hoped Dad was looking down on me.

Spoon World Cup Xmas celebrations

Shortly after the parade England had a fixture against the New Zealand Baa Baas at Twickenham and the rugby union decided to show off the World Cup again to the loyal rugby followers. A further opportunity for me to join in with the celebrations and say thanks to the England World Cup winning team and management.

I was very conscious that protocol meant that only the players and designated officials were allowed to touch the World Cup and resigned myself to just being close up to it. After the game the victorious England squad emerged from the tunnel with the Cup. Nobody from the RFU had given me any specific instructions, so I just stood at the entrance to the tunnel, nearly on the pitch.

I'll always remember, Lawrence D'allaglio came past me and shook my hands and said. 'All right Pete.' The whole team went onto the pitch and I thought, now what do I do? Nobody had said anything to me, so I decided I would follow the players onto the pitch. If anyone thought I was out of order, I knew they would tap me on the shoulder and say, 'oi Pete, what do you think you are doing?'

I set off onto the pitch and I will never forget, we were showered in thousands of confetti, which rained down from the sky. Martin Johnson stood for a moment in front of me trying to remove the confetti, which was ankle deep and clinging to the soles of his shoes. The team walked right out to the middle of the pitch, I followed them as discreetly as I could, dressed in a white top hat and tails with a bold red cross of St George emblazoned on it and holding a great big flag!

Soon, the players started passing the cup around amongst themselves and I found myself right in the thick of it all, celebrating as if I was part of the team. My heart was racing, it was like being in heaven. I was in the middle of the stadium soaking up the atmosphere as the players showed off the World Cup to all the fans who had stayed behind to witness the celebrations. It seemed there wasn't an empty seat in the stands as we walked back towards the tunnel area.

I followed the players and remember thinking to myself, that's it, they will be heading back down the tunnel now. As we walked back I seized what I thought could be my final chance of ever lifting the World Cup, I said to Jason Leonard, 'can I hold it?' 'Crossy', he replied, you're not supposed to, but go on then!' Jason and me held it together.

To my great surprise the players then started walking around the pitch doing a lap of honour. I was thinking to myself, I don't want to be pushing my luck here, so I just stayed a distance behind the players. People at home tell me that it looked like I was in the middle of the jubilant party. Maybe my flag did stand out a bit! When we reached the East Stand I was near to Lewis Moody. I have always got on really well with Lewis, I don't know how but suddenly I was holding the trophy with Lewis! Danny a steward who I didn't know at the time, but I know now, said, 'you cant do that', too late, I'd done it! It was awesome, it was spine tingling, similar to the Trafalgar Square experience, but with a full capacity stadium of pure rugby people.

Some time later The Wooden Spoon charity and in particular Bruce Priday got in touch with me and asked would I like to be involved in taking the Webb Ellis, trophy around Devon to show it off to all the Devonshire rugby followers. I happily agreed saying, 'it would be an absolute pleasure and honour to do it.' They proposed that as people lined up to see the cup, I could be stood alongside it and the fans could pay a donation to Wooden Spoon to have their photo with the World Cup and me.

The first morning we went to Plymouth Albion's clubhouse and the atmosphere was buzzing, with lots of families and young children wanting to see the World Cup and have their picture taken with it. On my arrival I noticed an orderly queue had already formed with enthusiastic people waiting to get their photo taken. At the end of the morning, Devon Wooden Spoon had organised for a military helicopter to pick the trophy up from Plymouth and fly it to Torquay's rugby ground. Meanwhile, I set off before the helicopter and made a hectic car journey to Torquay, putting my foot down to ensure I arrived in time. I knew the timings, but there's always a concern that there would be a hold up on the roads.

Arriving at Torquay's rugby ground on the seafront, where I had first started playing the game of union I love so much nearly forty years previously, was so special. I had so many fond memories of playing on that ground as a young man and now I was part of a reception committee ready to greet the rugby World Cup. (Well done Jonny, Martin, Richard, Jason, Lawrence, Clive, etc, this was what it was all about, you had brought the World Cup to England, fantastic!) It was an emotional time for me as I met many old friends, who I'd played with or against. I'd gone on memorable Pilgrim Father's tours with some of them. We reminisced together as we stood waiting for the helicopter to land on the centre of the pitch. The excitement of the families at Torquay matched the reception the World Cup had received in Plymouth. The atmosphere was amazing and I was still buzzing!

Next morning we visited Barnstaple and the town's famous pannier market where the atmosphere seemed to have gone up another notch or two, Barnstaple being at the heart of the North Devon rugby community. It seemed as if there were more people present than there had been at Plymouth. The atmosphere was terrific, I saw my nephew Tim's, Kiwi wife Sha and their two children, Peter and Phillipa, who had their photos taken, along with hundreds of others.

In the afternoon we drove to Bideford (another North Devon rugby stronghold) where even more large crowds were there to meet us at the Atlantic Village shopping complex. Finally, in the evening we travelled to Tiverton rugby club where the clubhouse was full to the rafters, amazing. I was absolutely shattered.

On the final day of our epic tour around Devon we took the Cup to Exeter where we had a breakfast reception at the Royal Clarence Hotel, which was hosted by Michael Caines (celebrity chef) and Andrew Brownsword (at the time the owner of Bath Rugby Club and of The Royal Clarence Hotel). After a fabulous breakfast with invited dignitaries and invited guests including the Mayor of Exeter and his wife, people lined up again to have their photos taken with the cup. Then we had a police car escort with armed police to take me and the trophy a few hundred yards to a civic reception at the famous magnificent 13th century Exeter Guildhall. I'd never been into the Exeter Guildhall. Hundreds of people stood in queues stretching out into Exeter high street, to join the cup and me inside, brilliant! Two ladies approached me and one asked, 'do you remember me?' I looked at her and said, 'yes, you're, Sylvie, Richard Hill's mother in law.' It was Richard's wife, Claire's mum who lived in Exeter and her sister, they said they had to come and see the World Cup that Richard had won!

In the afternoon we took the trophy down to another of my old stomping grounds, the Exeter County Ground. This was magic, I'd played there for quite a few seasons and knew loads of the hundreds of people present again. Finally, we finished the tour in the seaside town of Exmouth where masses more people came down to Exmouth Rugby Club to have their photo with the trophy. I was exhausted, but elated at the amazing numbers of wonderfully enthusiastic Devonshire people that had come out to see what was for the time being at least, England's World Cup!

In 2003, the year we brought home the World Cup, the official England Supporters Club was introduced. The RFU used my image to promote the launch and said on their literature, 'Peter Cross aka Mr England is one of England's greatest rugby fans and has travelled the world supporting the boys attending as many matches as is humanly possible. Not all fans go to the same lengths as Peter, but they are still just as important to us. That is why we have created the England rugby supporters club, membership is our way of rewarding your loyalty, benefits include access to tickets, player events and great rugby discounts.'

It's a great club, every junior member is entered in a ballot to be in with a chance to be a mascot at an England game. I love witnessing the winner enjoying his special day.

SWING LOW SWEET CHARIOT

Four years passed rapidly and England were tasked with retaining the World Cup in France. I had planned to fully attend the 2007 World Cup in France, travelling around the country in a car with my great mate Dave Williams, as we had in Australia 2003. Unfortunately, just before the tournament Dave's wife, Nina, was diagnosed with a serious cancer completely out of the blue. This was really terrible news and we totally altered our plans, ensuring Nina was uppermost in our considerations. However, as with me losing my dad in Australia, Dave and me stayed positive, altering our plan for the first two fixtures. Dave and I flew into Paris where we witnessed England being well beaten by South Africa, which was not good and then struggling to overcome the USA whilst not playing very well.

It was clear England were struggling in the early stages of the tournament. I remember bumping into Andy Gomersall's father at the team hotel in Paris before the Samoan game. I knew Andy's dad through a mutual friend. Andy Mcdowell, from Newton Abbot, was best mates with Gomersall's dad and indeed was Andy Gomersall's godfather. Andy Gomersall's dad told me there had been a bit of a player led revolt and some of the senior players were now dictating to the management that England should play a simpler game plan. I felt that if we were to progress this made sense and as it happened Andy Gomersall came into the team replacing Shaun Perry. He was more experienced, more direct and had a massive influence on the rest of our participation.

It was now vital that England won their final two group games to qualify for the quarter finals. Pre-tournament, both remaining games were seen as potential banana skins. We knew what the Samoans could do and Tonga were never easy because you never knew how they are going to play. I flew to Brest with Pam and took a few days vacation, enjoying the French countryside while travelling down to Nantes for the vital fixture. The reorganisation of the England team produced a positive reaction from the players and we duly beat Samoa in a physical game.

Pam and I then made our way to Paris for the final group game against Tonga travelling via the Loire valley and again enjoying a mini break. Having celebrated our final group stage win over Tonga, Pam and I travelled by Eurostar to Avignon to meet with my good mate Butch White and his French wife, Natalie. We were joined by Howard Warren another good friend of mine from Dawlish and his wife, Maggie.

A celebration weekend had been arranged in Jean Claude's home town in Provence to commemorate that he had been the French rugby mascot for twenty five years and we were all invited. I'm sure Jean Claude must have been stunned by the turn out for his party. The passion for rugby in the South of France is overwhelming and I'm convinced this is why there was such a marvellous turn out. Historically so much rugby has been played in the South of France. The relatively close proximity of the teams in the South ensures that players and supporters regularly mix and bond with each other. As a result, Jean Claude's celebration day turned out to be a spectacular occasion with so many famous old pros attending. I was tremendously proud and honoured to be invited.

A special match was organised for the afternoon with about thirty ex-French rugby internationals available to play against Jean Claude's hometown team. We all met in a bar at midday and enjoyed a superb lunch washed down with Pastis and wine. Sat on our table were a group of four or five French international rugby players. It was a wonderful occasion full of joie de vivre. After a very satisfying lunch, we went outside into the glaring sunshine and made our way to the match venue. Jean Claude had decided I should take the kick off to start the match and he had made sure I was in my full England uniform. You can imagine the scene as I kicked off, I tried my best to concentrate given the alcohol I had consumed. Fortunately I didn't make a pigs ear of it! Throughout the match ex-French International, Claude Spangaro, one of three famous

French international brothers was manning the bar and keeping the drinks flowing.

In the evening a full banquet was laid on in the Town Hall and we continued to enjoy even more glorious French hospitality. We were sat at the top table and we listened to numerous entertaining speeches in French by a host of ex internationals. Butch's wife Natalie translated some of the content, although by that stage, it didn't really matter what was being said! Looking around, I recognised so many famous French internationals and their wives. They were all ordinary, rugby people, having a great time, assembled in honour of Jean Claude. Frank from the Recruitment Bar in Paris had sent down one hundred bottles of Champagne to help Jean Claude celebrate. What a fantastic tribute the day was for Jean Claude. It sent a shiver down my spine when I thought of the esteem in which Jean Claude was held. When Claude Spangaro, the seventies rugby legend, landed face first in his dinner it capped off the entertaining evening off beautifully. Spangaro was totally pissed, his wife kept slapping him around the chops to try and stir him, it was hilarious. Incredibly, an hour later when he was due to make the main speech in honour of Jean Claude, after another almighty slap, he stood up and delivered a brilliant tribute. Everybody stayed and danced the night away until at least two in the morning. What an honour for Jean Claude!

The French public are really warm and cordial towards me as a mascot, Jean Claude is revered throughout France and the French people are massively supportive wherever I travel in their beautiful country.

A swift recovery was needed, because we were now heading down to Marseille for the Quarter Final against Australia. I visited the team hotel on the morning of the game and having sensed the mood in the camp, I just knew we would win. For me our front row would be too strong for them and sure enough that's how it turned out.

During the game we were lucky enough to be sat next to Jonny Wilkinson's mum and dad. Witnessing their emotions during the game was something I will never forget. It's almost impossible for me to describe the tension a parent must be feeling as they watch their son representing their country. Jonny's mum cannot bear to watch when Jonny has a kick at goal and spends a lot of the match looking away from the pitch. We really stuffed Australia throughout the match, but they kept kicking their goals and we hadn't managed to shake them off. Near the end of the game, Australia had a penalty kick and a chance to claim an improbable victory. Jonny's mum left her seat and went to the stadium concourse, while we all held our breath.

Australia missed their chance and we were all jumping up and down, kissing each other. I was hugging Jonny's dad. Jonny's mum came back over and said, 'did he get it?' Very funny. It was a magical feeling, I was so pleased for the Wilkinson's and all the other families sat around us, what a relief. After the game, our group was stood at one of the roadside bars outside the stadium and we saw the England team coach drive past. Team Manager, Brian Ashton, saw us and he was jumping up and down waving at us, celebrating like a youngster, it was brilliant! I had texted Brian before the game wishing him the best of luck. Thankfully we had got the result the whole country craved. Now for the French in Paris.

The Semi Final was in Paris, giving the French home advantage. Could they handle the pressure of an expectant nation? Jean Claude had arranged tickets for us and I was sat with him. Once again, we were not allowed onto the pitch because of World Cup regulations. Jean Claude had still never seen the French lift the cup despite them having some terrific teams over the years. Lets hope it stays that way, I remember thinking to myself. I'm glad to say that even though the French team were hot favourites and it was in their own back yard, they were not destined to get to the Final this time either. Jonny Wilkinson kicked England to victory and I spent the evening consoling Jean Claude. Yet again the English had ruined his dreams and to make it worse, in France!

When I was walking around the Stade de France stadium in Paris before we played South Africa in the World Cup final who did I bump into again? Dickie Evans and his wife. I asked how they were and Dickie answered, 'fine', he went on, 'Pete this is a good omen, we were together four years ago, we're together now. I've got the same hat on that I had on four years ago and the same shirt'. I chuckled, 'I can see that Dickie!' Dickie laughed, a wonderful man.

The RFU didn't have any tickets for me for the final, such was the massive demand, so I had to turn to my good pal John Hall from Gulliver's to help me out again. John told me he could get tickets for me at face value, no problem I thought! I ended up sitting behind the posts in seats that as it happened were quite close to Eileen and Vincenzo D'allaglio. Eileen was now sadly suffering with throat cancer, but she was still full of her usual enthusiasm and passion and we enjoyed a good chat before we took our seats in anticipation of a great game. South Africa were really strong but I think we could have beaten them. The game turned on a crucial decision not to award England a try just after half time, Matt Tait made a brilliant break, before Gomersall fed Mark Cueto who scored what I thought was a perfectly good try. I was sat right behind the try line and from where I was sitting it definitely looked as though Mark had grounded the ball. Unfortunately, the video referee spotted Cueto had a foot in touch and it was disallowed, leaving South Africa to finally come out on top 15-6.

MAD DOGS AND ENGLISHMEN

After a long flight of twenty four hours, with a stop at Brisbane, where we stayed with an old mate of mine Owen Sharrocks and his wife Ann, we were finally flying down towards New Zealand. Coming up over the Southern Alps, all of a sudden I had that tingling feeling looking down at the snow topped mountains. We were nearly at the World Cup, this was why we had worked so hard and saved all our money. As we began our descent to the airport runway you could just make out dozens of sheep in

Dunedin farmers World Cup support

243

Mad Dog

the fields that were covered in fresh snow. The landscape was all white and looked spectacular. We touched down safely and negotiated customs before picking up our hire car and beginning our journey to Dunedin. Suddenly, everything was All Black, farmers had positioned All Black banners all along the roadside, the bunting was All Black, All Black flags were everywhere. We were left in no doubt that the New Zealanders were up for this World Cup, it's their national sport, they are fanatical, fanatical. I will never forget the contrast of the all white approach in the skies to the All Black welcome.

This was the the 2011 World Cup and as we settled into Dunedin, a relatively small town on the South Island, we quickly realised that the rugby was going to be all consuming. One local farmer had painted the backs of five of his sheep with the flags of the five countries competing in Dunedin in England's group. Every district of Dunedin adopted one of the five countries to support too. As you travelled around Dunedin you passed whole areas, not just displaying the All Black banners and flags, but also the national flags of the country that their local district was supporting. This idea was replicated across the rest of the country. It was incredible, almost every farm, private residence or office was decked out in a nation's colours. In the stadium, the New Zealanders all supported their adopted country, waving flags and banners and cheering, when their designated team competed in the matches. It ensured all the early matches were well attended and the atmosphere in the stadium was brilliant. The local schools had competitions for the children to create things with anything to do with the World Cup. Lots of the children were encouraged

All Black World Cup fever

to research about the country they were 'supporting' and produce relevant items. One girl made five iced cup cakes featuring the flags of the five countries competing in Dunedin. It should come as no surprise to learn that she was the daughter of the farmer who had painted his sheep!

Jason Leonard summed up the passion the New Zealanders have for the game when he told a story about how when he was walking down a street in Auckland, two old girls with blue rinse in their hair stopped to talk to him and said you're Jason Leonard, England and British and Irish Lion. Jason

245

was surprised even to be recognised, they then proceeded to discuss his career with him. Amazed at their knowledge of the game and his personal career, Jason said to the ladies, 'you know more about my career than I do!' As Jason put it, 'It is that intense'

I'd seen the All Blacks play a lot over the years and I actually felt they could be beaten. They were massive favourites, but they could be beaten. The reason for my thinking? I felt it was that old thing again, expectation. I hoped it would weigh down the New Zealanders as it had done many times before.

It was quite interesting, back in 2003 thousands of English supporters were in Australia for the World Cup right from start of the tournament cheering on the team at all the early matches. Thousands of English supporters, ex-pats, backpackers and casual tourists, were down under. A wonderful carnival atmosphere ensued, many of the supporters were wearing costumes or had their faces painted it was fantastic. It had been similar in France in 2007, because the tournament was so close to home, there were English fans everywhere. I have to say I imagined it would be like that in New Zealand and I was really looking forward to it. When we got there, I was slightly disappointed; there were not that many English supporters around, certainly not to start with. I guessed this was just a sign of the times, the economic climate meant that many folk had to face difficult decisions regarding affordability. New Zealand is such a stunning, scenic country and was with no doubt a fantastic place to host the World Cup. The fact the party took some time to kick off was no reflection whatsoever on the hosts.

As far as the England team were concerned, their ill – fated World Cup campaign to New Zealand was a real shock to me. I was genuinely stunned that when I returned to the UK all that people questioned me about was the supposed ill discipline. England were originally scheduled to go to Christchurch for two weeks and Dunedin for just one game. The terrible earthquakes Christchurch had suffered meant the original plans had to be altered and all of England's group fixtures were moved to Dunedin.

I believe this had a massive impact on England's preparations. Martin Johnson had originally decided that all the wives and girlfriends could fly out to New Zealand, he didn't have a problem with that whatsoever. As it turned out, with the group games now being scheduled for Dunedin, few of the wives and girlfriends made the trip to Dunedin as it was a quite remote. I believe this forced change to the meticulous planning, that I know Team England would have carried out, may have had an adverse effect on the team in the early stages. I am convinced that the professionalism of the England team and their mindset was deeply affected by the change in schedule.

We were sometimes fortunate to be at the team's hotel after the matches and we would see at first hand how the families can have a positive effect. We witnessed simple things like Lewis Deacon coming down to the bar with his little girl and playing games with her. Pam commented to me later in the tournament how the wives and girlfriends were not the stereotypical WAGS, beautiful, yes, but also very down to earth, normal people. Lewis Moody's mum, Heather, was particularly friendly and she remarked to Pam one night that the players had been to museums etc during the day but they were finding it hard to kill time between matches. We had noticed when we first went out and about in Dunedin that a lot of the players were just sat around in coffee bars twiddling their thumbs.

Later, when I spoke to one of the management team over a beer he confirmed to me that the players were suffering from boredom and I could understand that. As a supporter, Dunedin was a wonderfully welcoming place to be, although during the day there was not a lot going on. At least we supporters were able to enjoy all the touristy things, like going up the mountains. In the evenings, we were able to relax, go out for some beers and a nice big meal as there were plenty of good bars and restaurants.

From the England player's point of view, you have to remember that they had been holed up in a training camp for about two months before arriving in New Zealand. When you put yourself in their shoes, it's easy to understand how creating a good team spirit amongst all the players in the squad is critical. Individuals are expected to live night and day with a player who might of hammered and abused them during the domestic season. The management somehow have to foster a spirit of togetherness amongst players from competing club teams. I believe the England team is always united and for me the importance of having their families around cannot be underestimated. A typical day for the England players in Dunedin probably consisted of some intense training in the morning and then lots of spare time for the rest of the day. These are young men, athletes, who are naturally energetic.

I'm in a lucky position where I've got to know a lot of the players over quite a long time. I can only say that every player I've met is true to the core values of rugby. They are nice guys who will always talk to people. They're not arrogant or up their own arses, they are on good money, but they are not on mega-star salaries. We expect certain standards from the players, but I sometimes wonder, romantically perhaps, why they can't enjoy their private lives as we did all those years ago, their social time is their time after all. However, I do recognise that England have raised the bar in terms of behavioural standards and these high standards have to be maintained to promote a healthy, competitive team spirit.

Being a rugby man through and through, I played a lot of rugby as a young man in the South West, where I was just a good club player. I loved the ethos of the amateur days of rugby. Nobody worried what you did at night. The rugby community stuck together. You knocked seven bells of shit out of each other during the game and got pissed with each other in the bar afterwards. I think that a lot of the rugby community, people who have played rugby and support England, still really like that ethos. Although the England players are superstars, internationally well known, we like them to be basic normal guys, just like they were in my day. I think all we ask as England supporters is for the players to earn good money and in return, we want them to be true to rugby values.

I always adore the early World Cup group stage matches, where players suss' each other out and you get all the nitty gritty, pure rugby. The first game in New Zealand left me feeling a little bit disappointed, I was really looking forward to mixing with all of the players families and yet unfortunately in New Zealand only a few were present.

At least we were joined inside the stadium by Lewis Moodys' mum and dad, (who we often socialised with during our stay), Toby Flood's mum and dad and Manu Tuilagi's mum, dad and brother. We all had players' tickets and Pam and I felt very honoured to be in that group which we privately called the 'Inner family.'

A day after the Argentinian game, the players went up to Queenstown for four days, which is when they did the notorious bungee jumping. In

248

Mrs England

the New Zealand press we also read bits and pieces about Mike Tindall, it wasn't big news. However when I returned to England after the final I was gobsmacked, everyone was asking me about England's behaviour. Dwarf throwing and bungee jumping.

On the night of the dwarf tossing incident, we didn't know what to do or where to go ourselves. If I had known that party was going on, even though I had Pam with me, I would have chosen to be there, it sounded like good fun! As it happened, we had gone to a small bar in Queenstown. It was a Boutique style place, a really unique establishment, where you had the chance to do some wine tasting. You were given a kind of credit card and you just went and helped yourself to a glass of small, medium or large wine from an optic. The machine recorded what you had had, we tried loads of different kinds of wine all night, all of them were brilliant. You were also able to buy titbits of food to eat with your wine, beautiful cheeses as well, it was just a brilliant social situation.

Purely by chance, Graham Rowntree was there with some of the fitness staff, Paul Cridgeon and Calvin Morris (a Tavistock man), amongst others. It was great to meet them in a non-working capacity. They were just socialising and were fantastic with Pam. For me it was really nice to meet them in that kind of situation, chilled out and relaxing. They never once mentioned anything about the likelihood of dwarf tossing going on within metres of where we were sat that night. If only they had known.

The players obviously let Martin Johnson down because they knew the media were looking for stories and they should have been more disciplined. We expect certain standards, but I think we expect them to be normal rugby players also. I think they had gone to Queenstown just to chill out, enjoy some different surroundings, do some outdoor activities and have a few beers. I would accept that as a rugby player at a World Cup you shouldn't be drinking too much. Traditionally, however, rugby players have enjoyed a few beers in the midweek and sometimes even the night before a game. Rugby has always had its own standards and ethics and it is still the same now, even if we are now in a professional era.

One day, when I was waiting to collect some tickets outside the team hotel in Dunedin after the dwarf tossing episode, there were loads of paparazzi hanging around. As I chatted with Mike Ford he said to me, 'Pete they have been here all night outside the team hotel', I could tell that it had really annoyed him. I later spoke to Dave Rogers and he said something along the lines of, 'Pete, it's sad isn't it, I'm here as a photographer just wanting to take photos of the team to go around the world and you've got these guys who are just looking for trouble.' Dave continued that he'd seen many interesting things over the years but he wouldn't dream of reporting on what he had seen.

Mike Ford was the England defence coach during the 2007 World Cup through to the 2011 World Cup and is still involved in the game as Head Coach at Bath. Mike hailed from Oldham the same as me, but unlike me, he'd played for Great Britain at rugby league. Mike's boys, Joe and George, both play union professionally and are very talented with bright futures ahead of them. George played in the England Under 20's team that won the World Cup in 2013 and won the IRB Junior Player of the Year in 2011. As I write George has been called into the full England squad. I've always got on really well with Mike and his wife Sally Ann and there other son Jacob who played rugby league for Saddleworth as I had done many years ago. I'm sure Jacob will be another member of the Ford dynasty to keep an eye on in the future.

During the World Cup, I had been using the players' complimentary tickets as agreed with the RFU. On the day of the game I would go to the team hotel to collect my tickets for Pam and me from Dave Barton the media manager. However, as the England team progressed through the tournament I was becoming concerned that I may not always have a ticket for a game. Mike Ford provided me with the reassurance I needed when he said to me one day, 'if you have any problems at any time, just give me a shout and you will have tickets for you and Pam.' Sure enough, I needed tickets for the next game and Mike sorted them for me.

I met Nick Easter at a restaurant in Dunedin one night before a game in which he wouldn't be fit to play. He saw me and Pam and came over to us. I asked him how his injury was and he said he had had this big injection, epidural in his back. He told us that for two days he could hardly walk, then all of a sudden I am much better today. I asked him, 'do you reckon you did it bungee jumping then?' He said 'Pete, I haven't got a clue, it could have been, it could have been training, or an old niggle just flaring up.' Nick continued, 'I can tell you, I bet at any given time, half the England squad have got back problems, it's the nature of all the knocks you take and the physicality of the rugby.'

Dylan Hartley, who also wasn't playing the next day, was at the restaurant too. He was sitting with four England fans on the table next to me and they were having their photos taken with him and chatting away. Dylan had not recognised me, so I went over to his table and said, 'you don't recognise me Dylan do you?' Dylan looked at me perplexed. I explained, 'normally I'd have a top hat and tails on.' Dylan said 'bloody hell, I've met you so many times!' I had watched as Dylan had gone over and talked to those two middle aged couples for fifteen or twenty minutes. How many other top class world sportsmen would do that? Virtually all the England squad come from grassroots rugby, they've either played mini rugby, junior rugby or senior rugby at ordinary clubs across the country. That's where we're all from, that's the soul of English rugby, people at the top level have come from where we are.

After the Queenstown trip and the Mike Tindall incident, I'd happily got our tickets for the game. When we got to the stadium, Zara his new wife was sat right behind Pam with two friends. Lewis Moody's mum advised me, 'Peter, we are all protecting her, she doesn't want to be on television or anything, she wants to keep a low profile.' Zara had a hat on and kept her head down and the 'England family,' wives, girlfriends etc supported her. It was brilliant, apparently only three photographers recognised her and they weren't going to give away their exclusive. At the end of the game she stood up and chatted to us all, it was lovely, we felt we 'the family' had done our little bit in protecting her from the press.

Before we had set off for New Zealand, the Autumn international against Australia coincided with the tenth anniversary of me being England's mascot. Coincidently, I'd made my first official mascot appearance when the Aussies were our opponents ten years earlier. Maureen Brewer had found out that it was my tenth anniversary and invited Jim Hickson and me to the after match reception. When we went in for dinner we found we were sat at the President's table. Jim was sat next to John Steele who was the Chief Executive of the rugby union. As Richard Appleby, the President, completed his speech he suddenly said, 'I would like to make a special presentation to a special person. Would Peter Cross like to come up and receive a gift from me?' I was shocked and nearly speechless, 'Jim, that's me,' I cried. I slowly walked up to accept my gift, passing most of the England and Aussie teams, as Richard informed everyone I had been the official mascot for 10 years. He presented me with a brilliant framed caricature of myself. I was elated. How had I come this far? When I thought about it afterwards in the cold light of day, I remembered The Rugby Union had been celebrating their 100th anniversary that season and I had been their mascot for ten years, a tenth of England's RFU history, incredible, awesome!

Later, I had replicas produced, I framed photocopies of the print and auctioned them off in aid of Devon Wooden Spoon. They sold a batch of 10 at an event I attended. Cleverly, Bruce Priday, the auctioneer asked people to stand, if they would pay the current asking price, as he raised the price step by step. Once ten people were remaining all willing to pay £100 he congratulated them all on owning one each, at a cost of £100 apiece, making an instant £1,000 for Wooden Spoon!

Back in New Zealand at the World Cup and we were on our way to our next group game against Scotland in Auckland. We had booked a stay

10th Anniversary award

in Hanmer Springs. On arriving we settled in and then in the afternoon Pam and I went up into the mountains before relaxing in the hot springs. As we sat in the spring, I looked at this guy and thought, he doesn't half look like the Aussie hooker, Stephen Moore. Then I definitely clocked the great big giant second row forward James Horwill. I realised that the Aussies must be in town. Sure enough, they were staying at the same place as us. Before we knew it there were six of them sat around us and we got talking. I explained who I was and then they recognised me. I'd got presented with the caricature commemorating ten years as the official mascot at the England versus Australia only a short time ago.

That evening we went out in town to eat and all the Aussie team were out in the bar with their wives and girlfriends, including Kurtly Beales and his best mate, Quaid Cooper and their girlfriends. I introduced myself to them all and they turned out to be brilliant company. There were plenty of English supporters and Australian fans there and the Aussie players were all happy to have their photos taken. I reminded Kurtly of the try at Twickenham, when Chris Ashton had skinned him and he just laughed and said, 'it was a great try.' Then I said, 'but you got your own back because you scored a fabulous fifty metre try.' Kurtly replied, 'yes I did, but what I remember most about that day was Twickenham, It was my debut game there. I was so honoured to play at Twickenham stadium because it is the one ground in the world where you want to play, even though we lost, for me it was a brilliant day.'

Having qualified out of our group we were matched up against France in the quarter final. Before the game, we had been touring around the Bay of Islands and on the Thursday night we booked into a motel. As it happened, the owner was a big rugby fan, who isn't in New Zealand?, who in conversation turned out to be the brother of Ian Jones the legendary All Black second row. Only days earlier, BBC New Zealand had asked me to appear on their nightly rugby show, hosted by Stuart Barnes and Ian Jones! The next evening I went down to the studio and the first person I saw was Ian and he came right over to me with a big smile on his face and shook hands. I don't know if his brother had spoken to him or not, I never asked, but I did mention I had stayed at his brother's motel the night before. The live interview was conducted outside on the waterfront with all the fans walking by as we spoke. The interviewer was Richard Turner,

England's youngest supporter in New Zealand

Chatting with Barnsey in BBC's New Zealand offices

Ex-New Zealand No. 8,
Richard Turner

New Zealand legend, Ian Jones

England v France. YES PLEASE!

an ex New Zealand number eight. He was just like Clare Balding and Ricky O'Shea, he made me feel so at ease and I was able to come across really well. Some of the England management saw me the next day and were really pleased with how I'd been so positive about our chances. I had said we would stuff France.

Sadly, I was wrong, France finally beat England at the World Cup but Jean Claude wasn't there to saviour the moment! Jean Claude was retired from work now and was getting on a bit and as a result he had decided not to fly to New Zealand.

Pam and I had tickets for the Semi Final between Wales and France. We had just settled in our seats when Pam cried, 'look Jean Claude's over there'. Sure enough, there he was sat about thirty seats away. I immediately rushed over to greet him and we had a chat, it was brilliant. Remarkably, a friend of Jean Claude's from the South of France had sponsored Jean Claude to fly out and watch the semi and the final. France reached the final, but yet again it was not to be for France or for Jean Claude, as despite a spirited performance, New Zealand beat them, 8-7.

The Tuilagi incident at the New Zealand World Cup reminds me of

With Sophia of New Zealand TV.
Another tough assignment

my touring days with the Pilgrim Fathers. Manu is a young man, twenty years old at that time, he had only been playing professional rugby for one season and did a crazy thing. I suspect he'd not been drinking, but for whatever reason he jumped overboard, high spirits? yes, stupid? yes, stupid to himself.

Years ago final Pilgrim Fathers tour had been to Vancouver. Memorably, one day we were on a ferry near Vancouver, amidst freezing Artic waters. We had always enjoyed the inevitable drinking games associated with rugby tours. All the players used to be given horrendous fines and forfeits dished out by our kangaroo court, a unique justice system inspired by Newport Rugby Club in South Wales and introduced to us by John Widdicombe.

On this particular day, a big prop forward of ours, Graham Edmunds, who had played for Devon was being given summary justice by the court when he suddenly threw himself off the boat, Tuilagi style, because he couldn't handle the court's verdict! It was a crazy thing to do, then again some of the punishments were severe! We later found out that Graham wasn't unique, many people had leapt off the ship before. The ship's Captain advised us that people had actually died in the freezing seas. Thankfully, this time the ferry turned around which took about half an hour and we managed to fish a very relieved Graham out.

John Widdicombe was a Torquay boy who would always be on the tours with us. John had played first team rugby for Newport in Wales and that is where he had learnt all about the kangaroo courts. At Newport it was Spike Watkins, a really fiery hooker and Welsh International, who used to be the judge. In his playing days John would travel up to Newport every Tuesday and Thursday from Devon to train and then travel up again on a Saturday to play if it was a home fixture. Similarly, wherever Newport were playing their away fixtures John would meet up with the team. John had been on the verge of playing for England one weekend, he'd been called up as a last minute replacement, but sadly he never actually got on the pitch. It was John that established the ideas for the kangaroo courts for our tours and he constructed all the fines and forfeits.

When we were on tour, it was John who was the self appointed judge. I remember I used to keep in the background when I knew there was trial about to begin. I'd witnessed two chaps who were handcuffed together for forty eight hours and I didn't fancy that idea. You can perhaps understand why Graham had ditched in the sea off Vancouver now? Another highlight of my touring days was when everyone was out together on shore. The court dictated that wherever we were, on the hour, every hour, we had to stand up and howl like wolves, regardless of what we were doing. (Maybe Jonno could have probably done with a bit of that kind of justice in New Zealand!)

Previously, I had been lucky enough to be invited to go on many tours with the Pilgrim Fathers. My first (and what was the second Pilgrim Fathers tour), was a two-week trip to the Caymen Islands, New Orleans and Miami. The touring team comprised mostly guys in their thirties and forties who had been first team players but was also bolstered by two or three younger guys. It was a great way of keeping fit and having fun while continuing to play rugby, albeit not on a weekly basis.

The principle was that the teams that we were playing would host us by welcoming us into their family home. When I arrived in the Caymen Islands I was delighted when I found out I was billeted with my great mate Dave Williams down at the Attorney General's residence! It was only a small house and Dave and I had to share a double bed! We quickly devised a system where I slept on the top of the sheets and Dave stayed safely under the covers! On our first day we were all on the beach enjoying a few drinks and having fun and I decided to go on a sailing dinghy with a mate. Stupidly, I burnt the top of my feet, had blisters and couldn't get my boots on the next day. The grounds in the Caymen Islands were coral based, rock hard, so I had no chance of playing, I had to sit out our first fixture.

We moved on and our next stop was New Orleans. This was a dream come true, we stayed in a brilliant hotel in New Orleans and partied on. The music was out of this world and the camaraderie amongst all us rugby boys was superb. In Miami we were billeted again. One of the great things about staying with a host family is you get to know the people really well and often make friends for life.

Two years later we toured Vancouver, Banff and the Rocky Mountains this was a two and a half week tour. The more we toured, the longer the durations became! Our first game was in Bellingham, U.S.A. South of Vancouver and I was billeted with a guy called Dave Hirschey who was a legend in the area, a real character. I developed a really good relationship with him. The following Christmas, Pam and I flew out to Vancouver and stayed with Dave. The Bellingham boys all looked after us and we had lots of house parties and barbeques, it was brilliant. Dave and a pal and his wife then joined us in Mexico. Dave's pal had business in Mexico and we spent a week there and visited Mazatalan, a big game fishing area on the west coast.

A year or so later, Bellingham brought a touring team over to the U.K. and one of their matches was at Torquay. Dave came and stayed with us and we reciprocated his hospitality. Many years later in 2012, Bellingham brought over their Colts team, I can't tell you how special that was, their coaches were guys we'd played against on tour. I went down in my England gear and had pictures and had a brilliant time reminiscing with them all. While visiting Devon the Bellingham Colts had a day out and in Dartmouth. We learnt they were terribly excited to bump into Martin Johnson who was staying at his holiday home in the area. Martin kindly had his picture taken with them all in the middle of a main street in Dartmouth!

For our third tour, we flew into San Francisco and made our way down to San Diego taking in the whole of the West Coast of California. The tour was based around a rugby tournament they have in Monterrey every year. When we arrived for the competition we were surprised to see that we had been seeded as favourites to win it! The last English team to play in the tournament was Loughborough College and they had won it. That was no surprise considering they had Clive Woodward, Simon Hardy and (as I found out years later my mate Bruce Priday from Wooden Spoon.) Even though we weren't a bad team we proceeded to lose two of our three matches, not surprising considering some of the teams contained current American internationals.

My final tour was brilliant we had a wonderful two weeks in Barbados, which is when I fell in love with the place and its wonderful people.

MADE IN ENGLAND

England's Six Nations campaign in 2013 commenced with the Calcutta Cup match against Scotland, which England duly won. After the game, in the reception, Kelly Brown the Scotland team captain had the honour of addressing the teams and the wider audience. For Kelly to be made captain of Scotland had to be the pinnacle of his career and just reward for years of hard work. It was well known throughout the game that Kelly suffers from a stammer and I am sure he looked forward to making his speech with a little trepidation.

When Kelly stood up he delivered a remarkably good speech, you could tell he had worked on it and it went down really well amongst the hundreds of invited guests, dignitaries and players. As it happened, the Rugby Union had changed the format of the reception dinners, in particular, utilising the brilliant hosting skills of Martin Bayfield as a compere. As Kelly sat back down no doubt feeling very relieved and pleased with himself, Martin announced that they were introducing a new segment to the proceedings. Kelly and Chris Robshaw, Englands captain, would now be invited to partake in a question and answer session. Kelly could not believe it and said, 'after just making that speech, with all the problems I have got, you are now going to ask me more questions, for which I haven't got a clue what the answers will be. I should be terrified, but I will give it a go!' The timing of the new initiative was incredible, it was just Kelly's luck, he should be the first captain ever to be asked to contribute more than a speech. Yet again, Kelly was brilliant as he answered the questions faultlessly, everyone stood up and gave him a

Launch of Supporters Club

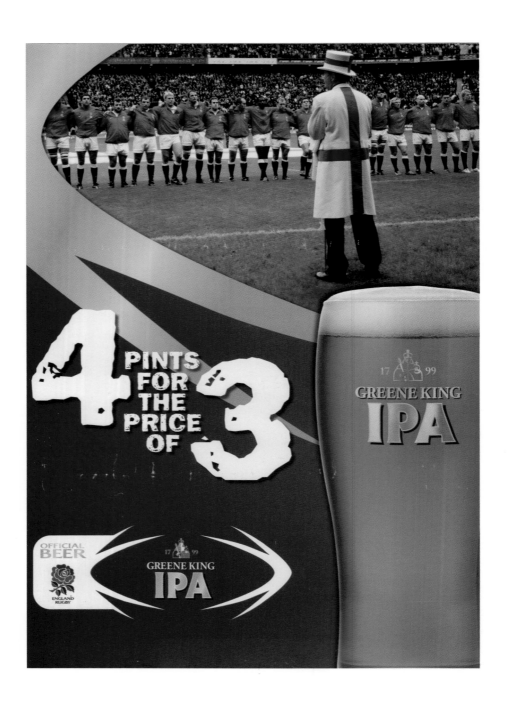

standing ovation. It was yet another inspiring moment that I was able to witness at an after match reception.

The French game is always special for me as Jean Claude and André always come over and stay with us at the White Hart. 2013 turned out to be another memorable weekend, not least because I was in demand! BBC Wales wanted to interview me for their Scrum V programme, which is shown on Sunday nights in Wales and O2 wished to interview me ahead of the game too.

The Friday night before was just like every other Friday before an International. Lots of good eating and drinking and bumping into familiar faces at the Sun Inn in Richmond. That night, as we were leaving the Sun Inn we had the bonus of meeting the French Legends team who were just arriving after participating in the annual legends fixture. They all knew Jean Claude and took great delight in shaking our hands and sharing a laugh.

On the day of the game, Ricky O'Shea, son of the legendary Welsh player, John O'Shea, the first Lion ever to be sent off in a Test match, was dispatched to meet me on behalf of BBC Wales. Ricky and his film crew arrived at The White Hart as planned to do some pre-game routines. BBC Wales were running an item where Ricky was an honorary England supporter for the six nations campaign, in order to give some balance to their coverage I guess!

With nephew, Simon, on O2 TV advert

The pub was full to the rafters. Initially they filmed me in my room getting ready, putting my hat on and doing all my preparations and then they filmed Jean Claude and me at the bar in our uniforms having a laugh together. I chatted with Ricky for a little while. He knew I was from the West Country and he told me how he'd lived in Mousehole, near Penzance until he was in his teens. I explained that I was in the gift trade and I knew a lot of people down that way. We discovered we had a lot of mutual friends, it was nice that we had a bit in common and it put me totally at ease. They then sat me down and Ricky interviewed me, for my mind it was a really good interview, Ricky had really made me feel comfortable.

That in hindsight was probably enough action for one day, but I also had my 02 commitments to think about, which I had agreed to do about an hour before kick off. In the meanwhile, I had a telephone call from Nick Sprague the owner of Frobrishers Juices, based in Exeter and shirt sponsors of Exeter Chiefs. Nick invited me to join him for lunch at a lovely pub restaurant in Richmond with his management team and staff. I said, 'I would love to Nick, but I've got quite a bit to do today and anyway I've got Jean Claude and his mate and three other pals of mine with me.' 'No problem Pete', Nick replied, 'bring them all, you don't have to stay for long!' What the heck I thought, this was a marvellous offer, we can all jump in a taxi and go for it.

We raced across to the other side of Twickenham and arrived at the Restaurant and the place was buzzing. It was packed out, Nick had a group of about twelve with him enjoying his hospitality and there were loads of corporate rugby fans soaking up the pre match atmosphere. Jean Claude and me were inundated with requests to pose for photos and we happily mingled with the punters who were pretty surprised to see the two of us stroll in! We eventually managed to find our seats and we all placed our food orders. Time passed very quickly and it was a bit of a blow that when finally some of our meals were finally served to our table. My meal wasn't amongst those that were ready! We'd arranged for the taxi to pick us up only an hour or so after arriving and it duly arrived before I'd had chance to eat. Oh well, I thought, at least I had enjoyed some brilliant company and some superb wine courtesy of Nick. Nick hastily arranged for my food to be served as a takeaway as we made our way back through the packed bar. We jumped into the taxi and half of us proceeded to eat our gorgeous food on the go. I hope Nick was not disappointed, we had been such fleeting guests, we'd had a brilliant time while it lasted!

We arrived back at Twickenham, in the nick of time to do the pre-planned O2 interview for the England supporters club. I then made my way to meet the team coaches, after negotiating some enthusiastic French followers who insisted I sampled their red wine and posed for photos with them.

Happily the game was straightforward, England ending up convincing winners over the French, thanks largely to some very strange tactical substitutions by the French coach, that didn't prove to popular with Jean Claude.

After the match, I met Ricky outside the stadium, Scrum V wanted to do an interview with Jeremy Guscott and me to get our reactions to the result and England's performance. Ricky started the interview by asking, 'ou est Jean Claude?' ('Where's Jean Claude?') it was such great fun as we'd beaten France comfortably and Ricky milked it for all it was worth. Ricky continued his interview by saying, 'there were 81,000 England supporters in the stadium today and I reckon you are the most fanatical England fan of them all', I smiled. Ricky then asked whether I would ever consider doing what he had done on behalf of BBC Wales and adopt the neighbours, Wales as my team? Although I'd had a long day I responded as quick as a flash, 'No! never!, that would be sacrilige, how could I ever do that!'. When I later watched the programme I saw they had edited the pub interview and after match interview really fairly, Ricky summarised the item saying, what have we learnt today? 'That Peter Cross is almost certainly England's top fan and a pretty good bloke'. I would say the same about Ricky, top bloke.

My nephew Simon, Jean Claude, Andre and I all walked back to the White Hart as quickly as we could to get changed into our Black Tie apparel ready for the evening reception. It was becoming noticeable that Jean Claude and Andre were lagging slightly behind by now, I guess the result hadn't helped. A quick change followed and we all set off again for the Stadium, pausing every now and again to wait for a now shattered Jean Claude!

The reception was fantastic as ever, if a little long winded. Tradition dictates that you never get to enjoy your meal until the speeches have been made. My experience of previous French fixtures pre warned me that it would probably be a long and drawn out affair as all the speeches would have to be translated. Because I had been rushing all day, I hadn't managed to get much fuel on board and I was becoming increasingly famished as the night wore on. It was comical to see some of the English forwards eating their soup rolls and craftily sneaking some of the delicious pate starter into their mouths when they thought no one was watching. Plenty of drink was consumed throughout the night to help compensate for our increasing hunger. By the time we had eaten and walked back to the White Hart Jean Claude had nearly come to a standstill!

Next up, England unexpectedly beat the Irish at the Aviva Stadium in Dublin. Ireland had comfortably beaten Wales at the Millenium Stadium at the beginning of the Six Nations season, consequently England were on course to win our first grand slam since 2003? I figured.

Beating Wales in Cardiff was the challenge that lay ahead to secure the grand slam. The English and Welsh players were not only competing for the Championship, there were also key battles ahead of the 2013 Lions tour of Australia selection. I thought we had been building confidence and growing as a team, but the truth of the matter was, on the day, Wales wanted it more. The Welsh bossed us in the forwards, their backs scored what I call really good quality rugby tries, good hands, good running, good lines and they deserved to beat us, you just couldn't argue with it. I am convinced that game was a massive learning curve for Stuart Lancaster, we would have to move on if we were to have any chance of winning the 2015 World Cup. He had seen our forwards totally dominated at the breakdown, knocked back and bullied by the commitment of the Welsh players and I think he would have realised you have got to have big forwards who don't take a step backwards.

My interview with O2 ahead of the French international wasn't the first time I had collaborated with one of the main sponsors of England rugby. Earlier the same year I had a call from the rugby union to ask if I could go up to Twickenham and participate in the filming of an advert with some England players. They informed me O2 were initiating a campaign of adverts that would go to air at peak times on a Saturday evening between the X Factor and I'm a Celebrity Get Me Out of Here. It sounded like it would be brilliant fun and without hesitation I volunteered to travel up to the stadium on the date agreed. The advert' would promote a competition for someone to have the opportunity of attending an after match reception with the players, something I have had the honour and privilege of doing myself on many occasions.

I invited my nephew Simon to travel up with me, as I anticipated the advert would be set in a hospitality environment, I figured Simon would be able to drive us home if drink was taken. We set off early in the morning, full of excitement and speculation as to what I would be expected to do and what stars may be present! As we travelled up the A303 around Sparkford in Somerset we had a blow out. Luckily, I was close to a slip road and I managed to pull over safely. The RAC guy had the right tools and quickly sorted the problem, ironically escorting us to the nearby Haynes International Motor Museum car park where we could test drive the car. We phoned through to Twickenham and informed them of our progress before continuing our onward journey and making it just in time.

There were around a hundred 'extras' already present, it was actually quite interesting seeing various wardrobe attendants dressing the extras to make them look like real fans! Simon, meanwhile was invited to be an extra too, he found it funny that although he was dressed in gear he would normally wear to a game, the wardrobe attendants insisted he change his top and added a pin badge to his jumper. The attention to detail was amazing. However, I was to wear my England uniform just as I do at every fixture I attend. We were invited to take our positions around the fully laid tables and quickly discovered that all the beer and wine bottles were in fact filled with non alcoholic beverages. Disaster! The Directors then told everyone where to stand and encouraged us to interact with each other as we would if we were at a real reception.

It was quite strange having conversations with complete strangers while being filmed from every angle. One of the extras we chatted to had featured in various 007 films and he informed us, in his experience, it was possible we could still be 'filming' until eight or nine at night. He went on to explain that it was not unusual to spend hours and hours being filmed only to discover that you were featured in the film or advert for only a second or not at all. What followed was pretty tedious. I was directed to walk in a zig zag direction amongst the tables, stopping and chatting to various people as I went. The England player's were not present during the early afternoon. Interestingly, body doubles wearing full England training gear stood in for each player until later in the day. We acted and re-enacted the same scenes over and over again for what seemed an eternity, each time we walked through the scene, the director's assistants would make minor adjustments.

Hours passed before in the late afternoon a group of players including Chris Robshaw, Alex Goode, Manu Tuilagi, Owen Farrell, Chris Ashton and Ben Morgan arrived after finishing training at Pennyhill Park. We were really excited to see the players at such close quarters and they all mixed and chatted with us all before getting down to business. It was very tiring and very repetitive, but the introduction of the players really lifted us and by now the main director had arrived too. We were ready for lights, camera, action! I was in a sequence with Chris Robshaw and by now I was totally confused, I'd zig zagged my way across that room so many times I was losing the plot, Chris nudged me, 'wake up, you've got to be over there!'

The finished production was shown on television during the Autumn internationals match coverage and on prime time Saturday night television. The quality of the advertisement was a testament to all the film crew and their assistants. No stone was left unturned in the compilation of the brilliant production. The realism of the thirty second advert was incredible and a fantastic advert for O2-proud sponsors of the England team. I was lucky to feature quite prominently and Simon even managed a second of fame, the time we had spent in the players company had made it all worthwhile.

Over time companies have begun to recognise the potential in using my image. Some time ago, I was preparing for the teams to come out of the tunnel at Twickenham, when a photographer pulled me aside and asked if I could rehearse a pose imagining I was lining up opposite the England players. I performed the rehearsal and then he explained his motives. Once the England player's were stood opposite me for real, he was going to take a picture of me from the side with the whole England team lined up in front of me. Weeks later the RFU contacted me and explained that the Greene King brewery and sponsors of English rugby would like to use the image in an advert they were planning. The RFU emailed a proof of the advert and I readily agreed, brilliant I thought! I have always considered the picture as an iconic image of me and I am very proud of it. The photograph appeared in all the Greene King pubs, in many magazines, on beer mats and posters all over the country. Brian Ashton the England head coach at the time was asked for a comment. Brian said, ' I think it is great that one of our sponsors have recognised Peter's unique contribution to England rugby over the last decade or so. He has played a big part in building a really good atmosphere at England games at Twickenham.'

LANCASTERS DAMBUSTERS

I have observed over the years that most England teams go straight back into the tunnel after the game, win or lose. Conversely, teams like Fiji, Tonga and Samoa who have invariably lost the game, always do a lap of honour, clap their fans, have a chat pose for some photos and sign a few autographs. I always thought that the England players should do that, in recognition of the brilliant English supporters. Some fans want to get close to the players. Youngsters and avid supporters like myself would really appreciate the chance to spend a little time in their heroes company. I have often mentioned it to the English hierarchy when I have been chatting to them.

When Stuart Lancaster took over the England team he pulled off a masterstroke. At the outset of his reign he asked the players to connect with the fans and communicate with them. They started walking around the pitch after games, saying thank you to the fans. It was a brilliant move by Stuart and for me it is so important that the supporters are right behind the team, especially at home games, it's massive.

England were looking for a coach after the Martin Johnson era and the media were talking about a big name coming in to take over England. Perhaps someone from another country like Nick Mallet. I thought Jonno had deserved to stay on but he had decided the time had come for him to go. I would have liked him to stay and get more experience and I am sure things would have got better. I believe he had a lot of respect from the players and we all know he's a winner.

I passionately believe that an English born coach should coach England.

Not only in rugby but in all sports, because it's part of the patriotism and desire. When the selection process was taking place I was reading in the press all these foreign coaches names and I was thinking, I don't know if any of these people are good enough for England. I am sure they could contribute in technical aspects, but for me, it's the wearing of your heart on your sleeve.

When Stuart got the job I didn't know an awful lot about him. I knew he was managing the Saxons and doing a good job there. He had been involved with Leeds, so he had a decent background, but there was no expectation on him really, he was only going to be a stop gap measure, a temporary appointment. In lots of ways he was not under so much intense media pressure and scrutiny. Therefore, he had the freedom to be himself.

The timing of Stuart's appointment was crucial. I am sure Stuart probably benefited from the perceived New Zealand debacle and the expectations of the England team had been lowered. In many ways, Stuart's knowledge of the players at his disposal was better than Sir Clive's when he first took charge. Stuart knew the personalities of many of the players in the England set up whom he had coached as young men and more importantly for the Saxons.

Cleverly, Stuart put together a strong core of coaches, retaining the excellent Graham Rowntree as the forwards coach and appointing Andy Farrell, a great man who played his heart out for his club and country. Andy has got a fantastic rugby brain having played at the highest level in both codes.

In my opinion, one of the key decisions made at the outset of his tenure was deciding to forsake the usual comfortable training base at the secluded Pennyhill Park in Surrey. Instead, by taking the players back to his old club in Leeds, the public could stand side by side with the players, reminding them of their grass roots of rugby. Stuart an ex school teacher, had the guts and vision to pick many players with the 2015 World Cup in mind. He was also a strong disciplinarian, who in the early days dealt with players like Danny Care in a strong and decisive manner while leaving the door open for a return.

Initially, Stuart was appointed as interim coach, taking charge of the England team for the Six Nations campaign in 2012. Stuart immediately installed Chris Robshaw as his captain, a brave move as it was only Robshaw's 2nd International cap. England defeated Scotland at Murrayfield in Stuart's first fixture. From the start, the emphasis appeared to be team unity and a strong defence. Italy then tested England's new found resolve in Rome, pushing Lancaster's team all the way. England were victorious by their smallest margin against the Italians to date. Despite succumbing to Wales' 20th triple crown success at Twickenham, England finished the championship strongly. First came a sparkling performance in a hostile Paris atmosphere. Three tries against the French, including a brilliant individual try by Tom Croft ensured a two point margin of victory. England signed their impressive campaign off in style with a strong display of forward dominance backed up by the impressive Owen Farrell as Lancaster's men eased to a 30–9 victory against the Irish.

The RFU had seen enough potential from the new England and Stuart was rewarded with the position of full time coach shortly after. Stuart's first challenge as head coach was an extremely tough assignment, a three test tour to South Africa in June. The first match saw England debuts for Tom Johnson of the Exeter Chiefs and prop Joe Marler and despite a fighting performance we went down 22–17. Despite many changes in the backs for the second test England again performed well despite losing the game and the series. The third test provided more encouragement and some momentum for Lancaster, a credible 14–14 draw. It was a positive end to the tour, Owen Farrell even missed a late opportunity to win the game, slicing his drop goal attempt wide. England ended a run of 9 straight defeats to South Africa.

In the Autumn, England were pitted against Fiji, Australia, New Zealand and South Africa in a daunting international schedule. It would be a stern test of Stuart's credentials, a challenge I am sure he relished. For me, the Autumn Internationals have become a regular fixture in my calendar; a chance to witness at close quarters the power and strength of the world's best as we test ourselves against the Southern Hemisphere's finest teams. It's an opportunity to meet some of the biggest characters in world rugby and to get to know them personally.

The Fijians were no match for England as we ran in seven tries in a comprehensive victory, the first for Stuart since taking permanent charge of the side. Next came the Australians, one of the top three sides in the world. However, the Aussies had been hammered 33 – 6 by the French only seven days previously, I was hopeful we would win. Leading at half time we unquestionably should have won, but we didn't. A significant setback for Stuart's rebuilding process.

Lancaster's men had now won just one of their last five matches with the tremendously powerful South Africans to play next and the World Champions New Zealand two weeks later. Unfortunately, England lost against South Africa by a single point, despite a spirited performance. On the day the Boks defence was so organised and committed. This was now a real test of Stuart's skills. We had succumbed to two consecutive defeats against two of the best teams in the world, yet the really strong performances left me feeling very positive for the future.

Finally, the World Champions, New Zealand came to town. During the build up that week everyone was writing us off. I knew that we had taken those other teams close without playing to the best of our ability. I felt we had a lot more to offer, although I wouldn't have put money on it! I reasoned we had a performance in that team and we needed to show everyone what we were capable of. However, the Kiwis were overwhelming favourites.

I just live in hope being an England fan that our boys can rise to the challenge. This time my optimism was rewarded with a victory. England got in their faces right from the kick off, knocked them back in the tackle and did not allow them to play. I've always felt if you can knock them back at the tackle, target their fly half, (Dan Carter or whoever they pick) and stop them getting go forward ball you can get on top of them. That is exactly what England did and they were excellent from the first minute to the last. When New Zealand came back at England just after half time, England had the strength to resist and soon started to dominate again. I believe Stuart Lancaster had installed in the players the belief and confidence that they were good enough and they proved it on the day.

At the end of the game we had beaten them fair and square, a record score for England against the New Zealanders. Our boys went around the pitch, thanking the fans for their magnificent support, everybody was euphoric. The coaches and management were all shaking each other's hands and giving each other high fives. I was buzzing. On the pitch amongst all this euphoria, the adrenaline was really pumping. Chris Ashton came over and I exclaimed, 'you've got that monkey off your back', he hadn't scored a try for ages and we'd talked a bit about it before. Chris got hold of me in a bear hug and I was thinking to myself, I hope you haven't got mud all over my white suit! Then Mike Brown, who was quite new to the team, came over grabbed hold of me and spun me around and around. I had only just got to know Mike who was relatively new to the team, but I had seen in Mike's eyes in the few meetings we'd had, that Mike had a passion for representing England.

Up in the members bar the buzz and the excitement was incredible. I was sharing the moment with so many excited England supporters who were saying things like, Pete, in time we will be able to say, I was there.

Later, I went into the after match reception where the players from both teams were applauded and the formal speeches and toasts were made. The New Zealand captain, Richie McCaw, stood up and delivered a remarkably humble and respectful speech, I will never forget it. Richie said that the best team had won on the day and that the New Zealanders just had no answer to the England team's intensity. He continued by saying 'England had got in our faces from the first minute and fully deserved their victory.'

The legendary Brian Williams, the prolific try scoring New Zealand winger, was New Zealand's President that year and his speech was brilliant, really, really good. He rounded it off by saying he would like to sing a little New Zealand ditty, a traditional New Zealand song and he asked Richie McCaw to lead the reply. After quite a disappointing result for the All Blacks, there I was, listening to Brian Williams lovely voice singing a beautiful verse and the whole New Zealand team, led by Richie replying with the next chorus, it was absolutely magic and a little surreal.

I read in the papers in the lead up to the 2013 Autumn International that the World Cup winning squad were going to have a big reunion in London to celebrate it being ten years since they had won the cup Down Under. I was thrilled to receive an email from the RFU saying the squad were going to get together for the first time since winning the World Cup in 2003, would I like to lead the team into dinner. Without hesitation I replied yes, it would be an honour! A week later, I received another email asking if I could arrive a couple of hours earlier and greet the guests when they arrived. Again, it was a no brainer, I love meeting people and at about £800 a head I suspected the guest list would be pretty special. Some fascinating people were bound to be in attendance.

The function was taking place on the night before the first Autumn International, against Australia. My friends Pete, Jim, Rob Vicary the Chairman of Teignmouth RFC, nephew Simon and myself left my home in Dawlish at 10.00am to allow plenty of time for the journey to Whitton. It was an horrendous trip, the traffic on the M5 was dreadful and we were diverted towards the A303 via congestion in and around Honiton. When we finally joined the A303 progress was slow, all the while I was looking at the sat-nav to check our predicted estimated time of arrival. The longer we queued the worse the ETA became, so we decided we wouldn't stop as planned to get some food. A six hour journey meant we arrived in Whitton at 4pm, I was due at the venue in Battersea at 5pm.

We hastily unloaded all of our gear into our rooms at the White Hart and I changed into some of my Mr England gear as quickly as I could, while frantically making sure I had my hotel details, dinner ticket, top hat etc. I then ran, arms full of gear to Whitton train station. Fortunately, we had learnt there was a train to Battersea via Clapham when we had driven past the station a short while earlier. I raced onto the platform just as the train appeared in the distance. I was glad I'd chosen in the rush to put my short – sleeved shirt on as I had worked up a bit of a sweat by now! No sooner had I sat down on the train and relaxed, safe in the knowledge the train would get me there on time, than an announcement came on the public address informing everyone the train would be delayed, because of a signals problem.

Fortunately, the delay was not too bad. I changed at Clapham and I was confident I was on track. I asked a guard if my destination, the Battersea Evolution was far from Battersea station and he assured me it wasn't. Good, I thought to myself, I wont have to worry about getting a taxi. As it happened the park was close to the train station, but the venue wasn't and I had to run across the park, just making it on time.

John Spicer showed me around the venue advising me as we walked of the plans for the evening. There was no mention of me leading the players in for dinner, I enquired, 'where would you like me to lead the players in from' The reply was devastating, 'oh, we are not doing that anymore,' my heart sank, 'we would still like you to greet the guests and meet the team.' I had been looking forward to the honour so much! I later learnt that because of the layout of the venue the players were going to come out from the wings of the stage one at a time and be introduced by a compere. I was shown the changing room I could use which I was sharing with the compere. As an aside, on the night the compere was brilliant.

The emails I had received had also mentioned that I would have a place at the dinner.

Out of politeness I asked whether I had a place for dinner and was surprised when I was told no! I was told I could eat in an area that was above the kitchens, when I viewed it, it was like a sweat shop. I was starving! Yet I thought, there's no way I am eating up here, I felt a bit numb at that point, I really should have queried the dinner plan, but I was in all my gear, it was very hot and I was tired from all the travelling.

I quickly gathered myself and went outside to meet the early arrivals. I was professional and immediately started to have some fun with the guests. When the England team arrived, all my disappointments melted away. The player's wives were in attendance and everybody was sparkling. To a man, every smiling England player came over and shook my hand and almost every wife gave me a kiss, I felt so proud. I wasn't bothered that I hadn't eaten since breakfast and I was no longer invited to dinner. This was what it was all about, I loved these England players and there partners, I wouldn't have missed this event for the world.

There was a champagne reception laid on and because I knew a lot of the council members who were there along with Trish Mowbray, I thought to myself, I might as well have a crack at the champagne. I decided I'd better eat something as I still intended to hang around for a while and see some of the presentations. I grabbed a quick bite in the room above the kitchens and went back down to mingle.

As I prepared to leave a little while later a council member I knew called Mike saw me and said, 'come and sit down with us and have something to eat.' I sat down with Mike and his friends, enjoyed their company and had another drink. It was turning out to be yet another memorable evening. I soaked up the atmosphere of the occasion and joined Sandy Le Good and Maureen Brewer at their table and enjoyed their wonderful company. One of the council members offered me the chance to travel back to Twickenham on the coach that had been laid on for them. I travelled back to Twickenham with everyone in high spirits and once the driver had dropped off all the council members at Twickenham he drove just me back to the White Hart where I rejoined my mates for the rest of the evening.

I later learnt there had been a place set for me, as I said, I should have queried it on the night, but I didn't and I blame myself for not checking the seating plan, I should have been a bit more savvy.

I was talking to Nicky Worsley inside Twickenham Stadium the next day. All the legendary players and their wives were having lunch before the game. I explained what a thrill it had been for me when all the team and coaching staff had come over and chatted to me and shook my hand the night before. Nicky replied, 'the whole team was always like one big happy family, when they had won the World Cup and we still are now', she continued 'and you are part of the family, in all of our eyes.' Brilliant!

England secured a fantastic victory against the Aussies that day in the first of the Autumn Internationals, a big leap forward in terms of the teams development for the 2015 World Cup. I believe Stuart Lancaster had learned from the final Six Nations game against Wales and changed his philosophy a little, picking amongst others Billy Vunipola who just doesn't take a step backwards. Despite Owen Farrell having a rare off day with his kicking, missing three penalties in the first half, the packed Twickenham crowd stayed with the team. The loyal England supporters were showing confidence in what Stuart Lancaster and his coaches were doing.

At half time, a parade with the 2003 World Cup winners walking around the perimeter had been arranged, the majority of the fans stayed in the stadium to acknowledge the legendary players. As in 2003, I had not been given any specific instructions, so I decided because of the genuinely supportive reception the players had afforded me the night before I would again join them on their lap of honour. I was so pleased I did. It was wonderful, the players were all having so much fun, passing the trophy around, waving to the crowd, giving live interviews, having their photos taken and having a laugh. As we went past the South stand Mike Tindall spotted me and beckoned me over and said 'grab a handle'. Mike and me were walking along holding the cup aloft. I chatted with Phil Larder, amongst others, as we all sauntered around the pitch together cherishing the positive atmosphere.

I am convinced that at the beginning of the second half, the positive vibe amongst the Twickenham crowd lifted the team. Mike Brown, the England full back, was exceptional throughout the game and thoroughly deserved his Man of the Match accolade.

The next weekend, I had arranged to meet Ken Evans a local engineer in Torquay outside the stadium before the Argentinean International. Ken had wanted to meet me the year before with his grandchildren and their friends so they could get a photograph with me. Unfortunately, because of a combination of circumstances, including their train being delayed and my pre-match commitments, we hadn't managed to meet and the kids had been left disappointed. This time, Ken made sure they arrived early. They were having a do in the South car park and I made sure I was in position outside the West stand to greet the team coaches earlier than usual, so we could get the photo.

We all posed for the picture, some of the children went to school in Torquay with my grandsons, it was very relaxed and the kids were looking really good in their England attire. Trish Mowbray, who edits the Touchline magazine, was passing by with a photographer from the Rugby Union. Trish spotted me with these smart looking kids and immediately asked the photographer to capture the moment. The children were ecstatic; I told them that it was a photographer from the Rugby Union and they were saying, 'whoa, thanks Pete!' What a bonus for them that they may feature in a magazine, the look on their faces was priceless!

England blew Argentina away in the first half and perhaps lacked a bit of motivation in the second half. Maybe their thoughts turned to the forthcoming All Blacks challenge. It was a difficult second half with only a late Ben Morgan try to warm the crowd. Nevertheless, the pack had stood up to the challenge presented by their Argentinean counterparts and the English substitutions were encouraging. It was a win and most importantly momentum was building ahead of the New Zealand game. England had remained unbeaten in the 2013 Autumn Internationals.

I was already suffering from pre-match nerves on the Tuesday before the game against the All Blacks. This was going to be one hell of a fixture on the road towards the World Cup in England in 2015. New Zealand are

The Exeter boys!

the best team in the world, by a mile. They were bound to be massively motivated after the defeat we had inflicted on them in 2012 and to cap it all, it was Dan Carter's 100th appearance.

Saturday was quickly upon me and for the third time in as many weeks I was stood waiting for the teams to arrive. Before the team coaches pulled up I kept thinking to myself, what is the New Zealanders head coach first name? Was it Alan? No, that was the football pundit, you idiot! I had a chat with one of the security guards as we waited for the coach to arrive, I asked him, 'what's their coach called, I know his surname is Hansen, but what's his first name?' To my horror, he replied, 'Alan?'

I couldn't believe it! I was getting desperate and beginning to panic, I always like to personalise my greeting. Only once or twice had I ever just said, Welcome to Twickenham. The name Alan was stuck in my head, the steward and I were thinking for what seemed an eternity, until one of us shouted, 'Steve!' What a relief, just in time!

When Dan Carter got off there team coach, he looked me in the eye and nodded, which was lovely. Many players are so focused or listening to their music that they don't always acknowledge you. I didn't have to wait long before, there he was, the New Zealand coach, Alan. I stuck out my hand and said confidently, 'welcome to Twickenham Steve, have a good day', you thought I'd forgotten, didn't you?

Prior to the game the press, public and bookies did not give England a shout, in fact New Zealand were 1/7 on favourites to win. I was realistic too, however, like in 2012 I thought, if we can get in their faces, cut out the supply to Carter, stop McCaw's influence at the breakdown, we would be in with a chance. If the All Blacks are able to play on the front foot they are wizards, I was as nervous as hell, I wouldn't have backed England.

In anticipation of the Ha Ka the whole of the stadium was alive with English fans singing Swing Low, Sweet Chariot. You could not hear the Ha Ka, it was totally overpowered and it sent shivers down my spine. Personally, I respect the Ha Ka and would never sing whilst it was being performed, but it certainly had set the tone for the day. Apart from the first ten minutes of the game, the atmosphere the England crowd generated that day was the best I can ever remember. They just encouraged the lads, non stop, it was an incredible feeling, a wave of positivity. I believe it was a real rugby crowd, I can't imagine many of the tickets distributed by grass roots rugby clubs being sold on the secondary market for that match.

New Zealand came out flying and scored a brilliant try in the first two minutes and were seventeen-three up in no time at all. I was concerned it could be a humiliation, a thirty or forty point defeat. Instead, our forwards produced a really gutsy response, there was no panic and we quickly secured forward domination.

England had a try disallowed, that I thought should have been given and then our forwards were finally rewarded for their endeavours with a well deserved push over try. In the second half, England established a lead. The crowd were tremendously vocal and thoroughly enjoying our supremacy. Our line outs were functioning superbly. However, with around twenty minutes remaining England made changes, some forced, some not. Geoff Parling, a recent Lion, came on and so did Tom Youngs to replace Dylan Hartley who was winning his 50th cap. Dylan was withdrawn suffering from concussion after making yet another big hit on a Kiwi, he had been immense.

England's line out domination was lost, we lost three line outs in

Dan Carter's 100th cap

quick succession. The changes affected our continuity and momentum considerably. Sensing blood the All Blacks stepped up a level and in the final period took a stranglehold, culminating in a brilliant offload by Ma'a Nonu and a stunning try to seal the New Zealanders a hard fought win.

Building towards the 2015 World Cup I thought it was a really positive performance and you could see we were moving in the right direction. The development of the squad throughout the Autumn Internationals had been noticeable. The amount of caps the New Zealand team had in comparison to ours was significant in my opinion. We could only get stronger, I reasoned.

I was on the pitch to witness the trophy presentations and Dan Carter was presented with his 100th cap. Dan conducted many interviews and posed for photos. The RFU allowed his dad onto the pitch which was a brilliant gesture. Dan looked so happy, the accolades were richly deserved. A short while later and we were up attending the cocktail reception for the players and guests prior to dinner. It seemed everybody wanted to chat or pose with Dan for a photo. Dan was brilliant, he had time for everybody and sported a permanent smile on his face. I had to go and say

Richie McCaw, New Zealand legendary captain

hello to him myself, I was dressed in my black tie evening suit for this special occasion and I was surprised that Dan immediately recognised me, a nice feeling. For years, England players and supporters who have seen me in my top hat have often failed to recognise me without my uniform. We had a lovely long chat about the game and I mentioned how proud I was of the England team's performance. Dan, Richie McCaw and the other Kiwi players I spoke to all appreciated how well England had played and were just as magnanimous in victory as they had been in defeat a year ago.

I asked Dan what his next step would be and he replied that he was having six months off. That to me was really interesting, the New Zealand Rugby Union have the ability to control the numbers of games the players play and give them rest periods to recharge their batteries. Our best players play a whole season, then go straight into a tour and are soon back playing Internationals and starting a new season in our professional set up. For New Zealand, their national team is their be all and end all, by far their number one priority. The English RFU have made excellent progress in recent times in limiting the amount of club rugby our players play, but maybe there is still room for some improvement?

GREAT EXPECTATIONS

I was massively looking forward to the Six Nations in 2014, for me England were coming of age under Stuart Lancaster's leadership. Stuart as all good coaches do, seemed to have learnt the lessons of the catastrophic defeat to Wales in 2013. Furthermore, looking beyond the Six Nations, to the 2015 World Cup, I was tremendously excited that Stuart had left the door open for the outrageously good, emerging young talent that England boasted. Stuart's bold selection of Exeter's very own Jack Nowell, plus Luther Burrell and Jonny May for the French game illustrated that perfectly. I was confident that others, like George Ford, Kyle Eastmond, Christian Wade and Marlon Yarde would soon be staking a claim to break into the squad too.

The first game of the tournament against France ended in defeat for England. We started disastrously, knocking on at the kick off. Before I knew it we had conceded two early tries and were trailing 16-3. Both tries were scored as a result of French kicks, the bounce of the ball eluding our defenders. I believe you create your own luck and the French certainly did. However, I took great encouragement from how we knuckled down, didn't panic and played our way back into the game. Our forwards got on top of the French pack and our three's, well led by Mike Brown, were well on top. Jean Claude, said to me with 15 minutes remaining, 'England will definitely win'. With a last throw of the dice the French brought on 19 year old centre Fickou in the 74th minute. He scored an outrageous try some three minutes later to secure France an improbable win. Although we had lost the game, I felt there were many positives to come from the game, not least, I knew the player's would learn from their mistakes and in future would close out the game.

Scotland at Murrayfield is always dangerous, as they always manage to up their game against us. In 2014 it was not to be for the Scots and we totally outplayed them. England retained the Calcutta Cup putting in a professional performance to ensure a comfortable victory. I felt we should have scored another 20 points, as we missed numerous chances. Mike Brown stood out again and was awarded the man of the match. Meanwhile Ireland had hammered the Welsh in Dublin, so I was really looking forward to England against the Irish at Twickenham.

The week before the Ireland game I was invited by my mate Neil Friend to his box at Sandy Park, Exeter to watch the Chief's play Bath. That week Bath announced they had signed Sam Burgess the Sydney Rabbitohs League superstar to add to their growing array of ex Rugby League talent. 'Slammin Sam' was outstanding for England in the 2013 Rugby League World Cup and is a tremendous talent. I think he will have an excellent chance of breaking into the England Union set up when he returns to England in the Autumn of 2014. Interestingly, Stuart Lancaster sees him as an inside centre, while Bath intend to use him at number 8, where we already have Billy Vunipola and Ben Morgan. Mike Ford commented on the radio that week that he would allow Sam to play his natural game and try not to change his style of play, believing ex league players had sometimes struggled to adapt quickly to Premiership Rugby Union.

In the past, some League players have found it really hard making the transition, players I thought would be a 'shoe' in for top International Rugby Union. Top quality players like, Henry Paul and Andy Farrell, (although it was late in Andy's career and he struggled with injuries to be fair) have struggled to make a lasting impact. Conversely, Jason Robinson was an outstanding success, Chris Ashton and Leslie Vianakolo haven't done too bad either!

After the Exeter versus Bath match I bumped into Mike Ford's son Jacob, who was with his his mum Sally Ann, watching his brother George represent Bath. We had a good chat. I'd met them both before at Twickenham and it was great to see them again. I couldn't believe how Jacob had shot up, I asked him, was he still playing for Saddleworth

Rangers? He wasn't, he too was now playing Union having been at Harrow school in London for the past couple of years. Soon Mike joined us, greeting me warmly and talking about the old times. Finally, George arrived too, it was really brilliant to see them all again. George was beginning to make his mark in Union at the top level, he had a great game for Bath that day and the following week he was selected in the England squad to face Ireland.

I mentioned how Stuart Lancaster had immediately set about encouraging the players to interact with the fans at Twickenham, particularly after matches, when he first took over as Head Coach. During his tenure I have been lucky enough to chat with Stuart and we both agree that harnessing the huge potential of the Twickenham crowd is imperative to England being successful. For me, with England hosting the 2015 World Cup it is a great opportunity for us to exploit that advantage to the full. Nobody can explain why home advantage is so important, but clearly it is often the difference between winning and losing.

To illustrate the point, England had suffered that defeat in Cardiff the previous year when the Millenium Stadium as ever had been a cauldron. After the game the Welsh players recalled their bus journey along Westgate Street and how they watched a video culminating with the words, 'Our Trophy, Our Stadium'. The sense of responsibility the players feel towards their own supporters is surely heightened by the anticipation felt outside their home ground.

Stuart decided to harness the English supporters fervour ahead of the Irish match. In the previous round of matches Ireland had convincingly beaten Wales, England would need all the encouragement they could get. The England coach stopped 20 yards further away from the Lion's Gate entrance than it normally would. The players disembarked from the coach and I welcomed them as I had before every game previously. It was noticeable, none of the players wore their headphones, but were fully focused on the job at hand. They could not have failed to be uplifted as cheers and shouts of encouragement rang out as they walked through the packed concourse. There was even a brief rendition of Swing Low, Sweet Chariot. As I followed the player's between the passionate ranks of fans, it was impossible not to witness the sense of excitement on everyone's faces. You could tell the supporters were ready for the battle, right behind the players. This was a rare opportunity for them to get up close and personal with their heroes and they were savouring every second. In turn, I am convinced the players must have been inspired to dig even deeper.

Inside the Stadium, the noise level was extraordinary and the atmosphere was intense. The more the players put their bodies on the line, the higher the volume of support became. The game was an extremely passionate affair and I am sure the commitment of the English supporters helped push England over the line. Yet again, just as he had been for the Scotland match, Mike Brown was declared, Man of the Match. After the game had ended with an outstanding English victory, all of the players did a lap of honour, thanking the fans for their support, just as I had always advocated. It was noticeable to me that more fans than ever stayed to applaud the team.

In the reception after the game I got talking to Mike Brown about the atmosphere that was being created and the positive vibe in and around the Stadium. Mike recognised how positive the atmosphere was becoming and agreed that it definitely helps. It could make the difference at the 2015 World Cup. Mike explained that the RFU were getting it right behind the scenes too. He cited that there was a new innovation in the changing rooms, the players hook for hanging their gear had the names of all the previous incumbents of their position. Although to some it was a minor detail, I could recognise that it was all to do with the history of playing for England, the pride of wearing the shirt and making the players feel at home. Mike was enthusing about the changing rooms and I said, 'corr, I haven't been in the new changing rooms.' Mike was flabbergasted, he couldn't believe it. Billy Twelvetrees, who was sat alongside us, immediately piped up, 'we've got to organise it for you.' When we finished our chat I headed back to my table to rejoin my pals. About five minutes later, Tom the Team Manager, came up to me and said, 'Pete, Brownie says you've never been in the new changing rooms, I cant believe it.' I replied, 'no, I've not been in them since way before they were refurbished.' Tom responded, 'leave it with me, the next game that it's possible, you'll be in.' I was absolutely chuffed that the players had spoken to the management to convince them that I should be part of everything that was going on. I later said to Tom, not to worry, I didn't want to put him in a difficult position. I know how busy those guys are on match days, I was just so proud to be thought of by the players. In fact these days, many of the younger players tell me that my image was one of their first memories of watching the England team.

The connection between the supporters and players had worked so well, it was no surprise when the same routine was followed for the Welsh match. The walk from the coach had increased numbers of fans spontaneously singing, Swing Low' and chanting, 'England, England. Inside and outside the Stadium the vibe was incredible, the crowd were increasingly responding to the player's commitment. England played superbly and were comfortable victors, with Courtney Lawes excelling, as the English forwards dominated. After the unfortunate defeat to France in the opening fixture, England had given themselves a chance of the Six Nations title on the final day of the campaign, whilst also securing the Triple Crown

After the post match dinner I got talking to Stuart and commended him on what he was doing. Stuart asked, how the atmosphere compared with previous eras, I replied, 'this was a massive occasion today'. Stuart continued, 'What about the Clive Woodward era, just before the World Cup victory? I replied, 'that without doubt, that was the best time for me . . . 'up until now!' I could not have offered a greater endorsement to Stuart and his approach. It's true, the crowd are definitely on side and believing in what England are doing. I sensed this season that the ante has been lifted, I can feel the enthusiasm all around me as I stand on or beside the pitch. The players are doing everything they can to connect with the fans. When the players are not available, I will do all that I can to provide that link.

Just as Sir Clive had previously recognised, Stuart understands the importance of installing a sense of obligation and patriotism into his players, without it being artificially forged. England's home, Twickenham, must develop into a fortress for the England players ahead of the World Cup. The team need to conjure up a ferocious early tackle, win a scrum against the head, or produce an early flowing move to lift the crowd off their seats. In turn the English crowd has a duty to create a passionate, intimidating and positive atmosphere to inspire the players. Hopefully, by 2015 the momentum will be with us and opposition teams will be daunted at the prospect of coming to Twickenham. I for one am totally committed to the cause, the team and the management.

I was inevitably in Rome for the decisive weekend, England needed to inflict a heavy defeat on Italy, while hoping that results went for them elsewhere. England managed to complete a comprehensive victory against the Italians, however the Irish, fittingly for Brian O'Driscoll, managed to win in Paris and were crowned the champions for 2014.

Before the Six Nations, I wasn't totally convinced that England were on track to win the World Cup in 2015, but now I believe that a lot of the young lads, like Courtenay Lawes, Joe Launchbury, Luther Burrell and Jack Nowell have really come on this season. Meanwhile, Danny Care, Owen Farrell and Mike Brown have developed rapidly. Considering we had a lot of players out injured for the Six Nations, I feel we pose a really serious threat now.

So, as we approach the 2015 World Cup to be hosted by the England Rugby Football Union, I thought it would be great fun to select my select England Rugby Team, from the players that have represented their country, since I was first appointed England Mascot in November 2000.

My immediate thoughts would be to pick the victorious 2003 World Cup winning squad. A, Because they were a bloody brilliant team, the first (and only) Northern Hemisphere team to win the World Cup and B, Because it would be a whole lot easier! That team was packed with talent and natural leaders throughout. It would be so easy to just pick this team, but many World Class players have represented England since, so, here are my elite England players, with apologies to all the outstanding, wonderful men I have left out, many I consider as friends.

No 15 Full Back – Jason Robinson (Billy Whizz). A lighting quick full back who in an instant could step off both feet. Whenever he got the ball he would instantly bring the crowd to their feet. He played 51 times for England and scored an incredible 140 points. Jason was comfortably the best convert from Rugby League. He was equally as dangerous when playing on the wing.

I seriously considered Mike Brown. Having regained his position during the Autumn 2013 games, he has put in many 'Man of the Match' performances and is now considered by many, including me, as a World Class Player.

No 14 Right Wing – Ben Cohen. A big man, with lightning pace. Ben was a fantastic ball carrier and great finisher. With 51 caps and 155 points he was a forerunner to the big brutes we are now seeing on the world stage.

No 13 Centre – Will Greenwood. The type of player every manager would want in his side. 'Greens' had great hands, deceptive power and pace and a great ability to create space in very tight situations. Will was often involved in many of his team's tries. He was a great support runner and scored many tries from such situations. A great leader and organiser.
I also considered Mike Catt, as he was massive talent. Mike was a great kicker, a fabulous passer, could spot the smallest of gaps and had the pace to get through them.

No 12 Centre – Manu Tuilagi. Relatively new in the England set up, Manu has already set the world alight with his pace and explosive power. Tuilagi can rip holes in some of the worlds best defences. He causes teams to double up on him, creating space for others. To maximise his ability to score tries, I believe he must also be given the ball in space, no matter how small. Should become world class.

I would have loved to have given this spot to Mike Tindall. Mike is a massive team player who shows tremendous power. He is big tackler and kicker, who always gave his all for England with a smile on his face. A top bloke.

No 11 Left Wing – Josh Lewsey. A versatile back three player, he gets my nod on the wing. Josh was a very powerful player, extremely fit, fast and a great defender. He could score tries out of nowhere. Won 55 caps scoring 110 points.

My 1st replacement for Josh would be Dan Luger. A fine athletic man with great pace and power and an uncanny ability to score tries.

I always liked Mark Cueto. He has pace, great feet, which give him the ability to beat defenders and he knows where the try line is.

A man I thought had tremendous potential, but didn't quite make it, Tom Varndell. Fantastic pace and ability.

No 10 Fly Half – Jonny Wilkinson. That drop goal to win England the World Cup put his name on everyone's lips. After that moment he became a world icon, but he had already made his mark as a world class player, with his dedication to perfection. Jonny could tackle with immense power and kick goals from anywhere. 91 caps and if he had not suffered so many injuries, he would have broken all records.

Owen Farrell, like Jonny, is an extremely likeable guy, with a super cool temperament. A clever player and communicator. An excellent goal kicker, with good hands and a solid tackle.

I was always a massive fan of Charlie Hodgson. A very good goal kicker, fantastic passer, and technician, who could put players into the smallest of gaps. It was a shame he couldn't always play his natural game whist representing England.

I loved Danny Ciprianni when he first arrived on the international scene. He seemed to have it all, literally! Maybe there is still time.

No 9 Scrum Half – Matt Dawson. Matt was always under massive pressure from that other World Class player Kieron Bracken, ensuring he had to be on top of his game to keep his place. A very reliable scrum half with a good boot, excellent pass and eye for a gap. A born winner.

Danny Care is starting to excel and has the potential to be a great.

No 8 Number Eight – Lawrence Dallaglio. A great man and born leader. Wore his 'heart on his sleeve' and would never take a step backwards. A consummate rugby player and true professional. Lawrence won 85 caps and scored 85 points. He was a winner of a World Cup in 15s and 7s and a European cup with Wasps, which says it all.

Although still a very young man, Billy Vunipola has a great career in front of him, with the potential to be better than Lawrence. Billy has already demonstrated that he is a powerful ball carrier, with a big engine. I am also a big fan of Ben Morgan. He has good hands, great feet and is difficult to tackle.

No 7 Neil Back – The man who was once not picked for England, as he was not big enough. His professional dedication to training and desire to be the best enabled him to be the best openside in the World. (At the same time as Aussie, George Smith was playing). He is the type of openside every international team in the World would love to pick.

A great linkman, Lewis Moody was high on my list of outstanding No 7s. Fearless, he would put his body on the line, whatever the situation.

I always hoped that Steffon Armitage would fill Back's vacated position. He had the potential, but decided to further his career at Toulon.

No 6 Richard Hill – 'The Man from The Woods' as the French called him. They never saw him coming, but he was always there. Richard is unrivalled as a number 6. Probably the best ever player for England, in this position. He was equally excellent in all back row positions. A World Class player, who never made a mistake.

Joe Worsley was a player who would have had many more caps had it not been for Richard Hill. He was a brilliant tackler, who would stop the very best dead in their tracks. He was also a big ball carrier.

I am very impressed with the work rate and leadership of Chris Robshaw and although he is currently leading England from openside, I think he could become an outstanding blindside.

No 5 Courtney Lawes – I am going for a man who I believe has got massive talent. Courtney is very athletic, powerful, with good hands, great stature and natural ability. He is a ferocious tackler who now knows when to put his body 'on the line'. Currently, the dedicated leader of the line out which has not only improved his work there, but has given him more responsibility and improved his all round game.

My second choice has got to be Ben Kay with 62 England caps. Great leader of the line out. Ben was an intelligent player, who was a great partner for Martin Johnson.

No 4 Martin Johnson – The enforcer. His style was brutish, direct and clinical. He led his team intelligently and never took a backward step. Martin had become a legend even before he lifted the World Cup.

Capped 84 times for England and 8 times for the British Lions, he also led both teams many times as captain.

Every pack needs a player of Johnson's calibre and my back up player, who was also a great enforcer, who never took a step backwards, is Danny Grewcock

No 3 Phil Vickery – The 'Raging Bull' Phil epitomised the rise of the modern athletic prop. At 6 foot 3 inches and 19 stone he had a genuine turn of pace and loved running at people. He was a great scrumager and had a good all round game. He won 73 caps and had the honour of captaining his country.

No 2 Steve Thompson – England's most capped hooker with 73. He converted from the back row to hooker, but never lost his ability to carry the ball. Steve was a big man who was fearless and loved a challenge.

My back up hooker is difficult. Mark Regan, reserve to Thompson during the World Cup, was extremely mobile and had played in the amateur days. It is noticeable that whatever team Mark played for, their results always improved. A good leader. I bracket Regan with today's England hooker, Dylan Hartley. Another hooker who is extremely mobile, is a consistent lineout thrower, never takes a backward step and a born leader.

No 1 Here I go, Jason Leonard – Mr Dependable, The 'fun bus' owing to his great personality, love of a good time and a laugh. He would be on every team sheet, as he could play equally well on both sides of the scrum.

The other prop I would choose is Andy Sheridan. A massive man, who had a reputation for being the strongest man in World rugby. He destroyed many an opponent and was a ferocious ball carrier.

To conclude I have to say that when I started this exercise, I said to myself that I would not just pick members of the World cup squad. The more I thought about it, the more I realised what an outstanding squad they were. They had leaders in key positions, and if there were weaknesses, the overall strength would cover them. To win the World Cup was unprecedented in Northern Hemisphere history. I still can't believe that the 2003 squad did not win the Tournament more emphatically. To me it shows how competitive World Rugby is and the pressure favourites are under. Always expect, the unexpected.

We have a number of outstanding younger players in the England squad, leading into the 2015 World Cup Finals. Although collectively they do not have a large number of caps, I can see rapid improvement in many of them. I can't wait for it all to kick off.

The anticipation, excitement and adrenalin will be coursing through my veins, as we approach each and every game.

The RFU in their eminent wisdom have made that man of the people Jason Leonard OBE, the President for Rugby World Cup 2015 in England. Just the right man to represent everything that is good about rugby and all the people that make up this great rugby family of ours.

Come on England, it's going to be a party. Can we win it? I think so, bring it on!

New Year's Eve 2013

A FINAL CROSS WORD

'Mr England' – Crossy to those of us who truly know the legend that is Peter Cross.

A man who loves all sport, and especially Rugby, nearly as much as he loves flirting with women (how do you put up with him Pam?).

I have spent the last 20 years giving 'Crossy' monumental stick. He loves it – he epitomises everything real and wonderful about the game. I once heard him say "if they weren't taking the piss out of me I'd feel hurt; like I didn't count".

He is the most naïve of men, in a bar in France once, excited to death because he was with his mate Jean-Claude 'Monsieur France' the French equivalent of himself, 'Crossy' was belly-laughing at all the jokes that Jean-Claude and his mates were coming out with. Except Jean-Claude and his mates from the South speak not one word of English and 'Crossy's' French is limited to 'Une Bier' and 'Euro'. He suddenly hands me his coat and asks me to put it on the peg behind me – then as a double take says "keep your eye on it, my passport is in the pocket" – he's been on loads of rugby tours why at his age would he not of realised the idiocy in that. We hear him on the telephone to his darling wife, Pam' nearly in tears, tired and emotional from 3 days on the 'pop' swearing he will jump the barrier at the airport rather then get left behind. We gave him his passport back in the taxi on the way to the airport – he'd been through agony once he 'realised' he had lost his passport 2 days before, we thought it was hilarious.

My best 'Crossy' story is when we're breakfasting outside a restaurant down by the water's edge on Circular Quay in Sydney just by the Opera House looking at the Harbour Bridge, a couple of days before the big day in 2003. The beautiful blond and tanned 'Aussie' girls were jogging and rollerblading by when 'Crossy' said God aren't they beautiful – look at their legs. I said what's your preference then 'Crossy' muscly, athletic ones or dainty slim ones – he replied he liked something in between, we were dying with laughter – he did not know what was funny.

Don't you just love him – the darling boy? A true Rugby man as his story tells.

Bruce Priday